Data D

D1254031

THE WORLD'S IRON AGE

THE MACMILLAN COMPANY
NEW YORK · BOSTON · CHICAGO
DALLAS · ATLANTA · SAN FRANCISCO

MACMILLAN AND CO., LIMITED
LONDON · BOMBAY · CALCUTTA
MADRAS · MELBOURNE

**THE MACMILLAN COMPANY
OF CANADA, LIMITED**
TORONTO

THE WORLD'S IRON AGE

By WILLIAM HENRY CHAMBERLIN

NEW YORK

THE MACMILLAN COMPANY · 1941

D
421
.C45

59541

This book is dedicated to those who have tried to prevent the coming to America of the Iron Age.

INTRODUCTION

SEVEN YEARS AGO I left Russia in order to be able to write an uncensored book. The title which instinctively suggested itself to me was "Russia's Iron Age." Russia during the last years of my stay had indeed lived through an age of iron, an era of terror and espionage, of famine and forced labor.

But I did not leave the Iron Age behind when I quit Russia. Germany, which I had known and loved when it was a free country, was already in the grip of a more formidable and efficient dictatorship than the one with which I was familiar in Russia.

My next place of residence was Japan and at first that old and physically very beautiful country was extremely relaxing after the grim strain of Russia. But the Iron Age came in full rigor to Asia when Japan, led on by the logic of conquest, pushed forward on the mainland of Asia and China, responding to the equally irresistible impulse of newborn nationalism, resisted.

Then I saw France fall. One of the most civilized peoples of Europe, unwisely, as I believe, pushed into a war for which it was neither materially nor psychologically prepared, went down before the shock of overwhelming superiority of mechanized weapons. The night that had begun in Russia had spread over the whole European continent. And during the last year I have seen the forbidding shadows of the Iron Age, especially those psychological qualities which are so inseparably associated with war and revolution, fall more and more darkly on America.

Out of these experiences I conceived the idea that modern civilization is experiencing a crisis which is more significant than any war and more profound than any revolution. I tried to analyze this crisis, to trace it to its sources, political and economic, intellectual and moral. The result of this study is the present book. What title could I give it except "The World's Iron Age"?

I should like to express my appreciation to the editor of "The Atlantic Monthly" for permission to incorporate in the book some material which has appeared in that magazine.

WILLIAM HENRY CHAMBERLIN

Cambridge, July 15, 1941

CONTENTS

THE WORLD'S IRON AGE

familiar in troubled and declining eras: an infernal cycle of war and revolution. War breeds revolution as the natural response to its miseries and dislocations. Revolutionary regimes in turn make for new wars. And the wastage of human, cultural and material resources during this infernal cycle soon eats up the indispensable reserves of civilization.

In discussing the collapse of a civilization one must define the norms of the order which has broken down. Now the Europe that existed before the World War was not a unit with a common background and a common set of historical values. It was a group of national states with strongly marked individual characteristics. Popular control over the direction of state affairs and respect for liberty tended to diminish as one moved eastward.

In Russia there was already a strong influence of Asia. This was not only because the empire of the Tsars included many Eastern peoples. It was because Russia, while it shielded Europe to some extent against the incursion of Turks and Tartars and other Oriental conquering races, absorbed into its own psychology and institutions much of the Asiatic spirit of unlimited power, of indifference to individual rights and callousness to individual sufferings.

Yet all Europe, including Russia, had responded to the impact of the liberalism, political and economic, which was one of the strongest characteristics of European society between the great upheaval represented by the French Revolution and the Napoleonic Wars and the still greater turmoil that began in 1914. The definition of civilization that would have met the most general acceptance among the educated classes of all countries would have been phrased in liberal terms.

Freedom of speech and press and religion and academic research. Freedom of travel and residence in foreign countries. Some form of elected national legislative body. Legal protection of persons and property against arbitrary imprisonment and confiscation. These would have been accepted

as the distinctive marks of a civilized, as contrasted with a
barbarous, state. Not one of these principles receives serious
consideration in the totalitarian states which have emerged
since the First World War.

Perhaps the best way to realize how far the collapse of civilization in Europe has gone would be to imagine trips across
the continent, from Madrid to Moscow, in 1911 and in 1941.
Such a trip in 1911 would have been a smooth and simple
enterprise. At the present time the difficulties and complications would be enormous, and not all these would be results
of the war.

Passports and finance would be two major problems of the
present-day traveler. Before 1914 one could cross any frontier, except those of Oriental Turkey and semi-Asiatic Russia
without a passport. And the money of any European country
was good, at a trifling discount, in any other.

Even before the beginning of the present war one country
after another had suspended freedom of currency exchange,
while travel without a passport has been impossible since the
end of the World War. From Spain to the Soviet Union the
traveler is obliged to exercise the utmost care not to carry
with him any money of the country which he is leaving when
he crosses a frontier.

The collapse of mutual confidence, of normal equilibrium
of trade and credit, reflected in this bristling barbed-wire en-
tanglement of currency restrictions is, of course, far more
important than the inconvenience to the traveler. It has meant
a general impoverishment, spiritual and material, a decline
from the progressive stage of European civilization when
goods and ideas and currency could move freely across frontiers as a matter of course.

Wherever one might travel, there would be a painful impression of deterioration of material conditions. In some countries the fall in the standard of living would be greater, in
others it would be less, depending largely on the amount of

equaled in its tragic history. After being one of the most badly devastated battlefields of the World War, after emerging later as an independent state, it has again been partitioned between its secular enemies, Germany and Russia. But former methods of Russian and Prussian oppression, while they seemed severe at the time, are mild indeed compared with those which have been employed by Hitler and Stalin.

A grievance of the Poles against Imperial Germany was the encouragement of buying up land in Polish regions for the benefit of German colonists. The Third Reich wastes no time on such formalities. It simply expels the Poles *en masse* from the regions which have been marked out for German settlement and dumps them penniless in the hungry overcrowded central part of Poland.

And the most ruthless Russian governor general who ever sat in Warsaw seems a mild and humane figure by comparison with Stalin's GPU agents who have been systematically "liquidating" the Polish population of the newly annexed regions by the method of mass deportations to Siberia and other parts of Russia. The number of victims of these deportations runs into hundreds of thousands.

Russia offers no exception to the general rule of declining living standards. Amid the fog of confused and confusing propaganda about Soviet social and economic conditions it is possible to discern two or three incontrovertible facts. Against a tenfold increase in paper money wages there has been a rise of at least fifteen times in the prices of food and manufactured goods. And the chronic shortage of supply, even at the high prices, leads to the constant appearance of queues, unknown in prewar Russia, before the shops which deal in scarce products. Another suggestive feature of Russian life is the offer of huge prices, in rubles, for the shoddiest castoff clothing that any foreigner may wish to leave behind.

That everyday life has become harder and poorer is only one aspect, and not the most significant or permanent aspect, of the transition from the relatively sheltered, prosperous, stable era that came to an end on August 1, 1914, to the present epoch of war and revolution. There has been a profound change in the cultural atmosphere and in the moral atmosphere.

If one should visit Europe today, after an absence of thirty years, most of the physical landmarks of the old continent would still be intact. But the institutions that formerly stood for creative thought, the universities, the cultural societies, the more serious newspapers and reviews, would be mere living corpses, in so far as they have survived at all.

One could traverse Europe from the Atlantic to the Urals without finding (except in two or three small democratic countries which still enjoy a precarious independence) a single publication which is not devitalized by censorship. One would find few universities where teaching and research in nonscientific subjects are not bound by dogmas more capricious and more far-reaching than those of the medieval Church. The scholastic thinkers of the Middle Ages enjoyed vastly more freedom of disputation and public speculation than the intellectuals of Soviet Russia or Nazi Germany.

The successor of Kluchevsky, one of the great imaginative historians of all time, is some Young Communist, accustomed to rearrange the facts of history whenever a new batch of executions requires a hasty rewriting of the records of the victims. Marching in goose step with the *Sturmabteilung* has become a prerequisite in Germany for holding the chair of Mommsen. Far removed are the days when that great historian could criticize the most powerful statesman of his age, Bismarck, and escape unscathed.

Europe today is faced with something that has never occurred in its history, except perhaps in the darkest period of confusion after the fall of the Roman Empire: the disappearance of its intelligentsia. The havoc among the older generation of the educated classes has been frightful, but some still which could easily have been given, as a punishment for their passive opposition to collective farming, and the process which was discreetly described as "the liquidation of the kulaks as a class." Reduced to human terms, this meant that great numbers of men, women and children were uprooted from their homes, packed into freight cars and dumped into Arctic wildernesses without adequate food, clothing or shelter. The weaker naturally died; the stronger survived as state serfs cutting down timber or performing other rough unskilled manual labor.

Or has any group of Germans been able to publish a protest against the maltreatment of the Jews or against the bestialities that have certainly taken place in some concentration camps? I know from personal experience that many Russians felt deeply about the cruelties of the Soviet regime and sympathized with the victims. I do not doubt this is also true of considerable numbers of Germans.

But one of the most diabolical features of the war of the totalitarian state on the free spirit of man is the blocking up of every channel through which moral protest might find expression. And in the youth a kind of callous indifference is cultivated, lit up by fanaticism in the few, animated by cynicism and apathy and desire for survival in the case of the majority. This is one of the gloomiest portents for the moral future of Europe.

The contrast between old and new in Germany is equally vivid and in some respects even more shocking. The Russian Communists inherited a governing system of violence, of arbitrariness, of contempt for personal liberty. They made this system much worse and they swept away certain mitigating features. But to some extent they were in the line of Russian historical tradition.

The ferocity which has marked the Nazi treatment of the Jews as a race and of their political opponents of all groupings was not an inheritance either from the Imperial regime or from the Weimar Republic. One would have to go far back in German history, perhaps to the Thirty Years' War, to find parallels for the systematic brutality of the concentration camp regime.

Germany in the nineteenth century was part of the general body of European civilization. Life and property were as safe against governmental violence there as anywhere else. The courts were independent; the universities were jealous of their tradition of academic freedom. The death sentence for political offenses, except in times of revolt and civil disturbance, as in 1848, was practically unknown. During the war of 1914–18 the leaders of the extreme revolutionary antiwar wing of the German Social Democracy, Karl Liebknecht and Rosa Luxemburg, were only held in prison, not put to death.

The Weimar Republic was one of the most humane governments that ever existed. A cynic might suggest that it was too humane for its own chances of survival. Not only did leaders of plots and armed insurrections, both Communists and extreme nationalists, get off, as a rule, without punishment or with short prison sentences, but the capital penalty for nonpolitical crime, such as murder, was seldom applied. So the roots of Nazi ruthlessness are not to be found in Germany's immediate past.

One of the many forces for European unity that have broken down in this turbulent age is the common cultural background which the ruling classes of all nations possessed a generation ago. If one reads the memoirs of a typical old-school German diplomat like Prince von Buelow one finds that he reads the same books, responds to the same classical allusions and historical associations, speaks the same cultural language, as an Englishman, Frenchman or Russian, a Sir Edward Grey, a Clemenceau, a Sazonov.

But in the Europe of the revolutionary dictatorships this common cultural language has vanished in a Tower of Babel.

Education under these systems is centered around the ideas and real or supposed achievements of the Communist, Nazi and Fascist revolutions. Old international cultural ties still exist for the middle-aged scholars of the dictatorships, harassed as they are by the suspicion that is always excited by the slightest contacts with the outside world. But the youth that is trained in the schools of the new regimes tends to become mentally isolated, cut off from association with other systems and other ideas. It was in much the same fashion, no doubt, that the dismembered provinces of the Roman Empire, under their barbarian rulers, gradually lost the old common language, the former facilities of communication, and became strangers to each other.

So what has happened on the continent of Europe, source of one of the world's most vigorous, creative and pervasive civilizations, is more serious and more significant than an unrelated series of wars and revolutions. It is nothing short of the collapse of a civilization, the predominantly liberal civilization of the nineteenth century.

Almost all the characteristic values, beliefs and institutions of this civilization are now repudiated over much the greatest part of the European continent. Freedom of thought has disappeared along with freedom of trade. Elections and parliaments have been turned into laughingstocks. If there is not a Fascist–Communist united political front there has long been an ideological front of these two forms of the totalitarian state—a front directed against all expressions of liberalism and individualism.

As usually happens, the fall of liberal civilization in Europe has been partly a revolt and partly a collapse. The postwar dictatorships have set about building up societies on entirely different foundations. But the success of these dictatorships is a proof and a sign of weaknesses and contradictions in an international social order where capitalism, nationalism, imperialism, militarism, socialist aspirations, the political awakening of colonial and semicolonial peoples, combined to create a far from harmonious ensemble.

The First World War, with its immense human losses and material dislocation, its intolerable psychological stresses and strains, turned what might have been a process of peaceful adaptation into a cataclysm of destruction, into the twilight, if not the night, of a noble civilization, into a tragedy of which the darkest hours are still to come.

In the face of such a disaster nothing is easier than to find a emotional release in a mood of crusading indignation. Nothing is so difficult as an objective scientific analysis of the causes and probable course of a great conflagration that is blazing up before our eyes. But it is the harder task that is the more necessary and the more challenging.

What were the elements of potential self-destruction in the old European culture and civilization and philosophy and politico-economic institutions? What was the appeal of the Communist and Fascist revolutions that thrust themselves into the vacuum of a crumbling civilization? What are the dominant forces of the future? Communism? Fascism? Democracy, as that term is conceived in the United States and in Great Britain? Sheer chaos? A synthesis of some elements of the old civilization with new forms and institutions of which we cannot yet discern the outlines?

Not one of these questions can be answered in terms of snap judgment and oversimplification. And the answers obviously depend in some measure on the issue of the war which is now in progress. But it is by persistent questioning along these lines that we may learn something of the malady that has attacked our civilization and our way of life.

Chapter Two

THE LIBERAL AGE

THE CENTURY WHICH ELAPSED between Waterloo and the out- *Nate* break of the First World War was probably the happiest and certainly the most creative in the history of Europe. Future historians may well give it a place comparable with that of the age of the Antonines in the Roman Empire. Four hundred and forty million people, about one fourth of the human race, lived on this continent at the beginning of the twentieth century. The increase of population during the preceding hundred years had been greater than the growth from the fall of Rome to the time of Napoleon.

And the 440,000,000 Europeans of 1910 were living much more comfortably than their 180,000,000 great-grandparents of 1810. Population pressure was and still is one of the unseen causes of wars, internal upheavals and migrations. But the accelerated pace of science and invention, the vast multiplication of the speed and facility of communications, seemed to confound the gloomy prophecies of Ricardo, Malthus and other prophets of an age of scarcity.

Emigration to the Americas and to other overseas countries was a valuable outlet. But Europe was able to sustain an ever increasing population on a standard of living that, with all its fluctuations, moved in a generally upward curve. New fields of employment were constantly being opened up as the age of steam unrolled its productive possibilities and was succeeded by the age of electricity. A combination of colonial expansion and conquest and overseas trade and investment brought the wheat of America and Canada, the coffee of Brazil, the beef of Argentina, the tea and silk of the Far East, within the reach of the European consumer.

Far distant seemed the days when the Black Death could sweep away half the inhabitants of Europe or when a man-made calamity like the Thirty Years' War could decimate the peoples of Central Europe. There was immense progress in the control and diminution of infectious disease. And Europe's liberal age, from 1815 until 1914, was significantly and happily free from major wars. The greatest conflict, the Franco–Prussian War of 1870–71, was a terrible shock to French national pride. It conveyed to the world a formidable impression of the disciplined power of a newly united Germany. But this war did not throw European civilization off balance and usher in a cycle of revolutions and subsequent wars.

After taking Alsace and Lorraine, Bismarck displayed moderation in victory. Germany was indisputably dominant in Europe from the fall of Napoleon III until the conclusion of the Franco–Russian Alliance twenty years later. But this was a period of peace and stability. No small countries were overrun; no new adventures were undertaken. Bismarck was slow to enter the general scramble for colonies and encouraged France to seek consolation for its defeat by building up a larger colonial empire.

The other wars of the liberal age in Europe, those which were incidental to the unification of Germany and Italy and the Crimean War, were mere skirmishes by modern standards. They caused no serious depletion of man power and national wealth and they did not create such dislocations as would undermine the social fabric.

There has probably never been a century and there may never be a century in any predictable future when the individual has been so free from direct external compulsions. The degree of freedom varied, of course, from country to country. But the trend was unmistakable. Parliaments during the nineteenth century came to be taken for granted in even the most backward European countries, although the reality of public control over state affairs differed in accordance with the political traditions of the countries and the prevalence of literacy. There was also a general tendency to broaden the franchise, and this went hand in hand with the spread of popular education.

England played a leading role in the European civilization of the century, and the British influence was generally liberal. This influence was not primarily political. It was a fairly consistent British policy to avoid involvement in the wars of the continent, or at least to keep participation within narrow limits.

But England was the workshop of the world, the first country which became predominantly industrial in character. The British achievements in production and trade inspired both envy and imitation. British thought, especially in economics, exercised a profound influence outside the British Isles.

And the trend of this thought was that the functions of the state should be confined within circumscribed political limits, that the welfare of the community in the economic field would be best served by a minimum of state restriction. Adam Smith, whose "Wealth of Nations" became the gospel of the liberal economic school, summed up the general moral position of the *laissez-faire* economists when he wrote:

"Every man is by nature first and principally recommended to his own care."

Smith was a consistent opponent of government intervention in economic relations. He opposed with equal and impartial conviction protective tariffs, trade combinations of capital and labor, monopolies and legislation on labor conditions. The negative attitude toward the state that underlies the classical liberal philosophy finds excellent expression in Burke's statement:

"To provide for us in our necessities is not in the power of government. It would be a vain presumption in statesmen to think they can do it. . . . It is in the power of government to prevent much evil; it can do very little positive good in this, or perhaps in anything else."

The nineteenth century liberalism that reached its most complete development and found its most general acceptance in England was a logical outgrowth of the two great upheavals that shook the framework of European society after the Middle Ages. The first of these was the Reformation; the second, the French Revolution.

Both of these crises, in their implications and in their consequences, went far beyond the disputes as to faith and ritual between the Reformers and the established Church or the overthrow of the old regime in France. Both were upheavals of European, of world, scope. Economic and cultural changes, nationalist and dynastic ambitions, were interwoven with the purely religious aspects of the Reformation. And some of the most important repercussions of the French Revolution were felt far beyond the borders of France.

French armies were spreading ideas of liberty in Germany, in Italy, in other parts of Europe, after liberty had ceased to exist in France. It was under the impact of the French Revolution that Prussia abolished serfdom and adopted the short-term conscript army. This was a weapon that favored France when it was the most populous country in Europe. It was to turn into a merciless boomerang when the balance of population shifted.

Now both the Reformation and the French Revolution

were favorable, on balance and in the long run, to the middle class which was emerging, with the progress of science and discovery, the growth of trade and industry, from the static noble-clergy-serf social order of medieval times. It was no accident that Protestantism usually found readiest acceptance in urban communities. And the final line of demarkation between Protestantism and Roman Catholicism in Europe coincided remarkably closely with the division between predominantly industrial and predominantly agricultural countries and regions.

The Protestant emphasis on freedom of inquiry and judgment was favorable to a rising class of merchants, lawyers, small employers. The traditional ban of the Church on the taking of interest was a handicap to commercial and industrial development in Catholic countries.

Huguenots in France, Puritans and Nonconformists in England, adherents of the reformed faith in the Netherlands, were the natural apostles of the new dynamic economic order against the static institutions of the Middle Ages. And, just as the Protestant entrepreneur was often against the restrictions of feudal times, against the guilds which restricted the number of operatives, fixed wages and otherwise limited freedom of economic enterprise, so circumstances often made him a rebel against the state.

Protestants, especially those of the more extreme persuasions, were often victims of persecution and discrimination. It is not surprising that they came to regard the state as an engine of oppression, as something hostile and alien, something to be resisted and, if possible, to be curbed.

So the Reformation was one of the harbingers of the liberal age, even though this age led to moral and philosophical innovations that Luther and Calvin would certainly have indignantly repudiated. Side by side with the leaven of the new ideas of the Reformation one could recognize the effects of growing trade and commerce as a result of the discovery of the American continent and the opening up of the sea routes to Asia.

Another powerful impetus to the flowering of liberalism was the French Revolution. It took place as the climax of an era of enlightenment and skepticism when the bases of order and tradition had been undermined by the searching, often satirical, criticism of such minds as Voltaire, Rousseau, Montesquieu, Diderot and the Encyclopedists. Its excesses sent many of its original adherents in France to the guillotine and chilled the early sympathies of liberals in other countries.

The French Revolution passed through more than one metamorphosis. Under Napoleon the revolutionary dream of "Liberty, Equality, Fraternity," already darkly stained with the blood of the victims of the Terror and made sordid by the corruption of the Directory, was exchanged for one of hero worship, of national aggrandizement, of glory. But when Napoleon fell there was and there could be no return to the old order. Feudal France had become bourgeois France. The final result of the Revolution had been to unleash the individual, to substitute for a system of fixed privileges and obligations one of unrestricted competition. The former system, as Taine has shown so brilliantly and so minutely, broke down because the privileges were exacted after the obligations had ceased to be performed.

The Reformation and the French Revolution did much to pave the way for the liberal age. Another important factor was the forward leap of technical and scientific progress. Between 1758 and 1785 a succession of new inventions, the carding machine, the spinning jenny and mule, the loom, transformed the British textile industry. The capitalist producer obtained an overwhelming advantage over the cottage artisan.

The introduction of railways in the first half of the nineteenth century multiplied the possibilities of trade and exchange and gave a further impetus to large-scale production. This advance in science, invention and productive capacity proceeded at an accelerated pace. The age of electricity followed the age of steam. An ascending spiral was created. Individual and national wealth grew rapidly as a result of the new methods of production. This wealth facilitated higher standards of education and research which, in turn, promoted new wealth-generating discoveries.

The pace of material development was unprecedented and breath-taking. The industrial revolution which had begun in England spread to the whole continent. Germany's advance after its industrialization had fairly set in was even more rapid than that of England. The forty odd years between the Franco–Prussian War and the World War may be considered the high point of the golden age of European civilization. Between 1870 and 1910 the annual output of coal in Great Britain increased from 110,000,000 tons to 265,000,000 tons, the output of pig iron from 6,000,000 to 9,000,000, while the rate of growth in other lands was still faster.

The German output of coal was up from 37,500,000 tons to 222,000,000 tons; the American, from 35,000,000 to 415,-000,000. Germany raised its production of pig iron from 2,000,000 tons to 15,000,000; America, from one and two thirds million tons to twenty-seven and one third million. Already Germany and the United States were being marked out as the industrial leviathans of the future.

During the same period capital investments in Great Britain increased from 35,000,000,000 to 70,000,000,000 dollars; in Germany, from 17,000,000,000 dollars to 70,000,000,000 dollars; in France, from 28,000,000,000 dollars to 53,000,000,000 dollars.[1] The mere piling up of wealth in the hands of a few millionaires would have been of minor social and cultural significance, might indeed have been regarded as harmful. But this liberal and relatively peaceful century was one of all-round progress in living standards.

[1] For an excellent summary of industrial, commercial and financial progress in the nineteenth century compare Carleton Hayes, "A Political and Cultural History of Modern Europe," Vol. II, pp. 207-220.

National wealth under the capitalist system increases at an average rate of about 3 per cent. The share of wages and salaries in this wealth remains pretty constant at about 68 per cent. So there was a steady if slow improvement in the physical well-being of the working classes. Indeed there is a very marked contrast here between the first and the second parts of the liberal age. Extremely bad conditions prevailed during the early phase of the capitalist system, which was one of primary accumulation.

But during the second half of the nineteenth century and the first decade of the twentieth there was a substantial amelioration as a result of several causes. The new industrial proletariat established very generally its right to organize trade unions and to strike. The general broadening of the franchise meant that governments could no longer be indifferent to the well-being of their poorer citizens. The march of technology made possible the combination of higher productivity with shorter working hours. The appearance of socialist and labor parties in almost all parliaments was a spur to social legislation along such lines as insurance against accidents and illness and old-age pensions.

Not only science, but literature, music, art, philosophy, history, experienced an intensely creative cycle during the liberal age. Comparative critical judgments are necessarily subjective. But achievement in most of these fields would compare favorably with that of any era of similar length. The increasing urbanization of life and the broadening of education provided larger literate audiences and also larger classes from which authors, poets, scholars, musicians and artists could be expected to emerge. The eternal problem of quality versus quantity was not solved altogether satisfactorily. Efforts at popularization often degenerated into vulgarization. The appearance of a large class of half- and quarter-educated readers was far from being an unmixed blessing.

Yet the cultural contribution of the liberal age was enormous, quite comparable with its advance in pure and applied science and in technology. Such features of the period as the absence of prolonged devastating wars and violent social revolutions were markedly conducive to fruitful effort in the fields of the mind and the spirit. French creative thought, for instance, was almost completely sterile during the storms of the Revolution and the wars of Napoleon, with their total mobilization of the nation's energies. The great figures of French culture in the nineteenth century, the worthy continuers of the tradition of Montaigne, Molière, Montesquieu and Voltaire, are all associated with predominantly peaceful periods—with the bourgeois monarchy of Louis Philippe; with the Second Empire, less exacting and less warlike than the First, until it foundered at Sedan; with the Third Republic. Among such names are Taine, Victor Hugo, Balzac, Stendhal, Renan, Anatole France.

A relatively high measure of prosperity and security helped to make the liberal age highly productive in the cultural field. There is no absolute relation between wealth and artistic creation. Periods of material progress are sometimes culturally sterile. And I should certainly not subscribe to the naïve economic determinism of the Soviet lecturer whom I once heard interpret the cheerful character of Glinka's "Russlan and Ludmilla" overture on the ground that Russian trade capitalism was prospering and capturing the markets of the Near East when the overture was composed. After all, there was no proof that Glinka owned shares in the profitable textile companies.

But the margin of leisure that increases during an era of peace and well-being is an important, almost an indispensable, element in cultural achievement. The leisure that is abused by many fools is still worth while for the few geniuses whose work it makes possible. Gibbon's "Decline and Fall of the Roman Empire" is far from being the only masterpiece which would probably never have been created if the author had not possessed independent means. A period of extreme turmoil, insecurity, poverty and physical suffering (the tenth century in European history, for instance, or Russia during the years of civil war and famine) is predestined to be a period of intellectual prostration and stagnation.

The great classical civilizations were economically based on slavery. The steam and electrical power of the liberal age created a broader as well as a more humane basis for the culture of which leisure and abundant opportunities for intellectual specialization are prerequisites.

Both the degree and the quality of European liberalism varied from country to country and from period to period. The triumph of the liberal theory of popular government was most complete in Great Britain and in France. Great Britain, ruled by a propertied minority of voters at the beginning of the century, had gradually enfranchised its entire male population. France, after several mercurial shifts of regime, had established republican institutions on a firm basis. It was in these two countries that the middle class had taken an active part in revolutions, had judged and cut off the heads of kings.

In Central Europe, in Germany and Austria, liberalism was a much less virile force. The landed aristocracy, which had always provided the majority of officers for the army and officials for the higher branches of the administration, retained its grip on the administration and there was no adequate system of control by popularly elected legislative bodies. There had been no successful revolutions in these countries. The unification of Germany and the vast development of trade, industry and national prosperity which followed had been, in the main, the work of a single man, Bismarck, who acted with scant regard for parliament. The German middle class, satisfied in its national pride and in its new opportunities for acquiring wealth, was content to leave the business of governing in the hands of the aristocracy and the bureaucracy.

The influence of liberalism in Russia, politically and ideologically, was pale and weak. And in Italy and Spain illiteracy and poverty, together with the absence of any orderly democratic tradition, deprived the constitutions of most of their reality and left authority in the hands of small cliques of politicians.

Still the century before the World War was liberal in terms of the general trend. Some kind of parliament was regarded as an essential part of every civilized government. Not only was parliamentarism the rule, however imperfectly it sometimes worked out in practice, on the European continent; it was the model for the Oriental peoples who were gradually feeling the impact of modern ideas.

Japan, most adaptable and most imitative of Eastern nations, sent its leading statesmen on missions of inquiry to study European constitutions and to find out which institutions would best suit Japan's national needs. It was to the British Parliament, to the French Chamber of Deputies, to the American Congress, that the young educated nationalists of China, Turkey and Persia looked for guidance and inspiration. It was with arguments drawn from the arsenal of British liberalism that the nationalists of India and Egypt took up the struggle against British imperialism.

And private capitalism, the economic expression of the liberal age, marched on with what seemed to be an irresistible sweep, constantly reaching new productive heights and drawing one country after another into its orbit. Along with the parliament went the bank, the stock exchange, the other outward symbols of a new, more artificial and more complicated system of international exchange. A transfer of paper values in London or Paris or Amsterdam could bring into operation oil wells on the shores of the Caspian, rubber plantations in the jungles of Malaya, railways to span the American continent.

Liberalism has always been under a cross fire from the forces of the past and from the forces which profess to speak for the future. Even when it was strongest it was by no means unchallenged. It was denounced as a dangerous, unsettling innovation by the Catholic Church, the conservative aristocracy, the upholders of authoritarian monarchy. And at the same time the rising revolutionary socialist groups attacked liberalism as a screen for the selfish interests of the well-to-do classes, as an excuse for the maintenance of an unjust social *status quo*. Now Communists and Fascists join in denouncing liberalism for much the same alleged failings: its identification with propertied interests; its lack of concern for public welfare; its irresponsibility; its lack of heroic fiber, of the impulse to sacrifice.

In these accusations, coming from so many and such varied sources, there is some element of truth. With the passing of absolute monarchy and the decline of intolerant clericalism, liberalism lost some of the fire that is kindled by persecution. It was exposed to the danger of becoming intellectually and psychologically fat and flabby. In retrospect it seems quite probable that the classical liberal economists tended to make absolute laws out of what were temporary interests of British economy. The growth of big, sometimes monopolistic, industrial and commercial and banking organizations and the parallel growth of powerful trade unions posed questions for which the early liberals, thinking in terms of a different society and economic order, did not always supply adequate and satisfactory answers. The unrestrained play of private interest did not always add up to public good with the mathematical certainty which Adam Smith and Jeremy Bentham anticipated.

But the liberal age has no reason to be ashamed of its fruits. Liberalism has been one of the most rational, tolerant and humane creeds that has ever acquired influence over the human mind. It has to its account no massacres, no persecutions, no proscriptions of human beings and burnings of books. Its yoke has been light; the number of its victims has been small. It was very probably the highest flowering of Western civilization. Never did so large a part of the human race enjoy so good a life as was made possible during the liberal age. Against the background of our own era, plagued with the double curse of war and revolution, the nineteenth century, with all its faults and weaknesses, may well loom up for a long time as a Promised Land of relative humanity and security.

While it is true that liberalism in politics and economics reflected the interests of the middle class that grew in numbers and in wealth as a result of the industrial revolution, it is also true that there is a strong element of independent idealism in the liberal philosophy. John Stuart Mill's "Essay on Liberty" was not written at the behest of any stock exchange. In the abolition of the slave trade and of slavery, in the humanization of prisons, in the extension of education, in the inauguration of social work among the poor, one can recognize the beneficent leaven of liberalism.

Perhaps its most signal achievement was in establishing the double principle that the minority should accept the will of the majority after an election and that minorities possess rights which majorities cannot properly abrogate. One has only to recall the record of dictatorship and civil strife, in former times and in the present age, to realize what an immense stabilizing and civilizing value this double principle possesses.

In the first years of the twentieth century European civilization, at a superficial view, might have seemed well poised and strongly buttressed against the disasters which had led to the decline and fall of civilizations in the past. The barbarian invasions which overthrew Rome and ravaged China seemed fantastically impossible in a Europe that had achieved overwhelming superiority over Asia and Africa in military and industrial technique. The specter of slave and serf revolts seemed to be laid in a society where the proletariat was becoming increasingly merged with the general body of citizens. Population pressure no longer seemed to be a threat when Europe was supporting two and a half times the number of its inhabitants of a hundred years before on a higher standard of living.

It is no wonder that, despite some voices of warning, the general mood of the liberal age was that of optimism, of faith in progress and human perfectibility. The condition of frozen stagnation that has sometimes marked the last phase of a great culture was certainly not a characteristic of the nineteenth century, when restless change was so predominant in every field, when new conceptions of the origin and destiny of man were being widely accepted, when the remotest corners of the globe were being explored, when the elements of time and space were being rapidly diminished. Yet since the French Revolution there had been no catastrophic social upheaval and the new industrial order was becoming more stable as it became more humanized. Since Napoleon there had been no cycle of all-devouring war.

Had the average educated European or American in 1900 been asked to draw up a forecast of the twentieth century he would probably have phrased it in hopeful terms. He would have foreseen new achievements in science and invention, a steady mitigation of poverty, perhaps the abolition of war through the general acceptance of some system of international arbitration and conciliation. Social problems there certainly were, but none that seemed insoluble in terms of the contemporary political institutions.

But in every rise of civilization there is inherent the possibility of a fall. Over every beginning lies the shadow of an end. In this liberal civilization there were, beneath the surface, deep-seated contradictions which the available sum of collective good will and intelligence failed to overcome. In these contradictions were the seeds of collapse. It is significant that the distinctive characteristic of the liberal age was the reduction to a minimum of external controls over the individual. Along with the virtues of freedom, spontaneity, originality, creative power, there was implicit in the philosophy of the time a kind of helplessness in the face of adverse unforeseen developments which did not lend themselves to direct scientific treatment.

One of the first and most obvious problems posed by the industrial revolution did not, in the long run, prove to be the most insoluble or the fundamental cause of catastrophe. This was the emergence of a new and ever more numerous class of workers in large factories, dependent on wages for their livelihood. The liberal thinkers of the middle class were generally disposed to accept this permanent labor reserve as something natural and desirable and regarded the maintenance of property as one of the main functions of the state. So Patrick Colquhoun wrote in 1806: [2]

"Without a large proportion of poverty there could be no riches, since riches are the offspring of labor, while labor can result only from a state of poverty. . . . Poverty, therefore, is a most necessary and indispensable ingredient in society, without which nations and communities could not exist in a state of civilization."

And the French revolutionary Barnave envisaged the task of the Revolution as completed when the aristocracy had been replaced by the middle class as the ruling power in the state. He did not anticipate that this middle class would in turn call into existence a new class with its own claims to a share in power—the urban working class.

The cruelty, squalor and poverty that accompanied the first decades of the industrial system excited more and more humanitarian protest and also inspired various ideas for alleviating the lot of the industrial workers and of the poorer classes in general. The Frenchman Fourier preached the idea of life in communist societies where there was to be an elaborate division of earnings as between labor, capital and talent. Marriage was to be abolished, as an unnatural restraint on human passion. The plan was nowhere successful when it was put to test of practice. But it became known beyond the

[2] Cited in "The Rise of Liberalism," by Harold J. Laski, p. 237.

borders of France. A Russian landowner, Petrashevsky, tried it out on his serfs; they promptly burned down the communal dwelling where he hoped they would live.

Another French pioneer of socialism was the Comte de Saint-Simon, who advocated a planned social order, to be controlled by industrialists and engineers, in the interest of society as a whole. Saint-Simon, the type of aristocratic radical which appears from time to time in all countries, introduced an element of Christian faith into his economic theories and committed himself to the formula:

"The whole of society ought to strive towards the amelioration of the moral and physical existence of the poorest class. Society ought to organize itself in the manner best adapted to achieve this end."

The more practical British businessman and reformer Robert Owen placed his faith partly in social legislation, partly in the development of cooperatives.

But the most formidable challenge to the capitalist system was sounded by Karl Marx. What he proposed was not a utopian scheme for personal living in communist fashion, but an allegedly scientific body of doctrine forecasting the supposedly inevitable fall of capitalism and its replacement by socialism. Of utopian schemes for ideal communities there was no lack in the nineteenth century. But almost all failed with the exception of a few which were supported by some common element of religious sanction.

Marx was a German Jew whose family had broken with the Orthodox Jewish faith and become converted to Christianity. His world outlook was affected by such varied influences as the Old Testament conception of relentless judgment, the aftermath of the French revolutionary ideas and the theories of the German philosophers of the early nineteenth century. His cast of thought was modeled on the Hegelian dialectic, with its conception of the constant clash of thesis and antithesis leading to a synthesis.

Marx applied this Hegelian idea to human society, which he considered a constant progression, through struggle, from lower to higher forms. Feudalism, for instance, was an advance over the slave society of antiquity. But it was reactionary by comparison with the bourgeois capitalist order to which it ultimately gave way. And the middle class, progressive and revolutionary in the struggle against feudalism, tended to take a reactionary position against the demands of the new, rising class, the industrial proletariat, for abolition of private property in means of production.

Marx predicted that capitalism would inevitably perish after it had run its appointed historical course as a result of insoluble internal contradictions. The development of capitalism, Marx believed, would produce an ever larger class of industrial proletarians, of men and women with "nothing to lose but their chains." Industry would become increasingly concentrated in the hands of a few magnates of capital; and agriculture would become industrialized, with the small farm giving way to the large estate managed on a capitalist basis with hired labor. During this process the rich would become richer and fewer, the poor more numerous and poorer.

Finally the capitalist structure would become so weak that it could easily be overthrown by revolution. Then it would give way to a socialist order, in which the proletariat would play the leading role. Marx's imagination did not carry him very far beyond the downfall of capitalism. Here, for him, was climax and apocalypse. The incessant process of conflict and change would apparently stop. The socialist order would be a kind of frozen paradise.

The systematic and superficially scientific character of Marx's teaching and its apparent confirmation by the growth and periodic crises of capitalism soon gave it a preponderance over all other socialist theories. It also possessed the distinct advantage of not being linked with any difficult experiments in communal daily living. As the questioning, dissatisfied in-

tellectual of the eighteenth century was a liberal, his successor
in the nineteenth century was apt to consider himself a socialist. The rising political labor movement, especially on the
continent, was largely identified with the Marxist viewpoint.

Yet as socialism gained in numbers and in respectability it
lost in revolutionary fire. As Socialist deputies multiplied in
the parliaments of Germany, France and many other countries, rank-and-file Socialists showed less disposition to raise
the red flag of revolt on the traditional barricades. Only in
Russia, where political despotism and, in the non-Russian
parts of the empire, nationalist discrimination complicated and
aggravated the economic issues between labor and capital,
could one find fiercely militant Socialists, ready to use the
bomb, the rifle and the revolver.

One very important reason for this gradual softening of
the revolutionary implications of socialism was the disproving
of Marx's theory of increasing misery for the poor by actual
experience. The increasingly mild, reformist character of
European socialism in the decades before the World War
cannot be explained, as extreme revolutionaries would like
to believe, by the tendency of individual Socialist leaders to
"sell out" the cause for Cabinet posts or other material considerations. There were some such cases, of course. But the
tone of the movement was mainly determined by the physical
and psychological condition of the workers who made up the
backbone of the membership. And these conditions were becoming more favorable. The worker, as a general rule, had
shorter hours, more protection against accidents and disease,
more money in the savings bank, at the end of the liberal age
than he had at the beginning.

But if the development of capitalism, contrary to Marx's
expectations, made for less rather than more friction inside
the national community this was unfortunately not true as
regards relations between nations. Capitalist economy in the

early and middle decades of the nineteenth century was based on the principles of free trade and free competition. There was an aversion to high military and naval expenditures and to overseas conquests.

This situation changed very significantly during the last quarter of the century. State regulation, protectionism, imperialism, became increasingly prevalent and increasingly popular. No individual, no country, was solely responsible for this shift. It was an inevitable accompaniment of the growth and spread of the industrial system.

Free trade was generally acceptable while England was the workshop of the world and the other European countries were predominantly agricultural. But the secrets of industrial power did not long remain a British monopoly. As factory smokestacks began to dot what had once been the European countryside the demand for protection of the young industries of the continental lands swelled in volume.

Characteristic of the general trend was the change in Germany, where a policy of free trade had prevailed until 1879. Then Bismarck went over to protectionism and an era of considerable prosperity followed. Riches, like power, came to Germany in a rush. The national income doubled between the accession of Wilhelm II and the beginning of the First World War. It was demonstrated that Adam Smith did not possess the only key to wealth. Germans began to be convinced of the rightness of their own economist, Friedrich List, who challenged the cosmopolitan economics of Smith and held up the opposed ideal of a protected, self-centered national economy.

Great Britain, with its belief in free enterprise and free trade and its profound distrust of state intervention, was the outstanding representative of early capitalism. Germany, arriving more tardily on the industrial scene, was the most conspicuous example of what might be called late capitalism. The German businessman was responsive to the idea of trusts and cartels, with their restriction of initiative for the sake of better all-round profit-making opportunities. In return for state subsidies he was quite willing to submit to state regulation. Germany was also the pioneer in the social legislation, designed to provide more security for the laboring classes, which is now a common feature of democratic, communist and fascist states.

Protectionism spread with industrialism and finally reached even a backward agrarian country like Russia, where there was a swift development of railways, mines and industries, stimulated by the inflow of foreign capital, toward the end of the nineteenth and the beginning of the twentieth centuries. The relation between protectionism and the threat of war varied in different parts of the world. The United States maintained high tariffs without exposing itself to attack or feeling any impulse to attack other countries.

But the position of the United States, as regards geography, area and natural resources, was singularly favorable. In the more interdependent European countries the nationally self-centered economy of which protectionism was a striking expression carried within it serious explosive possibilities. In an era of generally free trade it made little difference who owned sources of raw material or who controlled politically the colonial markets. Under a protectionist regime these questions were bound to present themselves with increasing sharpness, even to tempt an appeal to the sword.

Another threat to the security of the liberal age was the rampant imperialism of the last quarter of the nineteenth century. Here again profoundly impersonal influences were at work. Capitalism had justified one of Marx's criticisms. It failed to solve the problem of adjusting production to effective demand. There were periodic crises of so-called over-production which might have been more accurately described as underconsumption, since the standard of living in all the European countries offered abundant scope for improvement.

And so new untapped foreign markets were at a premium.

Imperialism was not merely a matter of commercial profits. Sentimental and emotional considerations were involved. There was the general instinct for national aggrandizement. There was the adventurous spirit that, in its varied manifestations, pushed the trader in search of profits, the missionary in search of souls to be saved, the explorer in search of regions where no white man had set foot.

But there were also four clearly recognizable economic factors in the sweep of European rule over what Kipling called "the lesser breeds without the law." These were the surplus of goods in the industrial lands, the much higher rate of interest which could be obtained in new enterprises in undeveloped countries, the improvement in means of land and sea communication, the growing industrial need for such tropical raw materials as tin, rubber, copra, palm oils and many others. As the natives were often unable or unwilling to produce these materials in sufficient quantities there was an irresistible impulse for the master races of the Occident to apply such measures as political control, economic persuasion and, when this failed, physical coercion.

Such barbarities as were practiced for a time in the Belgian Congo, where the whip and the gun were used mercilessly in order to force the unfortunate natives to turn out the quotas of rubber which were needed to produce vast profits for King Leopold, were uncommon. But there was much ruthless exploitation by such means as levying taxes which the natives could not pay in cash and had to redeem in labor service. Against such incidental benefits as suppression of some of the more barbarous native customs, modest progress in hygiene, the opening of a few mission and public schools, must be weighed the physical and psychological misery associated with the breakup of old tribal ways and organizations and the herding of large numbers of young natives into mines and industrial enterprises as unskilled laborers.

✓ Imperialism was a world-wide movement, perhaps unavoid-able as a consequence and a part of the industrial development of the liberal age. But it was in contradiction with the ideals of this age. If it reaped rich profits for its beneficiaries, if it erected an imposing structure of European domination over other continents, almost total in the case of Africa, very ex-tended in the case of Asia, it added substantially to the burden of competitive armaments. It created, as between the big im-perial states, half a dozen points of friction where one had existed before. It put in far greater danger the delicately poised equilibrium of international civilization.

Great Britain alone, during the imperialist last quarter of the century, added almost five million square miles of terri-tory, with a population of some eighty-five millions, to what was already the largest and richest empire in the world. France, under the prompting of statesmen like Jules Ferry, went vigorously to work to build up an overseas empire as a partial compensation for the loss of Alsace–Lorraine. The French Empire, mostly located in Africa, with a distant Asiatic out-post in Indo–China, finally accumulated an area of about four million square miles and a population one and a half times as large as that of France itself. Russia, negligible as a sea power, continued to press forward its land imperialism, some-times accompanied by colonization and settlement, in the Cau-casus, Central Asia and Siberia.

Germany was a late-comer in the colonial field. Even after the great access of national power that came with unification in 1871 Bismarck remained indifferent to the idea of colonial expansion. He refused to accept French colonies in lieu of Alsace and Lorraine. It was only in the eighties that the Iron Chancellor, falling in line with the general trend, began to sanction and sponsor German colonial enterprises. By this time the most desirable parts of the world had been preempted. Before the beginning of the World War, Germany had ac-quired a colonial empire of about one million square miles in Africa and in the Pacific. But the wealth and resources of this empire were not in proportion to Germany's military strength and industrial capacity. Even the self-contained United States joined in the imperialist game by taking over the Philippines and Puerto Rico after the war with Spain in 1898.

On a direct profit-and-loss basis, drawn up in terms of the national economy as a whole, imperialism has scarcely paid its way. For instance, as J. A. Hobson points out,[3] between 1855-59 and 1895-99 the share of Great Britain's imports from its possessions fell from 23.5 per cent to 21.6 per cent. The share of exports to its possessions rose from 31.5 per cent to 34 per cent. So there was a negligible increase in the total proportion of trade with colonies, despite the very great acquisition of new territory.

The British Army and Navy in 1873 took less than 24,500,-000 pounds of a budget of 65,000,000. By 1903 the proportion was about 79,000,000 out of 140,000,000. Not all this increase can perhaps be fairly attributed to imperialism. But the scramble for colonies and the staking out of spheres of influence which were not always well defined certainly did not make for international good will and may be considered a potent cause of the doubling of Europe's armament expenditures during the last thirty years of the nineteenth century. Here was certainly an ominous danger signal for the whole way of life of the liberal age.

The benefits of imperialism to national economies as a whole were perhaps questionable, when one considers the heavy, unproductive military and naval expenditures which were bound up with the maintenance of overseas empires. But the strength of imperialism can be understood only if one recognizes that certain individuals, classes and groups obviously derived wealth, employment and social prestige from

[3] Compare his very penetrating and well-documented "Imperialism," p. 29.

the process. John Stuart Mill once ironically characterized imperialism as a system of outdoor relief for the upper classes. The political and social influence of families with relatives in the army, the navy and the administrative bureaucracy, was no small factor in keeping up the system.

While the trading profits of imperialism were small, the investment profits were very substantial. Between 1884 and 1903 British income from foreign and colonial investments of a public and semipublic character practically doubled. As the French economist Paul Leroy-Beaulieu has pointed out, sums which would earn 2, 3 or 4 per cent in French railways and agricultural improvements would realize from 10 to 20 per cent when invested in undeveloped foreign countries. Imperialism, with its extension of foreign political control, often made it possible for the investor to have his cake and eat it too, to receive a high return, based on the idea of considerable risk, and to have this risk effectively neutralized by the presence of foreign troops and warships in the areas of investment.

As a result of this constant lure of higher profits abroad Frenchmen of property had placed fifty billion francs (then about ten billion dollars) in foreign countries by 1914. Great Britain, the richest investor, had sunk two billion pounds (about ten billion dollars) in British colonies and dependencies and almost an equal amount in other countries. German foreign investments were about twenty-eight billion marks (seven billion dollars).[4]

Another menacing force in the liberal age, the most fatal of all in its final effects, was unlimited nationalism. This was one of the fateful gifts to Europe of the French Revolution. Before this great upheaval the sense of nationality, especially in Central Europe, was not very strongly developed. It was no unusual thing for Germans, Magyars, Italians, Slavs, Flemings, to be subjects of a single prince. Great Britain and France had indeed evolved into compact national states. But

[4] Compare Parker T. Moon, "Imperialism and World Politics," p. 31.

Germany and Italy were divided into various principalities, which were sometimes at war with each other. Loyalty was often dynastic and religious, rather than national.

A passionate new sense of nationalism permeated the French masses at the time of the Revolution. It flamed out in the "Marseillaise." It carried the ragged, hungry soldiers of the revolutionary armies to victory after victory over the half-hearted forces of the old regimes which opposed them. As often happens, the French did not respect in others the principle which inspired themselves.

What had begun as a struggle of revolutionary defense against the onslaught of outraged reaction soon turned into a series of aggressive wars in parts of Europe to which France could lay no claim, on the basis of nationality. Many of these wars were little more than plundering expeditions in which the conquered regions were despoiled of everything, from money and food to art treasures.

It was just these wars of conquest that generated the spirit of intense German nationalism which was to recoil later on France with such terrible results when the balance of strength between the two countries shifted in Germany's favor. German national consciousness in the eighteenth century was at a very low ebb. French models were followed in literature and architecture. The first German prince and first soldier of the time, Frederick the Great, prided himself on his mediocre compositions in French and waited eagerly for the judgments of Voltaire.

It was out of the wars of liberation against Napoleon that a burning German national spirit emerged and found expression in the patriotic appeals of Fichte and the poems of Arndt and Koerner. And it was this newborn German nationalism that led finally to Sedan and to the union of the German states at Versailles.

It was not only in Germany that nationalism proved to be one of the dominant forces of the nineteenth century. The archconservative Prince Metternich, the Austrian statesman who played a leading role in the councils of Europe during the reaction against revolutionary ideas that followed the fall of Napoleon, recognized the explosive implications of the national idea and its special danger for a polyglot state like Austria–Hungary. But, with all his efforts, he could not dam the flood of national consciousness which swept into the most remote parts of Europe and inspired notable linguistic and literary revivals and more and more insistent demands for states organized on a basis of common language and nationality. The same national thought that was uppermost in the minds of such leaders of the Italian *Risorgimento* as Mazzini and Garibaldi inspired the revolt first of the Greeks, then of other Balkan peoples, against Turkish rule.

Side by side with the upsurge of German nationalism there was an awakening, political, racial and cultural, among the Slav peoples. Poland, divided between three great empires, proclaimed its will to freedom through the romantic poetry of Mickiewicz and the music of Chopin, both suffused with nationalist spirit. There was a similar Celtic renaissance in Ireland. Palacky and other scholars and men of letters revived the historical and literary traditions of Bohemia, which had been dormant since the crushing blow to Czech independence in the Thirty Years' War.

This awakening of nationalist consciousness was in many aspects in harmony with the spirit of the liberal age. It was part of the democratization of life, of the revolt against feudalism and absolute monarchy, of the common man's growing awareness of his part in the national community. In Italy and in the Balkans, especially, every generous and progressive spirit was instinctively enlisted in the movements against the cruel and obsolete Turkish despotism and the harsh, unsympathetic Austrian rule.

Yet nationalism was a principle both explosive and uncompromising. It was ill adapted to the spirit of "live and let live" that had to prevail if peoples in the many racially mixed areas of Central and Eastern Europe were to exist together on any tolerable basis. Like most crusading faiths, nationalism was most attractive when it was persecuted and not in power. The hunted nationalist, with the alien police on his trail, was often a hero. The same nationalist in power, when he had to deal with people not of his own race, was too often a persecutor himself.

Moreover, the spread of nationalism raised problems as fast as it solved them and created some issues which were scarcely capable of a peaceful compromise solution. The unification of Germany and of Italy was a natural process which caused no injustice to any other race. Alsace–Lorraine was a foreign enclave in the German Empire. But its annexation was a result of war, not of the union of the German states. And there was no racial minority of any consequence in united Italy.

But the principle of nationality, if carried to its logical extreme, demanded the breakup of Austria–Hungary, the further dismemberment of Turkey and a considerable diminution of the Russian Empire. There was small prospect that any of these ends could be achieved without war. The rigorous application of the nationality principle often conflicted with the requirements of economic well-being. The Austrian Empire, indefensible from the nationality standpoint unless organized on a federal basis, was an admirably well-balanced economic unit. The nationalism of minorities clashed with the nationalism of ruling majorities, each exasperating the other. An increase in conscious Russian nationalism under Alexander III led to an accentuation of unjust and discriminatory treatment of the Poles, Jews and other minorities; the Finns and Armenians had reason to complain of oppression under Nicholas II.

The conception of the sovereign national state was in contradiction with the growing cosmopolitanism of trade and finance. Perhaps the most important single cause of the catastrophe that finally overwhelmed European civilization was the failure to create, over and above the national loyalties of every people, a common conception of a European destiny, something in the nature of a European patriotism.

Along with such visible forces as imperialism, militarism, irreconcilable nationalism, there were more subtle spiritual and psychological factors that heralded and hastened the approaching end of the liberal age. The breathless speed, the constant change of a mechanical epoch, contained elements of brittleness and instability. If one contrasts the cathedrals and castles of the Middle Ages with the constantly altering means of communication and ways of life, as determined by new inventions, of the nineteenth century, one feels that the modern type of civilization, if more brilliant and many-sided, was less solid, likely to be more short-lived.

One can detect an element of rootlessness, the frequent precursor of the fall of a culture, in the thinking of the later phases of the liberal age. Every accepted moral idea, every established social and economic institution, was being critically dissected and called into question. Faith in an authoritative revealed religion had been undermined by scientific discoveries and research into Biblical history. But human reason proved unable to create a faith of equally wide appeal and binding validity.

The liberal creed, both in politics and in economics, bore the seeds of its own transformation, perhaps of its own disintegration. On the political side liberalism called for a steady widening of the franchise, culminating in universal manhood suffrage. This was bound to raise awkward questions as to how far the inequality of wealth which is inevitable in a society where private property is recognized could be reconciled with the equality of all citizens in making the laws.

Liberalism and democracy are by no means identical, even though the two words are often loosely used as synonymous. Liberalism placed the strongest emphasis on the rights of the individual. Its classical expression is to be found in John Stuart Mill's "Essay on Liberty," with its formula:

"The only freedom which deserves the name is that of pursuing our own good in our own way, so long as we do not attempt to deprive others of theirs, or impede their efforts to obtain it."

At first this right of the individual had to be vindicated mainly against tyrannical rulers and churches and was thus closely bound up with the struggle for political democracy and religious toleration. But when these goals were reached more complex problems arose. It was necessary to protect the individual, or the minority, against the tyranny of the majority. And there was always the danger that the majority itself might favor a dictatorship, especially under the stress of disorder, economic distress, or a temporary period of anarchical mob rule.

Contrary to the opinion of some superficial observers, fascism and communism do not belong in the same category with old-fashioned forms of undemocratic government, with absolute monarchy, aristocracy, oligarchy. They must rather be understood as demagogic perversions of the democratic idea. They are logical expressions of that "revolt of the masses" which Ortega y Gasset has perceived and analyzed with so much clarity and wit.

The typical nineteenth century liberal placed great faith in the saving virtue of education. But not all the contradictions of human inequality in intelligence, knowledge and wealth in a society based on equal suffrage were satisfactorily solved. The ideal democracy in which every citizen would possess an equal measure of intelligence, of public spirit, of information on questions of foreign and domestic policy, was very far from being realized, even in those Anglo–Saxon countries which proved best adapted to the working of a democratic political system.

Economic liberalism was also losing ground. That free play

of "natural" economic forces to which the Adam Smith school of economists attached so much value was being cramped by the growing power of organized capital and of organized labor. Free capitalism was giving way to what might have been described as bound capitalism, where the elasticity of wages, prices and profits was affected by trade unions, by monopolies, by tariffs. The middle class, which had been riding on the crest of the liberal wave, was to some extent being ground between the two millstones of great trusts on one side and powerful labor organizations on the other.

Yet these imperfections and new problems in themselves afforded no valid reason for despairing of liberal civilization. It possessed more adaptability than Marx's doctrinaire mind had foreseen. There were strains in the internal organization of society at the end of the liberal age, but these strains were not so serious as to portend the fall of civilization. This was to come about through another agency.

For over all the achievements of the liberal age, the relatively humane political and social institutions, the fruits of the culture that is often associated with leisure and tranquillity, the delicately balanced system of trade, production and exchange that made available on an unparalleled scale the products of the most remote parts of the world, there was always suspended a Sword of Damocles. This Sword was the coming of a great war, the scope and consequences of which almost none foresaw.

No civilization of which we know has escaped its cycle of rise, decline and fall. The maintenance of every civilization depends upon a very delicate balance between the extremes of stagnation and overrapid development. It is the destiny of some cultures to perish in the dry rot of a frozen political, social and economic order, where the creative faculties become atrophied. It is the destiny of others to go down in a turmoil of wars and social disturbances. It was this second fate that overtook the civilization of the liberal age.

Chapter Three

THE INFERNAL CYCLE BEGINS

ON THE SURFACE European civilization had achieved a substantial measure of unity in the first years of the present century. The increase in the world's wealth and the improvement
in means of communication had been most favorable to the
exchange of ideas as well as of goods. Scientific discoveries,
new books and musical compositions, new trends in artistic
style and philosophical thought, were quick to cross frontiers.
There were scores of international associations, based on such
common interests as science, scholarship, religion, social problems, business, exploration and sport, which frequently brought
together men and women of the various European countries.

Some of these associations were small and comparatively
unimportant. But others, like the International of Socialist
parties, counted its members in millions. The Interparliamen-
tary Union periodically provided a forum for spokesmen of
all the leading political parties. Yet, amid all this development
of international contacts, Europe, as events were to prove,
was no better safeguarded against war than it had been when
its primitive forests were inhabited by tribes of barbarians.

Of all the problems that called for solution if the relatively high moral, cultural and material level of existence was to continue, that of effective insurance against war was most completely neglected. There was no effective restraint whatever on the sovereign right of every strong state to make war whenever it might choose, although weak countries were occasionally cajoled or bullied into keeping the peace.

Minor wars between small nations and colonial wars of the great powers, however open to moral criticism, could take place without undermining the structure of European civilization. But to any farsighted observer in 1912 or 1913 a general European war, involving all the major powers, would have portended disaster for the common European cultural heritage, regardless of its issue. The growth of wealth and the tremendous advance of science, which improved the art of killing along with the industrial arts, increased enormously the prospective length and destructiveness of such a conflict.

It was only on the basis of a modern industrial and transportation system that huge conscript armies could be clothed, fed, armed and trained in peace and in war. The time had passed when war was an affair of volunteer and mercenary armies, fought out according to rules that were fairly generally observed and settled by the cession of a province or the payment of an indemnity by the defeated side, after which life would go on much as usual. The germs of that most horrible and suicidal conception "total war" were deeply implanted in the social and economic system of the early twentieth century.

There had been only one attempt to go beyond the resources of diplomacy in averting wars. Tsar Nicholas II of Russia in 1898 communicated to foreign powers a proposal for an international peace conference, declaring, with an unusual flash of insight: [1]

---

[1] Nicholas II was neither a humane nor a farsighted ruler. I have never seen a detailed analysis of how he came to conceive the idea, worthy of a greater personality and a stronger mind, of endeavoring to strengthen peace through international agreement.

"The economic crises, due in great part to the system of armaments, and the continual danger which lies in this massing of war material, are transforming the armed peace of our days into a crushing burden, which the peoples have more and more difficulty in bearing. It appears evident, then, that if this state of things were prolonged, it would inevitably lead to the very cataclysm which it is desired to avert, and the horrors of which make every thinking man shudder in advance."

The conference met in the following year and adopted a number of minor conciliatory measures. It set up a court of arbitration. It recommended mediation and the creation of commissions of inquiry to report on the factual questions involved in international disputes. It forbade "the launching of projectiles from balloons," an interesting historical note in 1941.

But when the Russian Colonel Gilinsky proposed a five-year stabilization of army establishments and of military and naval budgets there was a general refusal even to consider the suggestion. The little Boer Republic of the Transvaal, already threatened by British attack, was significantly not admitted to the Hague Conference to state its case. And the South African War commenced immediately after the conclusion of the conference.

Within its limited scope the Hague Court of Arbitration was a useful institution. But it judged only cases of minor importance which most probably would not have led to war in any event. The march of imperialism, as in the British conquest of the Boers or the Italian seizure of Tripoli, the fierce clash of hostile nationalisms, exemplified in the Balkan Wars, were not affected by the pleasant-sounding and well-intentioned resolutions of the two Hague conferences, the second being held in 1907.

Indeed the deeper and more irreconcilable causes of European conflict were scarcely susceptible to arbitration according to known judicial rules. Who could weigh fairly in the

balance the demand of the Austro–Hungarian Empire to
preserve its existence and the desire of Slavs and Italians
under Austrian rule to join their compatriots beyond the
border?

One reason why there was so little preparation *against* war,
as contrasted with the widespread preparation *for* war, was
the tendency, not restricted to any single nation, to glorify
war in the abstract as a school of manly virtue. Field Marshal
von Moltke, victorious leader of the Franco–Prussian War,
declared:

"Perpetual peace is a dream, and not even a beautiful dream.
War is one of the elements of order in the world, established
by God. The noblest virtues of man are developed therein.
Without war the world would degenerate and disappear in
a morass of materialism."

This is the viewpoint which one would expect in a Prussian
field marshal. But the distinguished French humanist and
intellectual Ernest Renan expressed a very similar train of
thought in his "La Reforme Intellectuelle et Morale":

"War is one of the conditions of progress, the sting which
prevents a country from going to sleep, and compels satisfied
mediocrity itself to awaken from its apathy. Man is only
sustained by effort and struggle. The day that humanity
achieves a great pacific Roman Empire, having no external
enemies, that day its morality and its intelligence will be
placed in the very greatest peril."

And Theodore Roosevelt once admonished his fellow
Americans, who had not experienced a thorough bloodletting
since the Civil War, in the following terms:

"We must play a great part in the world, and especially
. . . perform those deeds of blood, of valor which above everything else bring national renown. . . . By war alone can we
acquire those virile qualities necessary to win in the stern
strife of actual life. . . . In this world the nation that is trained
to a career of unwarlike and isolated ease is bound to go down

in the end before other nations which have not lost the manly and adventurous qualities."

More general, probably, than this attitude of positive praise of war was the tendency to accept it passively, fatalistically. There always had been wars; there always would be wars. Almost every European of military age was part of a war machine as officer or private. He had no means of controlling the forces that would set this machine in motion.

Even in England, classical land of liberalism, where sea power served as a substitute for conscription and where there was probably more theoretical pacifism than in any of the larger continental countries, democratic control had made the least progress in the field of foreign affairs. Parliamentary debates on foreign affairs were usually perfunctory and attracted a scanty attendance. Very few members of Parliament and a negligible number of British voters, even of the educated classes, understood the ramifications of Balkan racial feuds and the interwoven threads of Russian and Austrian intrigue in that troubled part of Europe or the background of the repeated Franco–German crises over the Moroccan question. Yet here were the sparks that might set off an explosion at any time.

A mistaken view of which Mr. (later Sir) Norman Angell was the principal sponsor was that war would not occur because it was irrational and because it would be unprofitable to the victor. On a basis of mid-Victorian ethics and economics Mr. Angell could and did make out a pretty good case for this theory in his book "The Great Illusion." But there were two grave miscalculations in his reasoning. The first was that he underestimated the irrational impulses that make for war, racial and national hatreds, considerations of so-called national prestige, lust for domination, sheer boredom with peaceful and orderly life. The second was that a conquering nation in time of war would observe the nice respect for private property that was enforced by law and custom under conditions of peace. The following citations from "The Great Illusion" sound like echoes from a far-off world:

"In our day the exaction of tribute from a conquered people has become an economic impossibility."

"If Germany conquered Holland German merchants would still have to meet the competition of Dutch merchants, and on keener terms than originally, because the Dutch merchants would then be within the German customs lines."

"Every financier in Europe knows that if Germany conquered Holland or Belgium to-morrow she would have to leave their wealth untouched; there could be no confiscation."

Along with the illusion that capitalist self-interest would prevent war there was the parallel illusion that the solidarity of the working class would achieve the same end. The growth of Socialist parties in the period before the beginning of the World War had been impressive. The Socialist vote in the German Reichstag election of 1912 had passed the figure of four millions. The German Social Democratic party mustered a million members and published ninety newspapers. Just because it was the typical land of late capitalism Germany was the country where socialism had won the largest number of professed followers. There had also been a pronounced growth of this movement in France, Italy and the smaller European countries. The British Labor party, while it was not doctrinaire in its adherence to Marxism, was broadly socialist in outlook. Most Russian revolutionaries and non-Russian nationalist rebels in the Russian Empire and in the Balkans considered themselves socialists of one kind or another.

The Stuttgart Congress of the Socialist International, held in 1907, passed a resolution to the effect that should the concerted efforts of the workers fail to prevent war "their duty is to intervene to bring it promptly to an end, and with all their energies to use the economic and political crisis created by war to rouse the populace from its slumbers and to hasten the fall of capitalist domination."

But only such extremists in the international socialist movement as Lenin, Rosa Luxemburg and Radek took these strong words at their face value. When the war crisis arose the international solidarity of labor proved to be a myth. Workers, members of Socialist parties, in the belligerent countries received and obeyed their mobilization orders like other citizens. For, although the nation-state had not become the formidable leviathan of our own time, it enjoyed vastly more power and authority than any force, whether of capital or of labor, that had grown up within its frontiers.

The anarchy of a European system under which nation-states were free to pursue their ambitions by all means, including war, without any international restraint, was the most obvious cause of the fall of liberal civilization. This fall was historically premature. The civilization of Europe in 1913 was neither decadent nor stagnant. Its creative and productive possibilities were still very great, as evidenced by its achievements in thought, in artistic creation, in science and invention and exploration. But collective intelligence and good will had failed to meet the apparently insuperable problem of imposing limitation on what was regarded as something absolute and untouchable, the unrestrained sovereignty of the national state. The penalty, when it was exacted, was a terrible one.

What maintained a semblance of order in the midst of the international anarchy was the system known as the balance of power. The great powers displayed a tendency to protect their interests by forming groupings and sometimes hard-and-fast alliances which served as checks and balances on each other. When there was a threat of war between small nations the Concert of the six Great Powers, Germany, Austria–Hungary, Russia, France, Great Britain and Italy, was sometimes able to check the threatened hostilities. When war actually occurred the Great Powers followed developments, keeping a suspicious eye on each other, and contrived at the end to effect some arrangement which would not seriously impair the existing balance of competitive national strength.

The avoidance of a general European war during the century which elapsed between Waterloo and Sarajevo was facilitated because Napoleon had no successor. His dream of uniting Europe under a single rule had failed so completely and proved so costly and so futile in retrospect that no soldier or statesman chose to repeat the attempt. There was certainly no question of maintaining in Europe the kind of frozen *status quo* of which Metternich dreamed. The map of Europe which was drawn up at the Congress of Vienna was changed beyond recognition. But such important events as the unification of Germany and Italy and the emergence of new states in the Balkans took place not, certainly, without bloodshed but without plunging the entire continent into war.

Points of friction between the Great Powers multiplied during the last predominantly peaceful generation that Europe was to know, the one between the Franco–Prussian War and the World War. The groupings of Great Powers, hitherto rather loose and shifting, were showing a tendency to harden into rigid alliances, which made compromise and retreat increasingly difficult in moments of serious international crisis. This system of hostile alliances, the German–Austrian against the Franco–Russian, with England on the outer fringe of the latter, began to contain the automatic destructive possibilities of a time bomb.

For some twenty years after the Franco–Prussian War, Germany was clearly predominant on the continent. The newly united Germany steadily outstripped its secular enemy, France, in population and in the pace of industrial development. Moreover, Bismarck assured his rear in the East by the policy of friendship with Russia which was reflected in the *Dreikaiserbund*, the alliance of the three conservative monarchical powers, Germany, Austria and Russia, which was concluded in 1873.

This alliance possessed an ideological cement, since the three sovereigns felt a common interest in resisting the rising tide of republicanism and socialism. So long as it stood it was a pretty solid guaranty of maintenance of the peace on the European continent along the lines desired by the three partners.

But it was not easy for Germany to maintain friendship simultaneously with Russia and with Austria. For the interests of those two powers came into conflict in the turbulent Balkans. The Pan–Slav tendency in Russia to regard all the Balkan Slavs as natural wards of Russia could not be reconciled with Austrian political ambitions in Southeastern Europe and with Austrian nervousness about the disintegrating effect of Pan–Slav propaganda on its own Slav subjects. A further difficulty arose later when Germany began to regard the Balkans and the Turkish Empire as natural fields of commercial expansion and investment of surplus capital—a sort of compensation for the lack of a rich colonial empire.

Because Austria–Hungary was mainly a German state, so far as its ruling class was concerned, Bismarck was obliged to treat it as the preferred ally. He concluded a separate alliance with Austria in 1879. But he was able to keep Russia out of any anti-German combination of powers by means of the Treaty of Reinsurance which was concluded between the three empires in 1881. This was a genuine achievement of secret diplomacy. Its existence became known only when the Soviet regime in Russia published the contents of the archives of the old regime.

Soon after the impulsive young Kaiser Wilhelm II ousted Bismarck as Chancellor he dropped the Treaty of Reinsurance. This helped to make possible the beginning of an encirclement of Germany which Bismarck had always feared and had pretty successfully counteracted. A military convention between Russia and France in 1892 developed into the Franco–Russian Alliance of 1894. Here was an extraordinary mating of the most reactionary with the most radical of the

Great Powers. Its irony was emphasized when Tsar Alexander
III, most uncompromising of autocrats, saluted the playing
of the "Marseillaise" when French warships visited the Russian port of Kronstadt. The "Marseillaise" was and remained a
melody strictly forbidden to the Tsar's subjects.

But it is a familiar historical experience that national interests, real or supposed, usually take precedence over more
sentimental considerations. At a time when men and women
were tortured, burned, hanged, imprisoned, exiled and otherwise persecuted for differences of religious faith it was no
unusual thing for Protestant and Catholic states and rulers to
form temporary alliances for the attainment of mutual political advantages.

Located in far-removed parts of Europe, Russia and France
had no important conflicting interests. To Russia the alliance
seemed to offer a counterpoise in the West to the German–
Austrian *Drang nach Osten.* To France the "Russian steam-
roller," as it was often but inaccurately called, seemed to be
at once a guaranty against German attack and a possible aid
in the recovery of Alsace–Lorraine.

There was also an economic background for the alliance.
Alexander III alienated the German agrarian interests by forbidding German purchases of land in the Russian western
provinces. In reprisal there was a boycott of Russian securities
on the Berlin bourse. Great Britain was cool toward Russia
politically and showed no disposition to open its financial
markets for Russia's benefit. So it was to France that Russia
turned for money. The savings of the French bourgeoisie
poured into the military and industrial development of the
vast Slav empire.

French Socialists and radicals often protested against the
Russian alliance both on moral and on economic grounds. It
was against the French liberal tradition, it was argued, to support a cruel and oppressive despotism. The soundness of Russia's finances was sometimes questioned, although criticism of

this kind was usually silenced by a more generous distribution of Russian funds to the proverbially venal French press.

There were old-fashioned Russian conservatives who distrusted and disliked mercurial revolutionary France and longed for the stability of the *Dreikaiserbund*. But the alliance successfully resisted the attacks of its critics in both countries.

The Franco–Russian Alliance destroyed Germany's unquestioned predominance in military power on the continent. The acquisition of Italy as an ultimately unreliable partner in the Triple Alliance was no compensation for the loss of Bismarck's cherished Russian connection.

Germany's position on the complex European political chessboard became still less favorable in the first years of the new century. Great Britain, hitherto aloof and independent in relation to continental combinations, began to swing more and more in the orbit of Germany's enemies. The personal antipathy between Kaiser Wilhelm II and his uncle, King Edward VII, helped to alienate the two countries. But a more fundamental cause was Germany's emergence as a formidable trade rival and as a threat to British maritime supremacy. As late as the end of the nineteenth century Joseph Chamberlain was advocating an Anglo–German alliance. But soon the traditional British opposition to the strongest single power on the continent began to direct itself, with unerring instinct, against Germany.

Two steps toward the inclusion of Great Britain in the anti-German combination were the *Entente Cordiale* with France in 1904 and the understanding with Russia in 1907. An important element in the *Entente Cordiale* was French recognition of the British dominant position in Egypt in return for British acknowledgment of French hegemony in Morocco.

The understanding with Russia was harder to bring about than the entente with France. Two of the chief aims of British foreign policy during the nineteenth century had been to check Russian designs on Constantinople and to safeguard India against the threat represented by the Russian advance in Central Asia. England had fought one war against Russia and several others had been narrowly averted.

But after Great Britain's new Oriental ally, Japan, had pushed back the Russian advance in the Far East in the war of 1904–05 there was a marked change for the better in Anglo–Russian relations. This found expression in the agreement between the two powers as to spheres of influence in Turkey, Persia and China in 1907.

Just as minor shocks usually precede a great earthquake, several minor wars emphasized the tension in international relations on the eve of the World War. There were no less than five wars between 1900 and 1914, the South African, the Russo–Japanese, the Italo–Turkish and the Balkan conflicts of 1912 and 1913. During the same period there were repeated international crises, centering around Morocco, where Germany unsuccessfully challenged French domination, and the Balkans.

One such crisis occurred when Austria annexed the Slav provinces of Bosnia and Herzegovina, over which it had formerly exercised a protectorate, in 1908. This offended Serbia, which considered itself the future center of a great South Slav state. There was considerable sympathy for Serbia in Russia. But Germany announced its intention to stand by its ally, Austria, and Russia, still weakened by the war with Japan, felt obliged to yield.

The Balkan Wars of 1912 and 1913 kept Europe in a state of constant alarm, because of the conflict of Russian and Austrian interests in that peninsula. Both these wars turned out unfavorably from the standpoint of the Central Powers. In the first one Turkey, where Germany possessed both political influence and economic investments, was severely defeated and compelled to give up most of its remaining territory in Europe. Serbia and Greece defeated Bulgaria in the second Balkan War, a result which was also distasteful to German and Austrian diplomacy.

The armament race which had been such a marked feature of the last quarter of the nineteenth century went on at an accelerated pace. Russia increased its peacetime army. France lengthened the term of compulsory military service from two to three years. Germany increased its army while the French proposal for longer service was still being considered by the Chamber of Deputies. All attempts to reach a naval building limitation agreement between Great Britain and Germany failed.

With the stage thus set for catastrophe, the inevitable spark to ignite the explosion was not long lacking. On June 28, 1914, the Bosnian student Gavril Prinzip killed the heir to the Austrian throne, Archduke Franz Ferdinand, and his wife while they were driving through the narrow streets of Sarajevo, capital of the recently annexed province of Bosnia. History cast a long shadow over the crime. It took place on Vidov-dan, the anniversary of the battle with the Turks at Kosovo which extinguished the medieval empire of the Serbs. The date was perhaps calculated to inflame the racial fanaticism of Prinzip, who, like many of the South Slav students of the Austrian Empire, hoped to see the breakup of the empire and the unification of his people with their kinsmen in Serbia.

In character Prinzip's act was a political murder like many others. In consequences it was one of the most fateful assassinations in history. Eight and a half million men lost their lives as a result of the tragic sequence of events let loose by the shots fired by a tubercular psychopathic young nationalist enthusiast.

There was symbolism in the fact that the Sarajevo murder was committed under the influence of the nationalism that was one of the basic forces of the nineteenth century. The participants in the conspiracy, of whom there were a number,

although Prinzip alone fired the shots, were Bosnians who
had been in contact with terrorist organizations in Belgrade.
The Sarajevo assassinations followed other terrorist acts in
Austrian territory which had been inspired by the *Narodna
Obrana* and other Serb nationalist societies.

The issues which were pushed into the foreground by the
shots at Sarajevo might well have baffled the sense of justice
of the most impartial tribunal. It was natural and inevitable
that the sense of racial solidarity which had led to the unification of the Germans and the Italians should also make itself
felt among the southern Slavs. It was equally natural and inevitable that the Austrian Government should have resented
a campaign of propaganda, terrorism and disintegration that
was being encouraged and to some extent directed from
Serbian territory.

Had the issue been left to Austria and Serbia it would have
been settled, temporarily at least, by the crushing of the smaller
and weaker country. But the European order had become
so delicately poised that even a small stone could not be dis-
lodged without precipitating an avalanche. Russia was unwilling to accept the humiliation and subjugation of Serbia.
Germany felt obligated to support Austria. France was bound
by its alliance with Russia. So the revolver shots of the obscure
young Bosnian whom fate had selected as the unconscious
gravedigger of European liberal civilization were soon transformed and magnified into the roar of cannon on the battlefields all over Europe.

The material on the controversial question of war responsibility would fill a large library. To discuss minute points of
evidence, to apportion precise degrees of responsibility, would
lie beyond the scope of the present work. There is, however,
an abundance of evidence to prove that no power had planned
the war in advance, or desired it. The German Chancellor,
Von Bethmann-Hollweg, said after the Sarajevo tragedy, "Of
course we shall quietly look on." When the German Secretary

of the Interior, Delbrueck, proposed to buy grain in Rotterdam, in July, both Bethmann-Hollweg and the Foreign Secretary, Von Jagow, opposed the idea as unnecessary and likely to cause alarm.

If there is no convincing evidence of premeditation in the case of Germany there is equally little in the case of the other Great Powers. Tsar Nicholas hesitated over signing the order for general mobilization as if he foresaw the cellar in Ekaterinburg where he and his family would be slaughtered after the Revolution.

"Think of the responsibility you are advising me to take," he cried out to his counselors. "Think of the thousands and thousands of men who will be sent to their death."

But the demands of high policy prevailed. The Russian mobilization was the reply to the Austrian invasion of Serbia. It was also the signal for the German mobilization, after which the subsequent declarations of war were little more than a formality. On August 1, 1914, a black day for all the values of European liberal civilization, the nightmare of a general war which had haunted the dreams of every farsighted statesman became a reality.

Before the conflict was ended thirty nations, including all the Great Powers, would have been drawn in. Eight and a half million men would have been killed, twenty-nine million wounded, captured or missing. There would be scarcely a family in Europe, apart from the few small neutral states, which had not lost at least one member. Hunger, disease and social revolution would complete the work of destruction begun by the war. Its direct financial cost has been estimated at 200,000,000,000 dollars, its indirect cost at 150,000,000,000. Behind these figures, so huge as to be almost meaningless, lies an almost inestimable amount of individual suffering and impoverishment, the result of direct war damage, blockade, inflation and confiscation.

One of the invisible casualties of the war was the liberal

spirit of reason, tolerance and humanity. Brutal and irrational itself, the war imposed a brutal and irrational stamp upon the revolutions which stemmed from it and upon the regimes which emerged from these revolutions. It is not psychologically surprising that the Russian worker or the Russian peasant, accustomed to mass slaughter, should sometimes have become a murderous Chekist or a participant in the wholesale killing of "bourgeoisie," of Jews, of any unpopular racial or social group against which he might be incited after the breakdown of the autocracy. It is understandable if the bitterness of defeat and the physical and mental consequences of the hunger which became acute in Germany during the last year of the war should have produced an unusual proportion of frustrated, embittered, abnormal, types, the natural leaders of the National Socialist storm detachments. Fascism in Italy would also scarcely have been possible without the sufferings of the war and the disillusionments of the postwar period.

Viewed in sober retrospect the World War of 1914–18 must be considered one of the greatest and most unmitigated calamities that ever befell the human race. The evil that it wrought was not exhausted or expiated by the marked and unmarked graves of the flower of the European youth who perished at Verdun and the other contests in mass slaughter. That evil, unexorcized and growing ever more powerful, went marching on through a series of social upheavals that, taken together, constitute a revolt against civilization, to find its terrible culmination in a second world war.

War was the Achilles' heel of European liberal civilization. In contrast to labor and social problems, where considerable progress had been achieved and the threat of social revolution and civil war had diminished, nothing had been done to abate the constant war menace. If Prinzip's bullets had gone astray there would soon, most probably, have been some other occasion for a crisis, leading up to the same fatal climax. For the causes of national friction were numerous and deep; effective machinery for dealing with these causes was nonexistent. The international anarchy must have ultimately borne its bitter fruits.

There was a general disposition at first in all the warring countries to underestimate the length of the struggle. It was not realized that the opposing forces were fairly evenly balanced and that the technique of war, as between countries of comparable military and industrial power, favored the static deadlock of trench warfare. There was also some survival of the delusion that it would be impossible to "pay" for a long war. This misconception overlooked the elasticity of the currency and credit system, the willingness of governments to resort to inflationary methods and the bedrock fact that purely financial difficulties have never meant defeat to a people with its heart in a war, so long as there were still men to be mobilized and food and raw materials to be rationed.

The amount of paper currency in circulation in the thirty principal countries of the world increased from seven to forty billion dollars during the four years of the war and there was also a gigantic credit inflation as a result of the lavish issues of war bonds. At the beginning of the conflict the governments, still under the influence of the liberal tradition, scarcely recognized their own powers. There were delays in the adoption of such measures as rationing and the control of prices and foreign exchange. Consequently prices rose steeply and stocks of foodstuffs ran lower than would otherwise have been necessary during the last years of the war.

All illusions of international solidarity vanished before the test of national war. The Socialist parties in the belligerent countries accepted the theory that the war was defensive and voted for the required credits. Individuals and groups opposed the war. But there was no mass resistance, no large-scale refusal to fight or to turn out munitions. The attitude of the

German Social Democrats was accurately summed up by an antiwar member of the party as follows: [2]

"The sacrifices imposed by the war were indeed borne with astonishing stoicism, but for the heroism of resistance to the war madness the necessary courage was lacking."

Passive acceptance of the war was probably the characteristic mood of the Socialist workers. Enthusiasm was more prevalent among the middle classes and the intellectuals. But a number of more or less prominent Social Democrats wholeheartedly accepted the war with expansionist aims. Paul Lensch, editor of a Social Democratic newspaper, declared that Germany was completing its revolution in the war. Germany, according to Lensch, represented a more progressive social principle than England, where the working class was backward and individualistic. Another Social Democrat intellectual, Konrad Haenisch, saw in the prospect of an Allied success "the victory of obsolete forms of capitalism over the most modern forms, of proletarian backwardness over proletarian socialism."

Early in 1916, when the military map was favorable to Germany, there was a conference of German and Austrian Social Democrat and trade union leaders in Berlin. The Austrian Social Democrat Karl Renner advocated Naumann's idea of a united Central European economic bloc, including the Balkans and Turkey. The German Social Democrat Emil Barth suggested that the Netherlands, Switzerland and the Scandinavian countries should be included in this bloc.

These expansionist ideas of German and Austrian Social Democrats are interesting for two reasons. They indicate how quickly antiwar ideals evaporate in the intoxication of victory. And it is ironical that these men, some of whom have probably been victims of Hitler's terror, should have anticipated Hitler's idea of a Europe economically and politically unified under German hegemony. Even within the old Social Democ-

---

[2] Compare Heinrich Stroebel, "The German Revolution and After," pp. 14, 15.

racy of Germany there were ideological germs of national socialism.

In the other belligerent countries there was also a marked tendency of former militant apostles of class war to become ardent supporters of the national cause. Indeed it was not infrequently those Socialists or syndicalists who had been formerly most violent in their expressions of desire to sweep away the capitalist system, by force if necessary, men like Gustave Hervè in France, H. M. Hyndman in England, Benito Mussolini in Italy, who became advocates of war to the utmost. Socialists of more moderate views, Ramsay MacDonald in England, Jean Longuet (the son-in-law of Karl Marx) in France, Filippo Turati in Italy, were more inclined to assume a negative or at least a critical attitude toward the war.

Psychologically this is quite understandable. War and violent revolution are emotional phenomena of very similar character and appeal. They evoke the same passions of fanaticism, of exaltation bordering on frenzy, of ferocious intolerance, of dogmatic assumption that a millennium at the end will justify all the immediate sufferings and hardships. The type of mind that is attracted by the idea of violent revolution is also likely to favor the short cut of war.

Soldiers, like statesmen, failed to anticipate accurately the character of the war. The issue of previous conflicts had usually been decided by pitched battles, by the number of men brought into the field and the skill of the generals in maneuvering. All these elements were reduced to a minimum on the Western Front, where armies of approximately equal training, skill and technical equipment became locked in an embrace of death, a gigantic deadlock from the Swiss frontier to the Channel.

After the first swift rush of the Germans across Belgium and into France had been checked at the Marne the war on the primary Western Front became a grim struggle of attrition, of exhaustion of man power and resources. There was none of the exhilaration that was associated with the swift movements, the decisive battles, of other wars.

In the race between offense and defense, which is as old as history, defense had obtained a clear margin of superiority in this most gigantic of all wars. The machine gun, combined with the system of deep trenches, strengthened by barbed wire, made frontal attack a costly and usually unsuccessful experiment which at best would bog down in blood-soaked mud after a microscopic gain of territory.

Of the new weapons which were later to turn the balance in favor of the offensive, the airplane was in its infancy and was more useful for reconnaissance than for destruction. The surprise value of the first use of tanks was offset by the failure of the British command to make proper provision for following up the original break-through. While the progress of medical science made it possible to reduce the incidence of disease and of death from wounds the terrific increase in the volume of artillery bombardment and the new use of gas as a weapon created new and terrible forms of casualties, listed under such headings as "Shell-shocked" and "Gassed."

So over a period of four years the younger men of three of Europe's largest and most civilized countries continued to slaughter each other on the fields of France and Flanders. Few civilizations have prepared for themselves such a terrible end.

In the other campaigns the vast superiority of the German war machine led to sweeping victories and large conquests of territory. The Russian armies, although they fought for a time with traditional stoical courage and won some important successes against the Austrians, were overwhelmed when the Germans began to launch great drives, with immense artillery preparation, on the Eastern Front. In the summer of 1915 alone half a million Russians were killed; a million were wounded; another million were captured. Serbia and Rumania were overrun. After the complete Russian collapse in 1917

German troops penetrated as far to the east as the Caucasus and as far to the north as Finland.

But these land victories over militarily and industrially weaker enemies were not decisive so long as the line held in the West and so long as Great Britain, controlling the seas, was able to apply the slow strangulation of the blockade. The use of a formidable new naval weapon, the submarine, gave Germany an opportunity to play havoc with Allied shipping. The submarine warfare was especially successful in the first months of 1917. In April, the black month of the submarine war for Great Britain, almost one million tons of Allied shipping were sunk. One ship out of every four leaving the British Isles failed to return. Food was short in England and rationing was introduced.

But Germany's submarine offensive was more than counterbalanced by the entrance of the United States into the war. The submarine campaign depended for effectiveness on its "total" character, on the sinking not only of belligerent but of neutral shipping approaching the British Isles. America had refused to admit this right of unlimited submarine warfare. Germany's announcement of the new policy led to a breach of diplomatic relations. Subsequent sinkings, together with the interception of an uncommonly stupid German proposal to Mexico to attack the United States, brought about America's declaration of war on April 6, 1917.

The vast resources of the United States, now placed unreservedly at the disposal of the Allies, and the large numbers of American troops which poured into France represented the decisive new force which broke what might otherwise have been a deadlock of indefinite duration. Germany's last gamble for victory, the four great offensives which Ludendorff hurled against the Allies in the spring of 1918, bent the lines, won territory and prisoners, but failed to achieve decisive success. The increase in the number of American troops in France from three hundred thousand in March to two million in November and the prospect of unlimited further reinforcements helped greatly to break German morale. As a German army report says in regard to the American soldier:

"Fresh, well fed and with strong nerves that had known no strain, he advanced against the German Army, which was exhausted by the unprecedented efforts of four years of war. In this and in the great numerical reinforcements which the Americans brought to our opponents at the decisive moment lies the importance of American intervention."

The first response of all the European peoples to the call to arms was calculated to discourage pacifists and to convey the impression that war is popular with the masses. Enthusiasm was general. Crowds in Berlin, Paris, London and St. Petersburg celebrated with equal heartiness. Adolf Hitler was not the only frustrated, maladjusted young German who found the day of the outbreak of the war the happiest in his life. The French syndicalists and extreme Socialists, deniers of "la patrie," advocates of no war but the class war, seemed to vanish overnight.

England, deeply torn by internal dissension about the thorny question of Ireland, closed ranks as soon as the war began. National unity in Russia had been undermined by revolutionary political struggle and by the grievances of the non-Russian minorities. But there was an ecstasy of demonstrative loyalty when the war began. Representatives of opposition groups in the Duma vied with each other in pledges of devotion. Veteran Socialists and anarchists like Kropotkin, Breshkovskaya, Tschaikovsky, Plekhanov, sympathizing with the more liberal systems of Great Britain and France, announced their support of the war.

Even in racially composite Austria, where patriotism was certainly at a discount except among the Germans and the Magyars, there was some genuineness in the cheers and celebrations that accompanied the outbreak of the war. Trotsky describes a scene which he personally observed in Vienna: the enthusiasm of a poor Czech apprentice at the beginning of the war. For this apprentice, as for many others, the war was something exciting and exhilarating, a break in the drab monotony of everyday life.

The peoples of Europe entered the great mass slaughter fresh. Not many of the conscripts, except in the Balkan countries, had taken part in actual fighting. The value of money was taken for granted; few people even conceived the possibility of inflation. It was also assumed that the regular supply of food and clothing would go on, in war as in peace. Every people cherished the illusion of a quick victory, to be won with slight sacrifices.

But as the years passed with no abatement of the struggle, as the casualty lists continued to mount and the rations became steadily shorter, the war turned into a supreme test of the collective national endurance of the participants. In such a contest it was the weaker political, economic and social organisms that had to go to the wall.

Russia was the first to collapse in this gigantic ordeal by fire. And this should have been no surprise to those who knew the clay feet of the Tsarist Colossus. Russia might have been called either the most backward of European Great Powers or the most advanced of Asiatic Great Powers. With its high percentage of illiteracy, its poor communications, its limited industrial development, it was predestined to defeat in war with a major military power like Germany. Defeat, as is frequently the case, meant revolution. And what began as the substitution for the autocracy of a liberal democratic government was soon transformed, again under the pressure of the intolerable strain of the war, into a social catastrophe of unprecedented depth and violence—the first act in the revolt against European civilization.

Italy at the time of its great defeat at Caporetto seemed to totter on the brink of a similar collapse. Italy's entrance into

the war was slower and less unavoidable than that of the powers which were drawn in during the first days of the crisis. It
remained aloof from the conflict for almost a year, while the
government was bargaining over the price of intervention.
Consequently there had been a chance for antiwar sentiment
to develop and crystallize. Such sentiment was especially strong
at the two social extremes: among the Socialists, who opposed
the war on orthodox Marxian grounds, and among the cleri-
cals, who disliked the association with freethinking France.
Morale was lower in Italy from the beginning than it was in
those countries where the governments could represent war
as the only alternative to hostile invasion. Moreover, Italy was
one of the poorest European countries in natural resources
and accumulated wealth. Morally and physically it was one of
the least able to withstand the strain of a prolonged conflict.

France had its dark moments in the spring of 1917, when
many regiments, sickened by the terrific wastage of lives in
futile offensives, left the front and started home on self-granted
leaves. It required a judicious mixture of shooting of ringlead-
ers and conciliatory measures toward the rank-and-file soldiers
to bring the French Army into order again. From that time on
the French commanders showed a tendency to be economical
with the lives of their men.

The French had not lost the soldierly qualities of their an-
cestors who fought in the armies of Louis XIV and Napoleon.
Their stand at Verdun was an epic of heroism. But they entered the war under two cruel disadvantages. The German
Army was better armed, better equipped and generally better
prepared—the result of the German genius for minute organization and of German industrial superiority. And there were
already more than three Germans to every two Frenchmen.
Had it not been for the increasing help with troops first of
Great Britain, later of America, France would have suffered
the disaster of 1940 at some time between 1914 and 1918.

Out of the carnage two nations emerged as clearly the

strongest in Europe, the predestined major combatants of the next war. These were Great Britain and Germany. England was forced to go far beyond the limits of its usual policy of waging war by means of sea power, money and small expeditionary forces. It placed vast armies in the fields of France and Flanders. On the sea it found in the submarine a more formidable challenge than Napoleon could ever offer. The British people met all these crises and endured with grim tenacity until victory was finally won.

Equally remarkable was the German achievement. With little help from Austria (often a military liability, rather than an asset) and still less from Turkey and Bulgaria, the Germans by the end of the war were fighting the armies, the industries and the food production of the whole world. Germany of course enjoyed some conspicuous advantages: unity of command, a central position, a high degree of military and industrial preparedness. Moreover, its enemies entered the war at various times. Still, after making all proper allowances and reservations, the German showing in the war, military, economic and moral, was remarkable. It recalled the days when Frederick the Great, with his comparatively small Prussian state, fought off the armies of Russia, Austria and France.

No one consciously planned or desired this greatest of all wars. And it could be pretty accurately described as the war which nobody won. The former governing systems of Russia, Germany and Austria collapsed during or after the end of the struggle. Italy was to experience its revolution and Germany was to go through the fundamental change which it missed in 1918 with the accession to power of the National Socialists in 1933. France won a reprieve from national disaster of less than a generation. And what is to come out of England's present ordeal cannot now be foreseen.

The true victors of the World War were not Wilson, Lloyd George and Clemenceau, the "Big Three" who wrote on shifting sands the forcible-feeble settlement of Versailles. These

victors were three other men, of whom one was entirely unknown in 1914, while the others were familiar names only in
small revolutionary circles.

At the commencement of the war Vladimir Ilyitch Lenin,
leader of an obscure revolutionary sect which few Russians
could have correctly identified, was living in exile in Austria.
As an enemy alien he could not remain there and he moved to
Switzerland, where he lived in great poverty, writing fierce
appeals to the workers to "turn the imperialist war into civil
war," which only a handful of people read. Then came the
breakdown of the autocracy; within eight months the obscure
exile was the victorious leader of a Russian revolution, which,
as he hoped and believed, would be only the prelude to a
world revolution of the proletariat.

Before the war Benito Mussolini acquired some notoriety as
an extremist leader among the Italian Socialists. Soon after the
outbreak of the war he broke with his party on the issue of
Italian intervention, which he advocated. He enlisted as a soldier and by the end of the war had built up a mixed, still small
personal following of nationalists, ex-Socialists, syndicalists,
lovers of direct action.

Of the three Adolf Hitler was the most obscure, the least
marked out for his subsequent amazing leap to world power.
An Austrian, he had volunteered for service in the German
Army because he passionately hated the easygoing, pleasure-
loving, cosmopolitan Vienna where he had been poor, friend-
less and unsuccessful. After a war record similar to that of
millions of other German soldiers he was lying gassed in a hospital and wept tears of bitter rage and grief when he learned
of the defeat.

These three men, the Russian revolutionary whose father
had been a provincial school inspector, the Italian blacksmith's
son, the Austrian housepainter who liked to talk and argue,
were to be the leaders of Europe's revolt against civilization.
Not one of them possessed advantages of birth or wealth. The

path for all of them was cleared by a war that was one of the most effective revolutionary agencies in history.

All the dreams that the war might be an agency of reconstruction, a means of ending war or making the world safe for democracy, were, I believe, foredoomed to frustration, even apart from the mistakes of individual statesmen and governments. A catastrophe of such proportions, with all that it meant in human suffering and psychological derangement, was certain to prove fatal to the liberal age. Vain were all the hopes of return to some form of equilibrium and stability.

Brutal and irrational in character, the First World War imposed a brutal and irrational stamp upon social changes which might have otherwise come about in a peaceful and orderly way. It ushered in a period of ever widening violence, an era of unreason to replace the predominantly rationalist age of the eighteenth and nineteenth centuries.

The World War of 1914–18 was not, like many lesser conflicts, an isolated event, bringing gain to some countries and loss to others and affecting only in slight degree the general trend of culture and civilization. It was both an end and a beginning. It was the end of liberal civilization. It was the beginning of an infernal cycle of wars and revolutions and counterrevolutions, of infectious and ever spreading violence and hatred and fear, of a descending spiral of humanity.

The golden age of European civilization passed with the World War. An iron age set in and gradually tightened its grip on every part of the world.

Chapter Four

THE RUSSIAN REVOLT AGAINST
CIVILIZATION

EUROPEAN CIVILIZATION cracked first in its weakest link, in Russia. In this vast Eurasian empire, so long the rear guard of European civilization, to quote the phrase of the great Russian historian Kluchevsky, the sun of Western liberalism had been reflected in a very pale and uncertain glow. The shield of Europe against Turks and Tartars, Russia, in fighting these Asiatic peoples, acquired some of their characteristics: ruthlessness, contempt for the individual, inability to conceive the state except as an engine of unlimited despotism. Shut off and isolated from the main currents of European thought, Russia almost completely missed the influence of those three European movements which promoted most strongly the sense of an individual human personality: the Reformation, the Renaissance and the French Revolution.

Until the nineteenth century Russian civilization, except in the fields of religious faith and religious art, could scarcely be said to exist. A thin veneer of imitative Western culture, mostly borrowed from France and Germany, had reached a small upper class of nobles and state officials. The general structure of society was Asiatic. The social pyramid was erected on a

76

base of peasant serfs who constituted the majority of the population.

The wild sanguinary uprisings of such Robin Hood peasant leaders as Stenka Razin in the seventeenth century and Emilian Pugachev in the eighteenth had ended in defeat. Weak and primitive and corrupt as the apparatus of the Russian state was, it could still crush rebellions of illiterate serfs.

To sail down the mightiest of Russia's rivers, the Volga, is to realize how poor the Russian Middle Ages were in architectural monuments, in color and variety. A similar trip on such a European river as the Rhine or the Danube would show a multitude of castles and churches and monasteries and old cities where the walls and gates, the decorated town halls and homes of the burghers, would recall an era of sturdy culture that possessed many links with the present age. But what strikes the traveler on the Volga is the absence of visible signs of the past. Now and then one catches sight of an old church or walled monastery and there is a graceful Oriental quality about the old citadel of Kazan, the former Tartar capital. But the typical Volga town has uncommonly little that would recall the medieval period in Russian history.

This relative emptiness of the Russian past impressed an unusually thoughtful Russian army officer of the early nineteenth century, Chaadaev. In a letter to a Moscow newspaper which entitles him to a place among the pioneer Russian intellectuals Chaadaev expressed the opinion that nine hundred years of Russia's existence represented a blank in the history of the human mind. Russia was a land without a past, with an aimless present and with no future to anticipate. It was under the reign of the stern reactionary Tsar Nicholas I that this pessimistic viewpoint was expressed. And punishment for such unbecoming freedom of thought was not long delayed. The newspaper was suppressed and Chaadaev was officially pronounced a lunatic.

But there was a large element of truth in his idea of the

comparative blankness of the Russian past. And, as Herzen, one of the broadest and most brilliant minds in the early revolutionary movement, recognized, this spiritual rootlessness of the Russian was a psychological factor in paving the way for revolution of the most sweeping type.

During the middle and latter part of the nineteenth century there was an extraordinary flowering of creative cultural achievement in Russia, especially in literature and music. Enthusiastic, if not always diligent, Russian students appeared at the universities of Western Europe. Russian intellectuals paid their devotions at the shrines of Western European civilization. And no doubt some of these intellectuals, like Dostoyevsky's Ivan Karamazov, felt more warmly about Beethoven and Rembrandt and St. Peter's and the Arc de Triomphe and the libraries and art galleries of the European capitals than the Germans and Frenchmen and Italians, who were more inclined to take these monuments of culture for granted.

The Russian thought of the nineteenth century, often revolutionary, was seldom liberal. As Nicholas Berdyaev, a modern Russian philosopher who is an admirable interpreter of the psychology of his countrymen, observes: [1]

"It is most important to note that the liberal tradition has always been weak in Russia and that we have never had a liberalism with moral authority or which gave any inspiration. . . . The Russian spirit is not prone to scepticism, and a sceptical liberalism suits it less than anything."

The Russian mind seems to turn instinctively toward absolutism. It possesses little sense of measure or relativity. It is perfectionist in character and hence prone to accept the specious argument that the end justifies the means.

The typical British intellectual figure of the nineteenth century was perhaps John Stuart Mill, with his highly developed sense of the value of individual liberty and his belief in grad-

[1] Compare "The Origin of Russian Communism," Geoffrey Bles, London, 1937, p. 37.

ual progress through education. The Russian antithesis to Mill, the typical spokesman for the young Russian culture of the same period, would be Dostoyevsky, social prophet as well as novelist, with his passionate God-seeking, his apocalyptic visions of heaven and hell in the human soul, his impatience with lukewarmness either in good or in evil.

Russia was the country of autocrats and of anarchists. The Russian character could appreciate and adapt itself to absolute power or to absolute absence of restraint. The liberal conception of ordered freedom was completely alien to it. And, as anarchy is less feasible than absolutism as a permanent condition of social existence, Russian history before and after the Bolshevik Revolution has been a chronicle of despotism, punctuated by short bursts of violent revolt.

Lenin, leader of the Bolshevik Revolution, and Pobyedonostsev, Procurator of the Holy Synod and strongest personality in the regime of ultraconservatism that prevailed during the reign of Alexander III, were at opposite poles politically. Either would have gladly signed an order for the execution of the other.

Yet fundamentally there was far more in common between these representatives of extreme revolutionism and extreme reaction than there would be between either of them and a Western liberal or moderate Socialist of the type of Jean Jaurès or Arthur Henderson. Both were men of simple tastes and personally kindly dispositions. Both were mentally steeled to authorize the commission of acts of terrible cruelty for the realization of their ideas. Both believed in the innate badness of man and consequently in the necessity for pitiless dictatorial rule. Yet both were inspired by a rather naïve faith in the mystical regenerative effects of a dogmatic formula. For Pobyedonostsev this formula was summed up in three words: Orthodoxy, Autocracy, Nationalism. For Lenin it was the dictatorship of the proletariat which was to lead, by some miracle, to the withering away of the state.

The revolutionary struggle in Russia, which became especially intense in the seventies and nineties of the last century
and in the first years of the present century, excited sympathetic admiration in radical and liberal circles abroad. And
there was heroic quality in the little band of men and women,
mostly of the educated classes, who deliberately chose to lead
the harassed, hunted life of the revolutionary agitator and
propagandist. Like every persecuted religion, the revolutionary movement possessed its quota of saints and heroes and
martyrs.

There was Prince Peter Kropotkin, a rich personality and a
many-sided intellect, whose social conscience was so tender
that he gave up what he considered the impermissibly selfish
delight of scientific research to take the hard road that led to
imprisonment and exile. There was the officer's daughter, Sofia
Perovskaya, moving spirit of the terrorist revolutionary society *Narodnaya Volya*, who went to her death after the murder of Alexander II with as much passionate devotion and
courage as she had shown during her life. One has only to read
the memoirs of Stepniak, of Kropotkin, of Angelica Balaba-
nova, to realize what a rare spirit of selfless dedication to what
must have sometimes seemed a hopeless cause prevailed among
these pioneer revolutionaries. More than once in Moscow,
when I noticed an elderly man or woman with particularly
fine and sensitive features, I would be told that there was one
of the few survivors of the revolutionary societies and circles
that multiplied during the seventies.

Yet some at least of these rebels, if one studies their records
more closely, were more admirable in exile or in prison than
they would have been in the seats of power. And in their ideas
there were germs of a new tyranny, along with ideals of freedom.

The famous critic Belinsky, for instance, was in some respects a prophet of the Bolshevik dictatorship. He would be a

tyrant for the sake of justice. He believed that people were so stupid that they must be dragged to happiness. What a contrast to John Stuart Mill's firm liberal faith that the most benevolent despotism can never be self-justifying! The young revolutionary Nechayev anticipated the Communist type of organized dictatorship, with all authority centralized from above and the country covered with a network of revolutionary cells. He expressed the view that it was necessary to promote and spread evils, so as to provoke the people to rebel, and declared:

"A revolution can be salutary for the people only when it extirpates all the elements of the state and eradicates all traditions of state order and all social classes in Russia. Let us unite with the wild world of robbers, the only true revolutionaries in Russia."

This same Nechayev persuaded some of his disciples to murder a fellow member of their organization, merely as a proof of loyalty. Along with its saints and heroes and humane idealists the revolutionary movement bred its full share of fanatics, cranks and psychopathic cases.

The uncompromising absolutism of the Russian spirit excluded any possibility of reconciliation between the autocracy and the rebel intelligentsia. A Tsar Nicholas I, who ruled Russia as if it were a huge penitentiary, with a spy and a gendarme at everyone's elbow, naturally evoked a spirit like that of Bakunin, the fantastic anarchist, who placed his hopes of revolution on the criminals and the poorest classes of the countries with the lowest standards of living, such as Russia, Italy and Spain.

In the same way the fierce fanaticism of the revolutionaries discouraged the few timid reforming gestures of the government. Perhaps the nearest approach to unity between the Tsar and the dissatisfied educated classes was attained during the first years of the reign of Alexander II, when serfdom was abolished, the zemstvos were created as organs of limited local administration, independent courts were instituted and conditions in the military service were improved.

But Alexander's reforms stopped short of what the ardent revolutionaries desired. Repeated attempts to assassinate him did not encourage further concessions. Yet a liberal minister, Prince Loris-Melikov, had obtained the Tsar's approval of a project for a consultative legislative body when the final attempt of the terrorists on Alexander's life, on March 30, 1881, was successful. The new Tsar, Alexander III, was a dull and stubborn autocrat. Loris-Melikov fell from favor and his experimental constitution never came into operation.

Before the nineteenth century the Russian state, weak, corrupt and backward as it was, survived recurring crises of foreign wars and frequent dynastic murders and palace revolutions for two main reasons. Russia was not in direct hostile contact with any very strong or stable state. Poland was more advanced, more in touch with European culture, than was Russia. But it succumbed after a long period of intermittent struggle, largely because of its incurable internal factionalism. The Turkish Empire and the Tartar khanates were in process of decay and disintegration. Sweden, after the vicissitudes of its martial sovereign Charles XII, relinquished dreams of martial grandeur and no longer disputed possession of the coast of the Baltic with Russia.

And while Russia's territorial expansion went on slowly, inexorably, like the movement of an advancing glacier, there was no serious challenge to the autocratic regime from within. The dense ignorance and illiteracy of the population furnished a guaranty against consciously planned revolution. When the peasants would break out in one of their fierce revolts, murdering the landlords and state officials on whom they could lay their hands, they would have no idea of changing the Tsarist system itself. They would dream only of placing a "People's Tsar" upon the throne.

But with the gradual spread of education and the truly remarkable growth of cultural achievement in the nineteenth century a dangerous ferment began to work within the body of the autocracy. Herzen and Bakunin, Belinsky and Chernishevsky, Mikhailovsky and Lavrov, Plekhanov and Kropotkin, revolutionaries of varying shades of thought, undermined Tsarism just as Rousseau, Voltaire and the Encyclopedists prepared the way for the French Revolution.

Russia became a country of profound contrasts and contradictions—one of the surest advance symptoms of impending social upheaval. Externally censorship was more severe than in any European country. But internally thought was remarkably free. The past exercised much less restraint on the educated Russian than on the German, the Frenchman, the Englishman, because Russia was almost without a traditional past in the field of thought.

A high level of culture and education for the few existed side by side with widespread illiteracy among the peasant masses. A moral and spiritual refinement that could rarely have been equaled in Europe coincided with gross corruption and savage brutality. There was no country where the contrasts of wealth and poverty were so vivid or where the upper class, which for a long time affected the use of French, rather than of Russian, was so isolated from the masses of the people. Even the radical intellectual was more apt to idealize the peasant than to understand him. Later another important social and economic contrast developed, between the large new factories, equipped with modern machinery and built with foreign capital, and the primitive peasant agriculture and handicrafts.

There was an evanescent, hothouse quality about the late flowering of culture in Russia. Nowhere could one find such a sense of self-abnegation, even of moral guilt, among the intellectuals, such a widespread disposition to deny that literature and the arts are ends worthy of pursuit for their own sake. Nowhere was there such a tendency to subordinate aesthetic to political, social and moral considerations, to make art serve utilitarian purposes.

The Russian intellectual was born with a curious instinct for self-depreciation, as if he anticipated the fate which would befall Russian culture when the revolution finally arrived. At first he was inclined to bow down before an idol in sheepskin in the shape of the peasant. The Slavophiles and the revolutionaries, opposed on most other points, agreed in extolling the peasant, who went his way indifferent to the concern which he was causing to the *barin*, as the peasants called anyone who belonged to the well-to-do or educated classes. The Slavophile saw in the peasant the exponent of the old Russian virtues which, as he believed, were being destroyed by alien Western ideas and institutions. The early revolutionaries looked forward to Russia as a country of free self-governing peasant communes. Later it was the manual worker, the proletarian of Marx's terminology, who was invested with a halo by the increasing number of revolutionaries who accepted Marx as their master.

Russia significantly produced more than the average number of prophets of a dark future, of an ultimate Catastrophe. Lermontov, one of Russia's two great lyric poets, voiced the following prediction in 1830: [2]

> The day will come, for Russia that dark day
> When the Tsar's diadem will fall, and they,
> Rabble who loved him once, will love no more
> And many will subsist on death and gore.

A minor author named Constantine Leontiev published a remarkably accurate forecast of the course of the Bolshevik Revolution a generation before it occurred. Leontiev foresaw that the revolution would be communist, not liberal, in its

[2] For this translation compare "The Origin of Russian Communism," by Nicholas Berdyaev, p. 92.

character; that it would destroy the radical and liberal educated class which helped to bring it about; that it would arouse old Russian instincts of submission and domination, would attract the peoples of the East and destroy the bourgeois world of the West.

At first Leontiev, who, like most Russian thinkers, disliked the middle class liberalism of the West, believed that an original nonbourgeois culture would be possible in Russia. Later he became pessimistic and expressed the conviction that the mission of the Russian people was to give birth to Antichrist.

The revolutionary movement in its first stages was kept alive by a small number of people, mostly of the educated classes. Russia was a country of small peasant villages, with few cities and large towns. Agitation had to be carried on secretly and the peasants were too ignorant and too suspicious of city folk to be easily reached. There were many cases when naïve young students went out to preach revolt to the peasants, who promptly handed them over to the police.

Peasant revolts of the Stenka Razin and Pugachev type had become impossible because of the improved organization of the army and police and the spread of such means of communication as the railway and the telegraph. So the revolutionaries of the sixties and the seventies were sustained only by the fervor of their own faith, not by visible evidence of support from any large mass following.

But toward the end of the century two factors tended to strengthen and expand the forces of revolt. Russia was becoming industrialized, largely with the aid of foreign capital. An industrial working class was growing up in Moscow and St. Petersburg; in the mining districts of the Donets Basin and the Urals; in the oil fields of Baku and in some Ukrainian towns, such as Kharkov and Ekaterinoslav. These workers, uprooted from their villages, exposed to the new influences and ideas of the towns, were much more accessible to propaganda than were the isolated country villagers. In Russia, much more than in Western countries, there was a constant ebb and flow between city and village. In times of slack industrial activity, the worker would go back to the family farm in his native village. Not infrequently he brought with him a few half-baked socialist ideas which he had picked up in the factory. And the peasants were often more willing to listen to one of their own class than to an outsider. So the increasing socialist agitation in the towns found some reflection in the villages.

As is always the case in a country which is in the first stage of industrialization, working conditions left much to be desired. Hours were long; wages were low; housing was squalid. There were exceptions to this rule; some employers were more progressive or more paternalistic than the general average. But the Russian worker was closer than the Western European to Marx's conception of the proletarian "with nothing to lose but his chains." So as he became partly educated he was more responsive to extremist teachings.

The other factor which stimulated the growth of unrest was the clash of national feelings that was mentioned in an earlier chapter. Russia was a heterogeneous empire, from the racial standpoint. More than half the population consisted of non-Russians, Ukrainians, Poles, Finns, Letts, Armenians, Tartars, Jews and many others.

Under the influence of such counselors as the archreactionary Pobyedonostsev and a nationalist publicist named Katkov, Alexander III, a conscientious but stupid and limited monarch, set out to press all this medley of nationalities into a mold of Russian nationality. Old restrictions on the Jews were revived and enforced; new ones were created. With a few exceptions Jews were forbidden to live outside the Pale of Settlement in southern and western Russia. They were generally excluded from the state service, forbidden to own land and limited as to the proportion of students in high schools and universities. Apart from these legal disabilities, the Jews were harassed by corrupt and arbitrary local officials and were sometimes the victims of mob attacks, accompanied by murder, pillage and outrage, known as pogroms.

The Jews, eternal objects of racial and religious hatred, fared worse than some of the other non-Russian minorities. But almost all non-Russians experienced some special grievances. A chief of education in Warsaw named Apukhtin in 1873 went so far as to forbid instruction in the Polish language even for inmates of deaf-mute institutions. The constitution which had assured Finland local self-government within the Russian Empire was abrogated by Nicholas II, and this normally peaceful and orderly country became a hotbed of unrest. The Armenians in the distant Caucasus were offended by the suppression of their national language schools and the confiscation of the revenues of their church.

All these racial and national grievances, superimposed on the general causes of social and economic unrest, won many recruits for the revolutionary movement. The number of Jews in all the Russian revolutionary parties, and especially in their leadership, far exceeded the proportion of Jews in the Russian population. Poland and Finland and other non-Russian regions also furnished more than an average number of rebellious spirits. Many of these, to be sure, were nationalists, rather than economic radicals, interested in obtaining independence or at least autonomy for their own country. But they represented an additional element of weakness and disintegration in the Empire.

Both the aims and the character of the Russian revolutionary movement changed perceptibly shortly before the turn of the century. It began to acquire a broader base of mass support. And it was to the industrial workers rather than to the peasants that the majority of the revolutionaries began to look for support. The towns were growing. Education was spreading. The industrial working class and the middle class, both very weak in the old Russia of nobles and serfs, were becoming larger and more articulate.

The early Russian revolutionaries had based their hopes on the peasant. They saw in the *mir*, the primitive peasant community, which had been preserved after the liberation of the serfs and where the land was periodically redistributed, the embryo of a future noncapitalist society. Get rid of the autocracy, give the peasants the land of the country gentry, set up schools and hospitals, and Russia would become a vast peasant social democracy. They hoped that Western capitalism, with its extremes of wealth and poverty, its mansions and slums, could be kept out of Russia.

But as capitalism made visible forward strides, as the factory smokestack and the mine shaft could be seen more and more frequently, the economic teachings of Marx won more and more disciples. There was much in Marxism that was congenial to the psychology of the Russian revolutionary intellectual, who was at once passionate and dogmatic. Marxism was professedly scientific. It set a revolutionary goal, the destruction of capitalism. Its materialism was in line with a tradition of dogmatic atheism that dates back to the Russian nihilists of the sixties, of whom Turgenev gives such a vivid picture in his character of Bazarov in "Fathers and Sons."

Two of the three principal revolutionary parties, the Bolsheviki and the Mensheviki, were avowedly Marxist in outlook. The other, the Socialist Revolutionaries, carrying on the tradition of the early revolutionaries, the Narodniki,[3] considered themselves primarily a peasant party and were looser and vaguer than the Social Democrats in their program of action. They preserved the romantic tradition of terrorism. Many ministers and high officials of the Tsarist regime fell before the bombs and bullets of the Fighting Organization of the Socialist Revolutionaries. The Marxists, on the other hand, with their impersonal emphasis on economic determinism, rejected individual terrorism as futile and distracting and placed in the

---

[3] There is no adequate or satisfactory English translation for the Russian word *narodnik*—which is derived from *narod*, the people.

foreground the organization of the working class with a view to the final capture of state power.

Bolsheviki and Mensheviki both acknowledged Marx and Engels as the ultimate authorities. But these two groups disagreed as to how these authorities were to be interpreted and applied under Russian conditions. The Mensheviki were the more orthodox Marxists; the Bolsheviki were the better practical revolutionaries.

For it was one of the stumbling blocks of the Marxist creed that there was no serious prospect of revolution just in those Western countries where capitalism was most highly developed and which, according to Marx, should have been the ripest for the transition to socialism. On the other hand there was such a prospect in Russia, where capitalism was in an early stage of development and which, therefore, according to Marx, would not be ready for socialism until capitalism had run its appointed course.

The Mensheviki, following Marx to the letter, arrived at the conclusion that Russia must pass through its capitalist phase before there should be any attempt at a socialist revolution. They were temperamentally suited to become a Socialist party of the West European type, moderate and gradualist in psychology and tactics. But for such a party there was no place in extremist Russia. Under Tsarism they were persecuted as too radical. Under the Bolshevik dictatorship they were outlawed as "counterrevolutionaries" and "enemies of the people." Their type of socialism could flourish only in a liberal political and economic system, such as never came into being in Russia.

Bolshevik policy, as worked out by its leader, Lenin, was dictated more by practical revolutionary considerations than by doctrinaire adherence to Marx's line of reasoning. Lenin was a devoted, a fanatical believer in Marx's ideal of replacing capitalism by socialism. But, like many an ardent disciple, he contrived to select from the works of the master just those passages which best coincided with his own conception of the needs of practical strategy.

So he laid tremendous stress upon Marx's phrase about the dictatorship of the proletariat. "The liberation of the oppressed classes," so Lenin wrote, "is impossible not only without a violent revolution, but also without the destruction of the apparatus of state power which was created by the ruling class." By means of this formula of the dictatorship of the proletariat Lenin attempted to justify every suppression of liberty that was required for the maintenance of the Soviet regime. He interpreted this dictatorship as something temporary and here again he found a justification for revolutionary terrorism. The state, as he conceived it, was merely an agency of class oppression, made necessary by the contradictions of capitalist society. Break up the bourgeois state, put the country through the regenerating process of the proletarian dictatorship and the state itself would wither away. It is characteristic of Lenin's mind, superficially rational but fundamentally irrational, like that of every fanatic, that he never apparently conceived the possibility that his "dictatorship of the proletariat" might become a self-perpetuating power machine.

To many orthodox Marxists the Russian peasant caused much worry. Here was a class of poor small proprietors who simply did not fit in with Marx's forecast of a "final struggle" between a pauperized urban and rural proletariat and a handful of magnates of capitalism. The existence of a peasant majority of the population seemed to the typical Menshevik irreconcilable with a socialist revolution. So he argued that such a revolution must be postponed until the country had passed through a process of industrialization and urbanization. Another prominent Marxist revolutionary, Leon Trotsky, took refuge from the inconvenient peasant in a theory of "permanent revolution," conceiving the Russian Revolution as the spark that would ignite the flames of social upheaval in the more advanced countries of Western Europe.

But Lenin found a phrase, "democratic dictatorship of the proletariat and the peasantry," which seemed to him to get over this difficulty. "Democratic dictatorship" was a contradiction both in terms and in actual practice. What actually happened in Russia was that a small band of professional revolutionaries seized power with the conscious support of a part of the working class and the more passive cooperation of soldiers who were attracted by the promise of stopping the war and of peasants who were lured by the prospect of looting the homes and estates of the country gentry.

But factual accuracy and even doctrinaire theoretical consistency were always subordinated in Lenin's mind to considerations of what would promote the success of revolutionary action. His historical greatness is that of a practical revolutionary, the first organizer of the modern style dictatorship. He was not an original or a brilliant theoretician.

In one of his first pamphlets—"What Is to Be Done?"—the Bolshevik leader stressed the importance of organization for the purpose of getting and holding power:

"Give us a revolutionary organization and we will turn Russia upside down."

The spirit of the man is well reflected in a message which he sent to the fighting organization of the Bolshevik party in St. Petersburg during the revolutionary turmoil of 1904–05:

"I am horrified, really horrified, I can swear to you, to see that for over six months talk has been going on about bombs without a single one being made. Form immediately and everywhere fighting squads among students and especially among workers. Let them arm themselves at once, as best they can, with revolvers, knives or rags soaked in oil for arson."

On the surface Lenin was a dry, plodding scholar who wrote abusive political tracts and one ponderous work on Russian economic history which was exhaustive rather than profound. But beneath this surface was a soul as wild, as passionate, as elementally rebellious, as those of the peasant insurgent leaders who spread havoc over the Russian countryside in the seventeenth and eighteenth centuries, Stenka Razin and Pugachev.

In the generally pacific atmosphere of Western Europe, Marx's ideas were tamed and softened by the Socialists who professed them. In semi-Asiatic Russia, with so many forces of popular ferment and discontent, the explosive effect of those ideas was tremendous. Indeed one may interpret Russian Bolshevism, the first phase in the revolt against European civilization, as the product of the crossbreeding of a Western revolutionary theory with an absolutist and largely Byzantine and Oriental historical tradition in which there was no place for such humanizing influences as freedom of individual judgment. The result was one of the most formidable outbreaks of destruction and one of the most complete tyrannies over the minds and bodies of men ever known.

The revolutionary movement of 1905 threw into clear relief the weaknesses of the old regime. Three of the forces that were to make for the success of the Bolsheviki—the militantly insurgent working class; the dissatisfied peasantry, ready to seize the landlords' estates; the resentful non-Russian nationalities—all found expression during the disturbances of that year. It was with good reason that Lenin called 1905 a dress rehearsal for 1917.

Another point of similarity between these two revolutions, one successful, the other finally suppressed, is that war was a powerful stimulant to both. Indeed Russian history affords a striking series of illustrations of the effect of war as an agency, now for speeding up social change, now for outright revolt. The uprising of the Dekabristi in 1825 was a direct outgrowth of the Napoleonic Wars. The Guards officers who participated in this unsuccessful conspiracy were influenced by the foreign ideas with which they had come in contact during their campaigns in Europe.

The Crimean War, with its revelation of the military incompetence of the iron despotism of Nicholas I, excited so much dissatisfaction that it must be considered an important factor in persuading Alexander II to decree the liberation of the serfs. The Russo–Japanese War brought widespread internal disorder, which forced Nicholas II to grant the first Russian Constitution.

This Constitution was emasculated as soon as the revolutionary storm had subsided and the autocracy again felt sure of its grip on the army and the other instruments of power. Tsarism enjoyed a respite between 1905 and 1914. The more active revolutionaries were in prison or in exile or were forced to flee abroad. Apathy followed the wave of strikes, riots and demonstrations that had swept over the country in 1905.

Material progress took off some of the edge of class antago-nisms. There was improvement in wages and working conditions. There was also an attempt to strike at the roots of peasant discontent by encouraging the growth of a class of well-to-do individual proprietors. Premier Stolypin sponsored a law which made it possible for the peasant to leave the *mir* and set up his own homestead. This was followed by a drift of the land from weaker to stronger hands. Under the former village organization every peasant family possessed land. But almost all lived on a very low level of poverty, because the more capable and progressive were prevented from adopting improved methods and planting special crops by the backwardness and prejudices of the majority of members of the *mir*, which controlled to some extent the activities of all its members.

Stolypin tried to introduce a new leaven of individualism into the Russian village. The more hardworking and capable peasant families were permitted and even encouraged to buy out the more poor and shiftless, who then became agricultural laborers or sought work in the towns. About 20 per cent of the peasant households quit the *mir* between 1905 and 1914. It is impossible to say with certainty whether this tendency, if it had gone farther, would have created a strong new bulwark against violent revolution by building up a class of fairly prosperous farmers, with the farmer's normal instinct for the maintenance of the rights of private property.

But Russia's involvement in the World War cast the die for the long-awaited and long-thwarted downfall of the autocracy. A conservative statesman, P. N. Durnovo, proved to be the truest of prophets when he foresaw, on the eve of the conflict, that "social revolution in its most extreme form" and "hopeless anarchy, the issue of which cannot be foreseen," would be the consequences of an unsuccessful war with Germany. The minor upheaval that accompanied the Russo–Japanese War was only a faint premonition of the social earthquake that was destined to engulf not only the Tsarist regime and the aristocracy but the whole Russian middle class and the great majority of the liberal and radical intelligentsia as well. The darkest prophecies of doom to be found in the poems of Lermontov, in the novels of Dostoyevsky, in the writings of Constantine Leontiev, were to be more than fulfilled.

At first the war seemed to go fairly smoothly. It was easier to stir up popular hatred of the Germans, who were known, than of the Japanese, who were almost completely unknown. The armies fought as well as their inferior equipment permitted. But after the German military machine crashed through the Russian lines in Poland and Galicia in 1915 a rapid process of internal decomposition set in—even more behind the lines than at the front. The colossal losses alone, estimated at from six to eight million killed, wounded and prisoners, with the resultant vast number of widows and orphans, for whom little provision was made, were calculated to inspire bitter and desperate resentment.

An old-fashioned despotic government depends for stability on inertia, on the maintenance of a certain social routine. But the war meant for the Russian people a gigantic uprooting, a disturbance of normal living habits. Over fifteen million men were torn from their homes and mobilized in a clumsy and useless effort to make up with sheer mass for lack of an adequate supply of modern weapons. Moreover, great numbers of people, losing all their possessions, were forced to flee as refugees before the German advance. Here were new elements of dislocation.

Although there was plenty of food in Russia, transportation was overstrained and distribution was bad. Great masses of peasants were taken away from the villages to work in munitions factories or were mobilized to fill the swollen rear garrisons. Both factories and garrisons became centers of spontaneous social revolutionary combustion. The continual defeats and the notorious semihypnotic influence of the amorous and adventurous monk, Rasputin, on the hysterical Tsarina and, through her, on the weak-willed Tsar, cooled off the loyalty which the upper and middle classes felt at the beginning of the war.

There were rumors of a palace revolution for months before the fall of the autocracy occurred on March 12, 1917. But no group was willing or able to assume the responsibility for such a step. So the revolution for which generations of rebels had worked and schemed and died came suddenly, spontaneously, like a thief in the night. It was a collapse, not a planned revolt. Food riots among the workers of St. Petersburg grew into large strikes and political demonstrations. The soldiers, summoned to fire on the demonstrators, joined in with them instead. And the revolution was there. So rotted out was the old regime from within, after almost three years of disastrous war, that not a regiment could be found to take up arms for the Tsar.

From March until November power was nominally in the hands of liberals and moderate Socialists. Actually Russia was in a state of steadily increasing anarchy. The real organs of authority, so far as any authority could be said to exist, were the Soviets, or Councils of Workers' and Soldiers' Deputies,

which sprang up all over the country as soon as the old regime
fell. Milyukov, Kerensky, Tseretelli, Chernov, the other figures in the frequently changing Cabinets of the Provisional
Government, would perhaps have been excellent ministers in
a sheltered Western country where law and order were taken
for granted. They were quite incapable of mastering the stu-
pendous double crisis of an unsuccessful war and an advancing
social revolution.

~ All the familiar disintegrating forces in Russian life leaped
into the foreground under the potent stimulus of the war and
the psychology of violence which the war promoted. The soldiers began first to question and disobey orders, then to strike
and sometimes kill officers, finally to desert and go home in
droves. Every minor nationality in Russia began to put forward separatist claims. The workers joined in the general
revolt. Food shortages, transportation difficulties, the increasingly visible effects of currency inflation, created an abundance of causes of labor disputes. Strike followed strike. In
some cases factory managers and engineers were ridden out of
factories in wheelbarrows, beaten or even killed. Authority
had vanished with the Tsarist regime. The efforts of the Provisional Government to effect results by means of persuasion
and conciliation met with little success.

The peasants, gradually sensing the fact that no troops or
Cossacks would be sent to punish them, commenced to seize
the coveted land of the country gentry. Beginning with petty
theft and refusal to pay rent, they steadily advanced to the
stage of wholesale spoliation, sometimes to an accompaniment
of violence and murder.

~ A focus of leadership in this tremendous surge of popular
revolt against the whole social order was found in the Bolshevik party under the leadership of Lenin. He had returned
to Russia, with other exiles, from Switzerland, crossing Germany in a sealed train. Ludendorff reckoned rightly that the
letting loose of a few extreme revolutionaries would paralyze

the Russian Army more effectively and more cheaply than any other means at his disposal.

Lenin was one of the very few men who had grasped from the outset the revolutionary possibilities of a major war. "Turn the imperialist war into civil war" had been the slogan which he cried from his lonely isolated place of exile in Switzerland. He viewed with equal contempt the Socialist majorities which fell in line with the war policies of their governments and the Socialist minorities which opposed the war on general humanitarian and pacifist grounds and favored a negotiated peace. The former, to him, were "social traitors." The latter were "social pacifists." In Lenin's opinion there was only one honest revolutionary attitude toward the war: to endeavor to exploit the ferment and bitterness which it might be expected to arouse in the workers of all countries for the preparation of social revolution. He attributed the war entirely to the capitalist system and especially to the imperialism which he regarded as the last phase of capitalism. He saw in revolution the sole salvation from an endless series of future wars.

Equipped with this viewpoint, and with a growing organized following in the Bolshevik party, Lenin was able to ride triumphantly the stormy waves of an upheaval that perplexed, dismayed and alienated many veterans of the struggle against Tsarism. The chaos, dissolution, breakup, which he saw all around him were to Lenin the birth pangs of a new order. He systematically encouraged every disintegrating tendency which the Provisional Government feebly and ineffectively opposed. For he was convinced that socialism must be preceded by a complete breakup of the old machinery of administration.

In a series of fiery pamphlets written in the months before the final leap to power in November he hammered home the ideas that the hour of revolution had struck, that the Soviets were the organs of the dictatorship of the proletariat, that the masses were with the Bolsheviki. Here he showed clearer insight than some of his associates and sympathizers, who were worried as to whether the proletariat might not find itself "isolated" if it should attempt to rebel. As the following citation shows, Lenin appraised at full value the revolutionary implications of nationalist discontent, of the peasant disorders, of the universal will to peace:

"The national and agrarian questions: these are fundamental questions for the petty-bourgeois masses of the Russian people at the present time. This is indisputable. With regard to both questions the proletariat is remarkably far from isolation. And the question of peace, that cardinal question of the whole of present-day life? The proletariat here steps forward as the representative of the whole people, of all that is alive and honest in all classes, of the vast majority of the petty bourgeoisie."

When the Bolsheviki (who subsequently called themselves Communists) struck for power in November, the process of social dissolution had gone so far that there was little immediate resistance, although some non-Russian parts of the country, such as Ukraina, Finland and Georgia set up nationalist governments which were not under Bolshevik control.

The first steps of the Soviet regime were the initiation of peace proposals, the abolition of private property in land and the establishment of workers' control in industry. (This workers' control, it should be noted, was not of long duration. It gave way to a system of very rigid and dictatorial state control after all the industries were nationalized.) With the passing of time every form of private property was destroyed with unparalleled thoroughness. Money was made worthless by unlimited inflation. Gold and jewels were confiscated. Stocks and bonds became mere pieces of paper because all industrial and commercial enterprises were nationalized. Private property in houses was abolished and working class families were moved into the flats and homes of the well-to-do.

The people who were unfortunate enough to be classified as bourgeoisie not only were plundered of their possessions but were subjected to every form of calculated insult and cruelty. They were given little or no food under the rationing system. They were excluded from military service and compelled to perform menial work behind the lines. They were liable to arrest on the slightest suspicion or merely as a measure of social reprisal. They were shot in batches with little pretense of a trial whenever there was an access of mass terror.

The term bourgeois, usually corrupted to "boorzhui" by the semiliterate proletarians, was a vague one at best. The more ignorant and ferocious Communists often regarded anyone of culture and education with a mixture of hatred, envy and suspicion. So it is no wonder that during those years of hunger, cold, hatred and terror between one and two million Russians, mostly of the well-to-do and educated classes, fled from the country. This was a political emigration of unprecedented scope. It meant the permanent elimination from Russia of a considerable part of the Russians who had come under Western influences. It was an unconscious victory of the dark, semi-Asiatic masses who, since the time of Peter the Great, had looked on European culture as something alien and hateful.

The infernal cycle that began in Russia when war gave birth to revolution continued as revolution led to civil war, with a frightful accompaniment of cruelties on both sides. During the years when civil war, hunger, disease and cold rode through the land like the Four Horsemen of the Apocalypse there was a reign of hatred such as even the somber genius of Dostoyevsky could scarcely have foreseen.

All the smoldering bitterness of the poor against the rich under the old regime was fanned into a constant flame by the systematic propaganda of the ruling Communist party. The new regime could not keep its promise to give the people bread and peace. But it could and did give them the satisfaction of trampling on the classes which had formerly been

regarded as superior. Along with the understandable dislike
of the worker, the peasant, the soldier, for the employer who
was greedy, the landlord who was oppressive, the officer who
was brutal, there was something more elemental and more
sinister. There was a revolt of the masses against civilization
and culture, a dull implacable hatred for everything that suggested intellectual superiority.

All the hatred was naturally not on one side. When the anti-
Bolsheviki, or Whites, as they came to be called, occupied
parts of the country they wreaked vengeance on all whom
they suspected of revolutionary sympathies. The traditional
Russian anti-Semitism assumed unheard-of proportions. The
number of victims of pogroms during the civil war exceeded
at least tenfold the number of Jews who had perished in such
disturbances during the previous course of Russian history.
This was partly because of the considerable number of Jews
in the Communist party; their co-racialists had to pay a fearful
price whenever the Soviet regime was temporarily overthrown. It was partly because of the stimulation of every
savage and brutal passion by the double influence of war and
revolution. The same mob that would plunder and kill the
"boorzhui" at Communist incitation was equally ready to
rob and massacre the Jews when the Whites gained the upper
hand.

There was hatred of city for village, of village for city. The
hungry people in the towns blamed the peasants for not feeding them. The peasants deliberately cut down their plantings
because they received from the cities not manufactured goods
but requisitioning detachments of soldiers and armed workers.
There was jealousy and bitterness between the nonparty
worker and the Communist, between the Communist rank-
and-file and the party hierarchy.

Finally peace and order emerged from this inferno of con-
tending passions. The outlines of the Soviet system, hitherto
obscured by extremes of propaganda, both favorable and hos-

tile, and by the difficulties of obtaining firsthand information, became clearer. The Soviets themselves lost all political independence after the first months of their tumultuous rule. Although they continued to function as executive organs of administration, all powers of initiative and decision were in the hands of the Communist party, which completely dominated the Soviets. And the Communist party itself was a tightly disciplined organization, in which the rank-and-file member's first duty, like the soldier's, was to obey, while all important decisions were taken by a small group of veteran leaders. Other Socialist parties, such as the Mensheviki and the Socialist Revolutionaries, were first harassed and persecuted and finally outlawed altogether. Membership in the Communist party was an unwritten requirement for high office. All the members of the Council of People's Commissars, the Soviet Cabinet, have been Communists since the early years of the Revolution. Major political decisions, however, are taken not by this body but by the Political Bureau, the inner steering group of the larger party Central Committee.

Communist leadership in the first period of the Soviet regime came from that class which was peculiar to Russia, the professional revolutionaries. Most of these, like Lenin himself, were educated men and women of middle class background, with a sprinkling of proletarians and an occasional aristocrat. The party rank-and-file were deliberately recruited largely from manual workers, who were considered the most politically reliable class in the population. According to the latest available figures a little less than two thirds of the Soviet Communists are manual workers; about one fifth are peasants; the others are state employees. Of the 1574 delegates to the last party congress, 659 belonged to the party bureaucracy; 230 were industrial managers, 162 Soviet and trade union officials; 283 were from the army, the navy, and the political police; 110 were from the transportation system, 63 from agriculture; and 35 were representatives of art and science.

This method of government by the dictatorship of a single party was an immensely important innovation that has already spread to many other countries. It differed from old-fashioned autocracy because it gave the new regime a band of organized supporters in every factory, in every office, in every military unit, in every village. And it set in motion a highly organized propaganda machine, utilizing the press, the schools, the theater, the radio, the moving picture, on a scale which had never been dreamed of under the sleepy bureaucracy which governed the empire under the Tsars.

At the same time there was no semblance of political democracy or of liberalism in the Soviet system. Wherever comparison is possible the repression of dissenting opinion has been more severe than it was before the Revolution. The promulgation of the new Constitution of 1936 made no difference whatever in the practical functioning of the dictatorship. While it provided for universal suffrage and for secret elections to the Soviets, only one set of candidates has been proposed for the voters' approval and the Soviet voter, in the elaborate instructions which are given to him as to how to cast his ballot, is warned not to write in any name which does not appear on the ballot. Arbitrary arrests and executions without public trial have been as frequent after the Constitution supposedly went into effect as before. No non-Communist political association is permitted to exist and no opposition magazine or newspaper is tolerated.

Politically, therefore, the Soviet regime is and always has been, despite occasional transparent attempts at window dressing, a dictatorship of the most absolute type, without any such distinctive signs of democracy and liberalism as freedom of speech, press, assembly, voting or trade union organization. At the same time this regime enlists a larger measure of popular support than an old-fashioned despotism, demanding purely passive obedience, might enjoy. The mere existence of the party creates a vested interest in the continuance of the system on the part of its members, who number between one and a half and two millions. Several million young men and women are enrolled in the Communist Youth organization and many Soviet children belong to the Young Pioneers, a Communist children's association of the Boy Scout type. The process of constant indoctrination with the dogmas of the ruling party, without any possibility of open dispute or contradiction, yields its results. And such measures as the forcible and violent changes in the old ways of living, the creation of many new industrial establishments, the placing of agriculture on a collectivist basis, appeal to some of the Soviet youth by virtue of their very novelty.

After Lenin's death on January 21, 1924, revolutionary oligarchy gave way gradually to personal despotism. Lenin was a leader who held his party together by prestige and force of personality, not by terrorism. He was in no sense a liberal and he would stretch to the limit the stern requirements of party discipline in order to keep opponents in line. Yet up to the time of his death no prominent Communist was executed, arrested or even permanently eliminated from public life.

Very different has been Stalin's method of governing. At the time of Lenin's death there were seven members of the powerful Political Bureau. Their names were Stalin, Trotsky, Zinoviev, Kamenev, Rykov, Bukharin and Tomsky. Zinoviev and Kamenev, Rykov and Bukharin, were shot after the curious treason and sabotage trials, involving so many old Communists, which took place from 1936 until 1938. Tomsky preferred to commit suicide. Trotsky was murdered in his Mexican exile in 1940. The crime might well have been signed with the initials GPU. Stalin is nothing if not thorough. The fate of his six former associates is only one vivid illustration of the technique of Russia's most sanguinary autocrat since Ivan the Terrible. It is not without significance, incidentally, that this psychopathically bloodthirsty Tsar has recently been restored to historical favor in the Soviet Union. The points of similarity between Ivan and Stalin are very numerous.

Soviet economics has been consistently based on the Marxian idea of eliminating private property in means of production, although methods and institutions have varied from time to time. During the period of civil war, from 1918 until 1921, every enterprise, from the largest to the smallest, was nationalized. The peasants were required to deliver up their surplus grain and other foodstuffs. In return they were supposed to receive manufactured goods. But in practice there was little exchange. The output of industrial products fell to incredibly low levels. The Communist economist Kritzman gives the following appropriate characterization of this era of war communism:

"Such a decline in the productive forces not of a little community, but of an enormous society of a hundred million people . . . is unprecedented in the history of humanity."

Under the so-called New Economic Policy which Lenin introduced as an effort to find a way out of the economic impasse in 1921 a fixed tax in kind (later replaced by a money tax) was substituted for the requisitions, and freedom of private trade within the country was again permitted. Private ownership of small enterprises was authorized and a number of concessions were granted to foreign firms for the operation of factories, mines and other establishments. These changes, especially the abolition of the requisitions on the peasants, combined with the end of the civil war, started Soviet economy on an upward curve and for several years there was a gradual improvement in living conditions.

A drastic economic change in an opposite direction occurred in 1929. All the concessions to private enterprise were swept away. A system of planned economy was inaugurated. The private traders were again expropriated. Trade within the country became a monopoly of state agencies and of state controlled cooperatives. A still bigger change took place in agriculture. The peasants were forced to sink their private holdings in so-called collective farms. The old method of a tax in kind was revived. The peasants were obliged to deliver up specific quantities of grain and other materials for nominal prices. The foreign concessions were liquidated.

Within the framework of this state-socialist or state-capitalist system there is a substantial and growing measure of inequality. The original self-denying ordinance under which a Communist, whatever his position in the state service, could receive only a moderate salary, a little more than the wage of a skilled workman, has been abrogated. There has been an increasing spread between the earnings and other material rewards of the higher classes of the Soviet economic and military bureaucracy and those of the workers and peasants. Among the workers themselves there is a greater difference in remuneration between skilled and unskilled labor than one finds under the capitalist system.

This socialist absolutism in Russia has succeeded in establishing new industries and considerably expanding the production of old ones. There has been a substantial increase in the use of electrical power. Agriculture has been shifted from a basis of the horse and plow and simple implements to the tractor and the harvesting combine. Huge canals, connecting the Baltic and the White seas and the Volga and Moscow rivers have been constructed.

But from the standpoint of human well-being there is little to be said for the Communist dictatorship. Real wages are low even by comparison with the wretched standards that prevailed before 1914. The acute shortage and low quality of manufactured goods are best proved by the high prices, in Soviet rubles, which the foreign traveler can obtain for his shoddiest castoff possessions.

The sufferings imposed on the Russian people by the Soviet economic experiments far exceed the worst cruelties of the early phases of the industrial system in other countries. Among these sufferings were the general malnutrition during the years of the first Five Year Plan, culminating in outright famine in 1932–33; the uprooting and forcible deportation of millions of people for social and economic reasons; the squalid and inhuman conditions which prevail not only in the numerous forced-labor camps but in many new industrial towns, where housing has been almost completely neglected.

Quality of production has remained amazingly low and is certainly no recommendation for turning over the whole of a nation's economic life to bureaucratic management. There are also continual bottlenecks in the productive system and some permanent grave disproportions in the national economic life. The expansion of the transportation system, for instance, has not been coordinated with the growth of industry. It must also be remembered that much of the technical progress in the Soviet Union is part of a world-wide process, has been duplicated or surpassed in other countries and would most probably have occurred in Russia under any political or economic system. It is certainly doubtful whether Russia's real military and industrial strength, in relation to other powers, has increased since the Revolution.

By a curious and ironical coincidence a revolutionary movement that began as the revolt of a Europeanized minority of educated Russians against the Asiatic cruelty, backwardness and corruption of the autocracy ended in a triumph of the Asiatic over the European elements in Russia's Eurasian culture. The Soviet Union at the present time possesses most of the characteristic qualities of the Asiatic absolutist state.

There is the unlimited, uncontrolled power of the despotic ruler. No Tsar of modern times ruled with so little restraint in the way of internal or international public opinion as Stalin feels.

Profoundly Asiatic is the secrecy which envelops every move of Soviet foreign or internal policy. The suspicion and espionage which surround the foreigner in the Soviet Union would be paralleled only in some very backward parts of Asia, in Afghanistan perhaps, or in Tibet.

In the Asiatic tradition is the complete absence of legal safeguards for the individual against the state. And in the same tradition is the equality of all Soviet subjects before their absolute master, Stalin. Like an old-fashioned Turkish sultan or Tartar khan, Stalin can (and often does) kill a highly placed Cabinet minister with as little hesitation as he would show in "liquidating" a recalcitrant peasant.

Asia's achievements have usually been in mass, in quantity, as opposed to quality. The Soviet Union has certainly conformed to this model. With all the emphasis on industrialization, one looks in vain for any important technical or scientific invention which can be associated with the Soviet regime. Its new factories and power plants have been constructed according to blueprints borrowed from abroad. And they have been built in the crudest and most painful way, by a brutal exploitation of serf labor.

Soviet military tactics in the war with Finland displayed the same lack of imaginative originality as Soviet industrial methods. The Red Army sustained a pitiful fiasco in every attempted operation which required some measure of skill, finesse and individual initiative, in dropping troops from parachutes, in adapting itself to the Finnish methods of carrying on a winter war on skis. Victory was finally won by the simplest method of piling up enormous masses of men and artillery and crushing the Finnish resistance at a tremendous cost in casualties. It was the barbarian horde against the civilized army.

It was Russia that supplied the impetus to the revolt against European civilization. Had there been no Lenin there might well have been no Hitler and no Mussolini. In two respects the first Bolshevik phase of the revolt against civilization paved the way for the second Fascist phase. Bolshevism supplied a new technique of government, the dictator supported by the single party and keeping himself in power by a continual process of propaganda and terrorism, which Italian fascism and German national socialism were quick to copy.

Moreover, communism, as a brutally violent challenge to accepted conceptions of legality, morality and humanity, elicited, by natural psychological law, a brutal and violent reaction. More than one social group could play at this game of dictatorship. If the proletariat, or that part of it which consciously sympathized with the Communists, could exterminate the propertied and middle classes socially, economically, to some extent physically, those classes in other countries were not likely to overlook this danger. The specter of Bolshevism, even when it was not very real, was effective in helping the Fascist dictators into power.

On the economic, as on the political, side Bolshevism anticipated many features of the subsequent Fascist regimes. The Soviet Union was the first large state which erected itself into a leviathan, asserting the most unbounded authority over the minds and bodies of its subjects while undertaking to supply all their physical and intellectual needs. It was the first European country to repudiate an international currency system.

Most significant of all, it was the first great power to secede from the community of European culture. Every new stage in the development of the Soviet regime meant a further recession from Europe. The first years of revolution and civil war drove into exile vast numbers of its Europeanized intelligentsia. Later came a further decimation of those educated men who remained in Russia on highly dubious charges of sabotage. Finally the more Westernized Communists themselves were "liquidated" during Stalin's merciless purges which began after the mysterious murder of his lieutenant, Kirov, in 1934 and went on for several years. The more prominent Communists who perished in these purges, in their great majority, were men who had been educated in the West. Stalin regarded them as out of place in his Asiatic despotism.

Under the impact of that great catastrophe of European civilization, the World War, Russia fulfilled the tragic destiny which some of its poets and prophets had foreseen. It tore itself to pieces in a social revolution of unprecedented depth and ferocity. And it became the focus of revolt against every ideal of Western liberal culture. Communism became a continuous running sore on the weakened body of postwar European civilization. Its direct propaganda, while it led to many strikes, acts of sabotage, murders and some riots and rebellions, represented only the lesser part of its share in the infernal cycle which commenced with the World War. More important were its stimulus, direct and indirect, to other forms of totalitarian revolt and Stalin's heavy share of responsibility for promoting the outbreak of the Second World War. As a force of sheer destruction Russian communism, that hybrid product of doctrinaire European revolutionism and the Asiatic elements in Russian society, has few rivals in history.

Chapter Five

ITALIAN FASCISM: MIDDLE CLASS BOLSHEVISM

AFTER NOVEMBER 7, 1917, when the Bolsheviki seized power in Russia, the next significant date in the revolt against liberal civilization was October 29, 1922, when another armed doctrine took possession of a large European country. The basic cause of the Fascist Revolution, as of its Communist predecessor, was the impact of the World War upon a weak political, economic and social organism. Yet the same cause, against a different national background, led to a different type of revolution, although the final outlines of the Italian leviathan-state were quite similar to the Russian pattern.

Italy was morally and materially one of the least prepared of European powers to withstand the ordeal of a great war. One of the poorest countries in Europe in natural resources, almost completely without the coal and iron and oil which are the lifeblood of the modern industrial system, Italy faced the problems of a proletarian nation. Its population tended to outgrow the meager means of subsistence at home. Emigration to the Americas provided only a partial remedy. Because its unification was achieved very late and because it was a second-class power in military and naval strength, Italy fared badly in the world scramble for colonial spoils. So it could not count on an overseas empire for assured markets, or as an outlet for surplus population.

Of the leaders in Italy's unification the statesman Cavour was a moderate liberal and the popular leaders Garibaldi and Mazzini were radicals. The constitution of the new Italy was drawn up along familiar liberal lines, with a monarch of limited powers at the head of the state. But the mere promulgation of a liberal constitution could not destroy the inheritance of centuries of arbitrary, despotic governments, often of foreign origin, tempered by occasional riots and insurrections. The high percentage of illiteracy, 69 in 1871 and 45 in 1901, especially in the South, was a serious obstacle to the functioning of a genuinely democratic form of government.

Suffrage was limited; less than 9 per cent of the Italian people could vote before 1913. Cabinet changes were frequent and the efficiency of the Chamber of Deputies was lowered because of the multiplicity of parties. The Socialist party was the only strong cohesive political organization before the war and it possessed practically no following in the backward, agrarian South. Regionalism, the natural consequence of the fact that Italians for many centuries had lived in separate states, slowed up the development of an effective sense of common nationhood. Another barrier was the schism in national unity produced by the irreconcilable attitude of the Pope, who refused to acknowledge the loss of his temporal power and considered himself a prisoner in the Vatican. Catholics were forbidden to take part in the political life of Italy until shortly before the outbreak of the war.

Italy had its share in the material progress of the liberal age. At the time of its unification the country was almost entirely agricultural. It built up its factories, its networks of railways. Between 1876 and 1911 the number of industrial workers increased more than tenfold. The 1,756 kilometers of railway lines in 1860 had become 17,649 kilometers in

1913. Foreign trade trebled in value between 1871 and 1913. And the Italian Government followed the trend of the time in relaxing punitive measures against Socialist and trade union activity and instituting some modest social reforms.

But the soil of Italian society remained as volcanic as Vesuvius. The combination of poverty with the excitable Latin temperament made for political violence. Such creeds of direct action as anarchism and syndicalism flourished. The second King of united Italy, Humbert, was killed by an anarchist and it was necessary to call out the army to suppress a revolutionary general strike in Milan in 1904.

One of the most active figures in the turbulent Italian labor movement was Benito Mussolini. The future Fascist Duce was the son of a village blacksmith who was something of a local Red and who named his son in honor of the Mexican revolutionary Benito Juarez. The young Mussolini grew up in the radical atmosphere of the village café, where the police, the Church, the army and other forces of conservatism were freely denounced. Largely self-taught, he became an elementary schoolteacher and then took up the wandering poverty-stricken life of the itinerant revolutionary. He went to Switzerland to escape conscription (later he took advantage of an amnesty to return and perform his military service). Here he almost starved and horrified the pious Swiss by going about and delivering public speeches against God.

Later he found a job on an Italian Socialist newspaper in Trent, then an Austrian town. He was soon expelled from Austria for suggesting in print that the existing frontier did not correspond with Italy's justified national aspirations. He then published articles in Italy ridiculing racial theories which exalted the Germans above the non-Nordic Italians.

Mussolini became one of the extremists in the Italian Socialist party. He was continually getting himself arrested for incitement to violence and he made no secret of his disgust with the moderation of the party leadership. When Italy attacked Turkey to obtain Libya, Mussolini threw himself into the fight against the war and stirred up a mob to obstruct troop trains which were carrying soldiers to ports of embarkation. During this radical apprenticeship he unconsciously pronounced a most devastating judgment on the very type of system which he was one day to establish:

"Imagine an Italy in which thirty-six million people should all think the same, as though their brains were cast in an identical mold, and you would have a madhouse, or rather a kingdom of utter boredom and imbecility."

So Mussolini's career until 1914 was that of an apostle of violent insurrection of the masses against the ruling classes. He might have seemed to be Italy's predestined Lenin. But in education and temperament there were decisive differences between the Communist and Fascist leaders. Lenin knew no teacher but Marx. His references to non-Marxist economists and philosophers are expressed in terms of stereotyped unimaginative polemical abuse. He possessed both the strength and the limitations that come from seeing life entirely through the prism of a single dogma.

Mussolini, on the other hand, read and thought widely, if superficially. He was influenced by Nietzsche, the lonely philosopher of the superman, and by the French syndicalist Georges Sorel, who despised parliamentary socialism as "bourgeois," extolled violence as an end in itself and condemned the middle class as smug and decadent. From Bergson and William James he derived a sense of the relativity of moral values. And Mussolini was temperamentally impatient of the constraint of the Marxist dogma. So, while he was certainly a revolutionary in the sense of being a man who craved change, who disliked "bourgeois" order and stability, he was a revolutionary of the free lance type, on his own, not anchored to the mooring of any fixed theoretical creed.

So Mussolini's attitude in strongly favoring Italy's intervention in the war on the Allied side is psychologically understandable, despite his previous record as a passionate anti-militarist. Some of his critics have suggested that French money had something to do with his change of heart. All the belligerents were spending money freely in an attempt to influence opinion in neutral countries. A radical like Mussolini who, in opposition to general Italian Socialist opinion, was in favor of intervention, would have been a logical candidate for a subsidy.

But it is doubtful whether money was the chief consideration in Mussolini's interventionism. The man's intense desire for action at any cost made it uncongenial for him to adopt a passive, negative attitude of aloofness from Europe's greatest war. So the former rebel and deserter from military service went to the front as a volunteer and justified his advocacy of Italian action with the following arguments:[1]

"Whoever thinks too much of his own skin to go out and fight in the trenches will not be found in the streets on the day of battle. We must act, move, fight and, if necessary, die. Neutrals have never dominated events. They have always been overwhelmed by events. It is blood which gives movement to the resounding wheel of history."

Italy had been deeply divided about the wisdom of entering the war for reasons which have already been described.[2] There was little popular enthusiasm for the conflict and a correspondingly bitter crisis of disillusionment and resentment after the fighting was over. The war had cost Italy six hundred thousand dead and a million wounded and cripples. The internal debt was six times higher than before the war. Prices had risen far above the prewar levels as a result of inflation and went on rising during the years after the peace. The poverty of the country aggravated the problems of reconstruction. The returned soldiers often found it hard to find jobs.

[1] Cited in "Mussolini's Italy," by Hermann Finer, p. 103.
[2] Compare Chapter III, pp. 71, 72.

There was also a sense of national frustration at the Peace Conference. The Italian claim to the city of Fiume, with a mixed Italian and Slav population, on the Dalmatian coast was sternly resisted by President Wilson, although Italy finally obtained the city after a coup by the romantic poet and playwright Gabriele d'Annunzio. Italy obtained practically nothing in colonial spoils. Its chronic difficulties as a proletarian nation, dependent on freedom of trade and freedom of emigration, were enhanced because of the increasing tendencies all over the world to impose restrictions on trade and immigration.

To be sure, Italy completed its racial unification by acquiring the districts around Trent and Triest, which were mainly Italian in population. It also obtained the solidly German South Tyrol and some Slav territory to which it had no ethnological claim. But grievances bulk larger than acquisitions in a mood of afterwar disillusionment.

A mood of sullen discontent swept over the peninsula. The antiwar parties and groups had their revenge. There was an impulse to repudiate everything associated with the conflict. Officers could not appear in uniform without being exposed to insult and assault. During 1919 and the first part of 1920 it seemed that the Russian experience of war leading to social breakdown, economic chaos and, finally, to revolutionary dictatorship might be repeated in Italy. The Socialist party, with 156 deputies, emerged as much the strongest single group in the Italian Chamber of Deputies after the election of November, 1919. Mussolini and his small group of militant nationalist supporters were completely beaten in this election. The Socialists in Milan held a mock funeral of Mussolini as part of their election celebration.

About half the cities and towns of Italy came under the control of Socialist councils. Red trade unions, in city and countryside, became more and more aggressive. There was a long succession of strikes and interruptions of public services, accompanied by some riots and violent street fights. The cli-

max of this wave of social disturbance was reached in August
and September, 1920, when workers, in response to a lockout,
occupied a number of metallurgical plants and commenced to
operate them on their own account. The Premier at that time,
a cunning old politician named Giolitti, refused to call out
troops and finally persuaded the workers to leave the factories
without bloodshed.

The lesson of these two years of unrest in Italy is that it
is dangerous and very often fatal to play at revolution. Italian
socialism, which won so much popular support after the war,
fell between two stools. There were too many extremists in
its ranks to make possible a policy of cooperation with the
more liberal "bourgeois" parties on a program of moderate
social reform. Yet the Socialist leaders, unlike Lenin and
Trotsky, were not willing, perhaps not able, to risk everything on a bold stroke for power. The middle classes were
irritated and alienated without being crushed. Fascism was the
beneficiary of this situation.

There were several reasons why Italy never fell over the
brink of the proletarian revolution on which it seemed to be
poised. The Italian temperament was milder and less uncompromising than the Russian. Giolitti once reassured the British
Ambassador, Sir George Buchanan, who had seen the coming
of Bolshevism in Russia and was fearful of a similar development in Italy, with the remark:

"You have never seen one of our olive trees in Russia, Sir
George? No more will you see Russian Bolshevism here."

Moreover, the social order in Italy, while it had been shaken
by the war and its aftermath, had not been destroyed, as was
the case in Russia. Crown and Church, army and police, continued to exist. Soviets did not crowd out other political institutions. Italian socialism was weakened by the secession of a
Communist minority in 1921. The Communists devoted much
of their energy to attacking the Socialists.

It was Mussolini, the former Socialist militant, who rode

into power on the crest of the anti-Socialist reaction. He organized his followers into combat groups (*fascio de combattimento*) at a meeting in Milan in 1919. The *fasces*, or rods of the Roman lictors, became the symbol of the movement. Its uniform was the black shirt.

It was a miscellaneous group that Mussolini rallied around him at this time. Many were ex-soldiers, "the proletariat of the trenches" as he called them. A few, like himself, had seceded from the Socialist party on the issue of the war. There were syndicalists and there was a considerable and growing element of young men of the upper and middle classes who welcomed fascism as a means of fighting socialism and who were bored by the stodgy side of "bourgeois" life. The program which was adopted at the Milan meeting in March, 1919, was radical on the economic side. It called for state ownership of some industries, for a capital levy, for the creation of economic councils with legislative powers, for the abolition of the conservative Senate.

At this time Mussolini was the leader of a small minority group. But fascism gained ground rapidly as the proletarian revolution sputtered but failed to strike fire. The number of the local Fascist groups increased and they began to launch brutal counterattacks against the Socialists. In the constant clashes between Fascisti and "Reds" the former, who were often supplied with army weapons and trucks and who received more and more financial support from the well-to-do classes, were consistently victorious. Radical leaders were beaten, dosed with castor oil, killed. Trade union and cooperative headquarters were sacked and burned. The same fate befell left-wing newspapers.

The backward swing of the political pendulum did not and could not stop with the restoration of conditions as they were before the wave of postwar unrest began. There was a rush to join the Fascist ranks. Mussolini hastily dropped or pushed into the background the economic radicalism of his original program. He found a basis of agreement with the Italian Nationalists, a conservative party which had always repudiated *laissez-faire* liberalism and favored a strong state.

The former rebel agitator came into power with the appeal of "restoring law and order," suppressing strikes, composing class differences within the framework of the strong national state. The decisive date was October 29, 1922. Tens of thousands of enthusiastic Blackshirts were converging on Rome. The Premier, a colorless politician named Facta, asked the King to declare a state of siege. But King Victor Emmanuel, knowing that there was a good deal of sympathy with fascism in the army and disliking the prospect of civil war, refused to sign the requested decree. He invited Mussolini to come to Rome and form a new Cabinet. So the *coup d'état* assumed the form of a peaceful and technically legal transfer of power.

Mussolini faced a double problem: to impose his will upon the nation against the remnants of Socialist and liberal opposition and to establish his position as the supreme authority in the still tumultuous and undisciplined Fascist party. At the time of the seizure of power the Fascisti were a small minority group in the Chamber of Deputies. This situation was soon rectified.

An ingenious election law was passed, providing that the party which polled the largest number of votes should receive two thirds of the seats in the Chamber. An election which was held in 1924, with an accompaniment of much violence and illegality, gave the Fascist list a comfortable majority. All non-Fascist parties were made illegal in 1926 and subsequent elections have been mere farces. One thousand candidates for the four hundred seats in the Chamber of Deputies are drawn up by the executive committees of the syndicates, which represent both employers and workers in various industries, trades and occupations, and by other public bodies. This list is sifted by the Fascist Grand Council, an organization similar in general functions and character to the Political Bureau of the Communist party in the Soviet Union. The Grand Council's list of four hundred is then presented for a plebiscite vote of the whole people. Naturally, under existing political conditions, the list is invariably ratified by an overwhelming majority.

Inasmuch as Fascisti predominate in the executive organs of the syndicates, the Fascist control of elections is complete to the last detail. This control is doubly assured because there is no freedom of speech, of press, of assembly, of publication. Here, as in many other respects, the political likenesses between Fascist Italy and Soviet Russia are so numerous as to be positively startling, despite the antipathy which these two systems have professed for each other.

Mussolini is thoroughly eclectic and he may have consciously borrowed some of the institutions and methods which proved effective in the hands of Lenin and Stalin. It is probable, however, that a single party dictatorship, quite regardless of its origin, is subject to certain uniform laws of self-preservation. It becomes increasingly totalitarian in character. It is driven first to exterminate the last vestiges of independent thought and expression in the nation. Then the ruling party itself tends to fall more and more under the unreserved domination of its chief.

This trend has been very visible in Italy. Fascism in its first phase was a typically Latin movement, impulsive, violent, loosely organized. There was at least one important occasion when Mussolini was overruled by his subordinates. This was when he concluded a peace pact with the Socialist and trade union representatives in 1921. The current of violence was too strong to be checked and the *rases*, or local Fascist chiefs, carried on their punitive and wrecking activities without regard for the pact.

After the March on Rome, however, Mussolini more and more turned the Fascist party into an obedient instrument of his personal rule. The party was gradually fused with the state. It became an unwritten law that higher administrative posts, as a rule, should be reserved for Fascists. Just as the Communist party and the Soviets function side by side in Russia, so the prefect, the government official, and the *ras*, or Fascist local boss, carry on together in Italy. A centralized authoritarian regime prevails both in the state and in the party. The most important administrative officials, the prefect, or governor of a province, and the *podesta*, or mayor of a municipality, are appointed. The Fascist party is also organized on a hierarchical basis, with the Secretary General appointing the provincial secretaries, who, in turn, supervise the lower party units.

Mussolini has endeavored to create a corporative state, where class collaboration would replace class struggle and where the state would be recognized as superior both to capital and to labor. Nationalism and syndicalism, two of the strongest tendencies in the dictator's thought, both find expression in the institutions which he has created.

Strikes and lockouts were outlawed. Employers and workers in all large branches of industry, commerce and agriculture were encouraged to form syndicates, whose executive boards were recognized as authoritative spokesmen for their groups. Collective contracts were signed between these employers' and workers' organizations. Minor disputes are subject to compulsory arbitration and larger questions are sometimes referred to the Ministry of Corporations.

Like every revolutionary and dictatorial regime, Italian fascism has been the object of extravagant praise by its propagandists and of exaggerated denunciation by some of its enemies. It certainly achieved no economic miracles. Italy remained a poor country where the rewards of labor are less than they are in more favorably situated lands. On the other hand there has been no breakdown of the country's productive forces. The Fascist regime gave more impetus to public works,

such as road building and the draining of marshes, than might
have been possible under a government which was more committed to the principles of commercial profit and *laissez-faire*.
Italy became more disciplined. Begging, petty theft, slackness
in daily life, diminished. The price, of course, was the loss of
freedom and of much of the easygoing charm of pre-Fascist
Italian life.

Fascism did not and could not save Italy from the difficulties of the world economic crisis. During the Great Depression of 1929–1933 foreign trade declined by two thirds
and unemployment increased from 193,000 in June, 1929, to
1,229,000 in February, 1933. Before this period of world-wide
distress Italy had suffered from some of the familiar consequences of deflation (lower wages, depressed trade and generally "hard times") because Mussolini insisted on stabilizing
the lira at a higher value than economic considerations warranted. More recently Italy has gone over more and more to
a war economy, with its familiar accompaniments of full employment and shortage of consumption goods, as a result of
the invasion of Ethiopia, the intervention in Spain and the
preparation for and participation in the Second World War.

Fascism has been denounced by critics of the Left as a
mere strikebreaking device, a scheme of the capitalist class
to insure its domination over labor. And it is true that the
well-to-do classes were inclined to sympathize with and support the Fascists during the period of postwar radicalism.

But the conception of fascism as an insurance agency for
protecting the privileges and the dividends of capitalists is
both superficial and inaccurate. It is rather a form of Caesarism. It is an assertion of the superiority of politics over economics. It is a vehement repudiation of those ideals of peace
and social stability which intelligent capitalists have favored
and under which the capitalist system flourished most successfully. Fascism is anti-Marxist. But it is also antiliberal and anti-
bourgeois. It is middle class Bolshevism.

The restless extremist agitator in Mussolini did not die when he donned the toga of a new Roman dictator. When he talked to captains of industry and finance it was to give orders, not to receive them. And he endeavored to train a new generation in ideals of constant struggle, of physical and spiritual hardness. As he said in 1934:

"Anti-fascism is finished. But one peril may yet threaten the regime. This is the peril of what is commonly called the bourgeois spirit, of satisfaction and adaptation, a tendency to scepticism, to compromise, to a comfortable life, to careerism."

Fascism possessed no recognized body of dogma, such as communism acknowledged in the writings of Karl Marx. It was based on feeling and action, not on reflection. The properly disciplined Fascist did what he was told and let "il Duce," the title which was generally bestowed on Mussolini, do the thinking for him. It was Mussolini who interpreted and rationalized the ideas of fascism in an article which he contributed to an Italian encyclopedia in 1932.

Fascism is represented by its leader as something more than a political system. It is a philosophy, a way of life, militant, active, austere, contemptuous of such values as peace, security and personal happiness. There is a prodigious exaltation of the state which alone, according to Mussolini, can resolve "the dramatic contradictions of capitalism." Fascism is obviously opposed to the liberal idea of the state as a necessary evil, which governs best when it governs least. But Mussolini also dissociates himself from old-fashioned despotism when he writes:

"A state founded on millions of individuals who recognize it, feel it, are ready to serve it, is not the tyrannical state of the medieval lord. It has nothing in common with the absolutist states which existed before or after 1789. In the Fascist state the individual is not suppressed, but rather multiplied, just as in a regiment a soldier is not weakened but multiplied by the number of his comrades."

Mussolini affirms the "irremediable, fruitful and beneficent inequality of men" and contrasts fascism with democracy, "which equates the nation to the majority, lowering it to the level of that majority." At the same time he makes out a rather confused claim that "fascism is the purest form of democracy, if the nation is conceived, as it should be, qualitatively and not quantitatively, as the most powerful idea (most powerful because most moral, most coherent and most true) which acts within the nation as the conscience and will of the few, even of One."

Fascism, as Mussolini declares, believes neither in the possibility nor in the utility of perpetual peace. War alone, he thinks, brings all human energy to its highest tension and places the stamp of nobility upon the peoples who meet it. Mussolini speaks scornfully of "the equation of prosperity with happiness, which would transform men into animals with one sole preoccupation: that of being well fed and fat, degraded to a merely physical existence."

Unlike communism, fascism is not avowedly antireligious, although it repudiates the humanitarian and pacific implications of Christianity. Fascism, according to the former militant atheist Mussolini, "respects the God of the ascetics, of the saints, of the heroes and also God as prayed to by the primitive heart of the people."

It was in conformity with this attitude of respect for the traditional religion of the Italian people, Roman Catholicism, that Mussolini took steps to heal the breach between the Papacy and the Italian state which had existed since 1870. Under the Lateran Agreement of 1929 the Pope was recognized as the sovereign of a miniature sovereign state, the Vatican City, and Roman Catholicism was pronounced the official religion of the country. There were subsequent disputes be-

tween Church and State over the training of the youth and
Mussolini declared:

"The child, as soon as he is old enough to learn, belongs to
the State alone. No sharing is possible."

After a period of strained relations and some violence, committed by Fascists against Catholic Youth organizations, a
compromise was effected. The state maintained its exclusive
control of the education and training of the young. But the
Church was given some facilities for imparting purely religious instruction.

A Latin dictator, Mussolini has not been unmindful of the
old Roman maxim of statecraft: *Panem et circenses*. Bread he
has not been able to give in larger quantities. But he has been
lavish with circuses. Color and drama are infused into every
ceremony connected with the Fascist party. National and
local festivals are celebrated on every possible occasion, with
bands and flags. Events that would pass off as a matter of
course under other systems, the payment of old-age pensions,
for instance, are dramatized and celebrated and made a means
of glorifying the regime.

From the age of eight, when he may be inducted into the
children's organization, the Balilla, the Italian child, in and out
of school, is under conscious Fascist influence. From the
Balilla he is passed on to the Avanguardisti, which is for children between the ages of fourteen and eighteen. Then he
may become a Young Fascist. Finally, if his application for
membership is accepted, he becomes a party member and
takes, with appropriate solemnity, the following oath:

"In the name of God and of Italy I swear to execute the
orders of the Duce and to serve with all my powers, and, if
necessary, with my blood the cause of the Fascist Revolution."

Just like the Communists in Russia, the Italian Fascists, after
they came into power, were confronted with the problem of
how to make their new ruling class a genuine elite, how to
keep out the swarms of careerists and job hunters who will

always attach themselves to any successful movement. Early adhesion to the Fascist cause is considered a fair guaranty of sincerity. Apart from a few of its members who indulged in too much independent thinking, the Fascist "Old Guard," the men who took part in the thousand street fights and village brawls which conquered Italy and who took part in the March on Rome enjoy a privileged position in the party, like the Bolshevik "Old Guard" until Stalin's ruthless purges.

Like communism and national socialism, fascism is distinctly a youth movement. The age of its officeholders is below the average in democratic countries or in pre-Fascist Italy. The whole atmosphere of fascism, its emphasis on action rather than thought, its swing and color, is calculated to appeal to the young. Its marching song, "Giovinezza," contains a tribute to "youth, youth, springtime of loveliness." And, as Hermann Finer, one of the best informed and most discerning foreign observers of fascism, observes:

"Youth has all the qualities of energy, generosity, enthusiasm, readiness to follow decided leadership, plasticity, which tend to action, and none of the qualities of knowledge, balance, reflection, self-criticism, experience of the margin between the ideal and real, promise and performance, which would cause it to ask inconvenient questions of its leaders."

Fascism has been no more successful than any other dictatorship in creating a leadership of the genuinely elite. It has devised no scheme for assuring moral and intellectual superiority, fitness for leadership on the part of its new haphazard ruling caste. Its methods are those of Soviet communism: systematic indoctrination of the young with its ideas and control over party members by means of censorship and purges.

By comparison with the bolshevism to which it was, in some degree, a reaction and which it imitated, consciously or unconsciously, in much of its political technique, fascism was a milder form of rule. Between 1927 and 1932 seven persons were condemned to death for political offenses, 257 to terms of ten years' imprisonment or more and 1,360 to terms of less than ten years.[3] These figures may well seem shocking to countries with a liberal tradition. But there have been few, if any, single years of the Soviet regime when these figures of Fascist repression for a period of five years were not very considerably exceeded.

The olive tree to which Giolitti referred in his conversation with Sir George Buchanan may have exerted a softening effect upon the Italian dictatorship. Still more important, perhaps, is the much smaller amount of human and material destruction which was involved in the Fascist type of revolution. Russian bolshevism was an enormous and continuous process of social upheaval which involved the expropriation, banishment, even death, of great numbers of persons merely because they belonged to certain proscribed social or economic classes. In Italy, on the other hand, the man who was not an avowed anti-Fascist could usually go about his business as before. The number of Italians who felt impelled to quit their country was negligible compared with the number of Russian émigrés, although it includes some of the finest and most generous minds and spirits of the country.

Mussolini's experience has been that of many other absolute rulers. His first years of power were his most successful. Arising in a period of turmoil and of great weakness, almost paralysis, of the legal government, fascism infused an element of vigor into Italian national life. Some internal reforms and improvements were pushed through. There was at least a negative economic advantage in the steady functioning of the industries and public services. Despite much bombastic talk, Mussolini, except for the bombardment of Corfu, committed no serious excess in the international field until 1935.

Mussolini began to live dangerously, in his own phrase,

[3] These figures (cited in Finer, *op. cit.*, pp. 242, 243) are taken from the Italian émigré newspaper, *Giustizia e Liberta*, which would certainly not be inclined to understate the severities of Mussolini's regime.

more dangerously perhaps than Italy's human and material resources warranted, when he followed up the conquest of Abyssinia with intervention in the Spanish civil war and finally entered the World War. It is not impossible that Mussolini's regime, which originated in the First World War and the sense of frustration, the physical and spiritual dislocation, which it brought to Italy, may perish, in one way or another, as a result of the second. The ordeal of war to which Mussolini has appealed so often and so vaingloriously may prove fatal to his personal power and to the welfare and independence of his people. All the wishful dreaming and calculated strutting in the world cannot make Italy a great military power. And it is only by a rare combination of skill and luck that second-class powers come off well by participating in major wars.

But it would be a mistake to underrate the significance of fascism as a political, economic and social system merely because Mussolini overestimated the military possibilities of his own country. Fascism, regardless of what form it may take or what name it may adopt, is a Damocles' Sword suspended over the neck of every industrial democratic country. There are three circumstances under which the threat of fascism is most likely to become a reality.

The first of these is unsuccessful war. The second is involvement in war which, even if it ends without defeat, leaves behind a heritage of social, financial and economic difficulties which defy the relatively slow processes of constitutional democracy. The third circumstance which brings fascism into the foreground of political possibilities is prolonged economic stagnation, accompanied by mass unemployment. For a country where capitalism has struck deep roots and where there is a numerous middle class, fascism is a far more probable expression of revolt against liberal civilization than is communism of the Russian type.

This has been vividly demonstrated in Germany. And the

triumph of Hitler's national socialism, with the tremendous consequences which this unloosed, was the final proof that an era not of stability, but of an infernal cycle of wars and revolutions, had arrived.

Bolshevism, despite its own claim to represent the vanguard of an international revolution, could have been dismissed as a Russian phenomenon. The Soviet regime was too weak and inefficient to expand by means of conquest, although the virus which Communist propaganda injected into the intellectual veins of democratic countries was perhaps more serious than was generally recognized. Italian fascism, considered by itself, might have remained just another of the personal dictatorships in which Latin countries have been so prolific. Italy could not, with its own limited strength, upset the European balance of power.

But when Germany, far and away the strongest nation on the continent in industry, in applied science, in every element of potential military strength, embraced the crusading revolutionary faith of national socialism it was clear that no reconstruction of the old Europe was possible. A tremendous impetus had been given to the all-devouring cycle of war and revolution that was rapidly destroying the last remains of the edifice of liberal civilization.

Chapter Six

THE GERMAN POWER MACHINE

GERMANY WAS THE pivotal factor in the struggle to restore European civilization on the bases which had been so tremendously shaken by the first World War, upon foundations of law, of freedom of persons and property, of common ethical standards. Without positive German cooperation there could be no stable order in Europe. With German collaboration it would have been possible to erect a strong Eastern barrier against the spread of Asiatic Bolshevism, to create a genuine European community of nations.

The Germans, after the Russians, were the most numerous people in Europe. There were at least eighty millions of them, reckoning the population of the Reich, of the truncated and purely German Austria which existed after the peace treaties, together with the three and a half million Germans in Czecho-slovakia and the smaller minorities in other countries. In its cultural contribution Germany stood very high among the nations of Europe. Easily first in music, it shared only with Great Britain and France, among the larger powers, its eminence in science, invention and philosophy. In industrial production, in organizing efficiency, in potential military prowess, it was easily the first power in Europe.

Analogies are seldom wholly accurate. But the policy of holding down Germany by means of a coalition of East European states, some entirely new, some greatly enlarged, all racially unhomogeneous and enormously inferior to Germany in military and industrial power, was almost as unreal as would be an attempt to restrain a temporarily disarmed United States by means of a combination of Mexico, Brazil and some other Central and South American states.

The story of the collapse of the Versailles settlement and the failure of all the postwar attempts at reconciliation is reserved for a later chapter. Here, in discussing the origins and background of national socialism, the reasons for Hitler's rise to power, one may merely observe that the victorious powers failed to adopt either of the alternatives which might have made for a longer, if not for a permanent, epoch of peace.

They did not carry out a root-and-branch dismemberment of Germany. But they lacked both the will and the power to adopt the boldly imaginative good will policy that *might* (no one can assert or deny with certainty that it *would*) have made the German Republic a contented, loyal partner in a society of nations. As André Maurois has said, with his French gift of epigram, the Treaty of Versailles was too mild for its sternness and too stern for its mildness.

Defeat in a major war usually brings about the fall of the government in power. Moreover, the Allies, following the ideological lead of President Wilson, had virtually made the abdication of the Kaiser a prerequisite of peace. So the Armistice was preceded by the proclamation of a Republic in Germany and by the disappearance of the Kaiser and of the Kings and Princes who ruled in the German federal states.

This German Revolution of November 9, 1918, was one of the tamest and mildest in history, and just for this reason its vitality and authenticity might well have been suspect to a thoughtful observer. Here was no uprising of an indignant people, animated by a sense of oppression and a determination to wreak vengeance on its rulers.

No representative of the former ruling class was killed or maltreated or even imprisoned. Councils of workmen's and soldiers' deputies came into being in the atmosphere of political breakdown and military defeat. But they were very different from the Russian Soviets. The efforts of the small Spartacist group, the nucleus of the subsequent German Communist party, to use these councils as the steppingstone to a German Soviet Republic foundered on the hard fact that the members of the councils, in their great majority, did not wish to assume power. As the German Left Socialist Heinrich Stroebel remarks in this connection:[1]

"In their opposition to a decisive revolutionary policy the Right Socialists had behind them not only the entire bourgeoisie, the whole of the officers' corps and the officials, but also by far the greater part of the soldiers and the socialistic proletariat."

This is not to say that there was no insurrectionary ferment in Germany during the postwar years. The blockade had brought about a state of acute undernourishment in the industrial centers. The collapse of the currency and the constant rise in prices, which kept ahead of the increases in wages, led to frequent strikes. And sometimes, in the strained atmosphere of the time, these strikes were accompanied by armed clashes.

There was severe street fighting in Berlin in January and March, 1919. In April of the same year there was a short-lived Soviet Republic in Munich and southern Bavaria. This politically very amateurish experiment, which was largely under the leadership of bohemian café radicals and alien Russian Jewish agitators, had effects in Bavaria which were out of proportion to its importance. It created in Bavaria, formerly a rather easygoing region of Germany, where the people dis-

[1] Compare "The German Revolution and After," p. 97.

liked Prussian stiffness and regimentation, a mood of fanatical nationalism and strong anti-Semitism. It prepared the soil for the work of Adolf Hitler.

When a small group of officers and former officials, enlisting the support of the reactionary Baltic Division, carried out the so-called Kapp Putsch in March, 1920, this reactionary revolt was successfully suppressed by means of a general strike, called by the trade unions. As a sequel to this there was some Leftist unrest and government troops clashed with insurgent workers in the Ruhr mining and industrial region. There was a feeble Communist uprising in central Germany in the spring of 1922 and an isolated Communist revolt took place in Hamburg in the fall of 1923, when the sense of national humiliation and the economic distress as a result of the Ruhr occupation were at their height.

But all these Leftist insurrections were foredoomed to failure. Not one of them assumed the proportions of a broad national movement. They won the support only of a part of the industrial working class and were easily put down by the trained troops at the disposal of the government. Even after the loss of the war the necessary conditions for a social revolution of the Russian type did not exist in Germany. The German peasants, for instance, were unshaken in their conservatism. The middle class, hard hit by inflation, was more disposed to embrace some form of violent nationalism than to seek a remedy in Marxist socialism.

The German Social Democrats, the largest political group which supported the Republic, proved sadly lacking in fire, imagination, willingness to press forward to revolutionary change, just the qualities which were needed if the vacuum created by the fall of the Kaiser was to be filled. With its leadership largely recruited from stodgy trade union bureaucrats, with a sprinkling of Marxist intellectuals, the psychology of the Social Democratic party had grown old before its time.

From the beginning it was hampered by splits within its own ranks which had their roots in differences of opinion about the war. Immediately after the war there were three main tendencies in German socialism. The Majority Socialists, who had supported the war as long as there was any chance of winning it, favored and practiced a policy of political co-operation with the more liberal "bourgeois" parties. This meant that socialism was watered down to mild progressivism. Then there were the Independent Socialists, who had opposed the war and who maintained the position, theoretically defensible, perhaps, but sterile in practical results, of refusing to cooperate with the middle classes and yet opposing an attempt at armed working-class revolution. Finally, a small extremist group, headed by Karl Liebknecht and Rosa Luxemburg, both of whom were murdered after the uprising in Berlin in January, 1919, were in favor of a German Soviet Republic. This group, very small at first, swelled into a mass party after the majority of the delegates at the Halle Congress of the Independent Socialists, in August, 1920, voted in favor of affiliation with the Communist Third International. The more moderate members of the Independent Socialist party later rejoined the Majority Socialist party.

While the Communists polled about five million votes in the last relatively free German election, in March, 1933, and obtained a considerable following in some industrial centers, especially among the younger workers and the unemployed, their political strength was never really formidable. Many Germans voted Communist not because they seriously expected to set up a Soviet Republic, but merely in order to express disapproval of what they considered the weak and compromising policy of the Social Democrats in defending labor interests. After the Hamburg revolt of 1923 the Communists made no further serious effort to organized armed uprisings.

They suffered from the handicap, a very grave one in a

country where the sense of national pride was as strong as it was in Germany, of being open to the charge of acting as agents of a foreign power and taking orders from Russia. Their leaders were arbitrarily shifted whenever Stalin chose, and the quality of their leadership steadily deteriorated until it became as wooden and unimaginative as that of the Social Democrats themselves. After all, Lenin would probably never have led a successful revolution if a Communist International had been in existence, giving him instructions from a distance, in 1917. Objectively, although not intentionally, the chief role of the German Communists was to pave the way for the coming of Hitler. During the last years of the Republic they directed almost all their propaganda not against the Nazis, but against the Social Democrats. So they drove a deep wedge into the German labor movement and destroyed any chance of organizing a united working class front against Hitler's seizure of power.

The Republic was proclaimed under singularly inauspicious circumstances, in a moment of great national disaster. Psychologically it was very unfortunate that the German signatories of the Peace of Versailles were two obscure Social Democrats and not some distinguished representatives of the Imperial regime. The responsibility for the military and diplomatic preparation and conduct of the war and hence for the defeat rested with the leaders of the Old Germany. Had they been compelled to recognize this responsibility by signing the peace treaty the psychological attitude of the people toward the Republic might have been different.

As events turned out, the politically immature German (and political maturity is not a German characteristic) tended to associate the national prestige, the order, the relative comfort and well-being, of the prewar years with the Imperial regime. The Republic, by the same token, was blamed for civil strife, inflation, impoverishment, humiliation, all the consequences of the lost war.

Germany made its first experiment in liberal democracy with the republican constitution which was drawn up at Weimar. The electoral inequalities of the Imperial regime were swept away and the principle of Cabinet responsibility to the Reichstag was established. Hitherto the German Chancellor had been responsible only to the Kaiser and had not been obliged to retire if the Reichstag passed a vote of lack of confidence. The utmost requirements of theoretical democracy (to the detriment, incidentally, of the practical efficient functioning of the Reichstag) were met by the adoption of a system of proportional representation which made for a multitude of parties. The eight-hour day was made a legal enactment and a system of works councils (*Betriebsraete*) was applied in the factories with a view to protecting the interests of the workers.

The administrative policies of the Weimar Republic were liberal and humane, if one excepts some instances of ruthless repression of Leftist uprisings by the military. There was complete freedom of speech and press, from the extreme Left of communism to the extreme Right of militant nationalism. Political offenders, including Communists and extreme nationalists who took part in armed rebellion, usually got off pretty easily.

But the virtues of the Republic were negative rather than positive. It was conspicuously lacking in strong compelling leadership; Gustav Stresemann is the only figure of the Republican period who could be considered a first-rate statesman. The Social Democrats were especially lacking in distinguished personalities. The system of proportional representation proved very badly suited to German political needs. It produced a ridiculous number of parties and imparted a character of anonymous irresponsibility to the decisions of the government. It also tended to erect a wall of separation between the voters and their representatives, because members were elected on national lists and not by local districts.

About the Republic there was always something timid, colorless, apologetic. There was little effort to purge the administration of known enemies of the new regime. Liberalism often degenerated into apathy and weakness. There was almost a complete failure to appeal to the youth by giving the sense of national unity and purpose which Germans crave more than most other peoples. The mood of this youth unquestionably found expression in the following criticism of the Weimar regime by Moeller van den Bruck, one of the most brilliant of the younger intellectuals who helped to shape the thought of the German postwar generation:

"To the end of time the German Revolution will be characterized by the total lack of personality among those who carried it out; not a man of them stood out by his stature above the mediocrity usual among German politicians. . . . Revolution and Republic have begotten no geniuses, but only compromisers, wait-and-see men, not men of action; anvils, not hammers; they have shown patience, not daring; *laissez-faire*, not enterprise; in no case creativeness."

Germany after its defeat faced social and economic difficulties and crises which called for strong governmental action. And this action was not forthcoming, partly because of the disabilities imposed by the peace treaty, partly because of the paralyzing contentions of class and group and party interests. The total destruction of the value of the currency, for instance, was a revolutionizing agency comparable with war itself. It pauperized the middle class which would normally have been the strongest barrier against adventurous and violent experiments. There is certainly a connection between what seems to be the unmotivated brutality of the Nazis and the indescribable bitterness and frustration of the great numbers of Germans who saw their modest savings in government bonds, bank accounts, mortgages and securities melt away and become so much waste paper.

A stronger government could not have altogether avoided

this social catastrophe, but it might have found ways of mitigating it. And when Germany's second great postwar economic disaster, the mass unemployment that began in 1929,
came on it, the resultant sweep of national socialism might
have been arrested if the government and the trade unions had
cooperated in a bolder credit policy that would have facilitated work-creation schemes.

A bad omen for the future of the Republic was the fact that
the victims of nearly all the political murders and attempted
murders of the period were men of the Left, Socialists, liberals,
Jews. This showed that the fighting fanaticism was all on the
other side. The strong conservative bias of the courts was
reflected in the very different measure of punishment applied
to political crimes of the Right and of the Left. It has been
estimated [2] that of 318 political murders committed by the
Right only one was punished; sixteen political assassinations
committed by Leftists were followed by eight death sentences
and the imposition of long terms of imprisonment.

Another development that threatened the existence of a
liberal regime in Germany was the growth of anti-Semitism to
almost pathological proportions. This hatred of the Jews was
not a creation of Hitler, although he exploited it and spread it
by all the propaganda means at his disposal. Nor was it, except
in minor degree, an inheritance from Imperial Germany.

There was social and racial prejudice against the Jews in
Germany before 1914. They were seldom admitted to higher
government posts and almost never given officers' commissions
in the army. And Germany turned out a ponderous weight of
theoretical anti-Semitic literature, perhaps more than one
could find in any other country.

Yet the German Jewish community of some five or six hundred thousand persons was prosperous and, in the main, as-
similationist in character. The majority thought of themselves
as Germans of Jewish faith and race, not as Jews who hap-

[2] Stroebel, *op. cit.*, p. 260.

pened to be living in Germany. Jews were prominent in business and finance; in the professions; in literature, art and science. It was not uncommon for members of the nobility and of the well-to-do classes to intermarry with wealthy Jewish families. Jews throughout the world did not instinctively look on Germany as an enemy in the First World War; Tsarist Russia was the only avowedly anti-Semitic great power.

War is a natural stimulant of violent and irrational passions, of hatred for everything that can be represented as alien. And the curve of international anti-Semitism tends to rise in times of suffering and emotional stress and to fall in sheltered and prosperous periods. So some increase in afterwar dislike of the Jews in Germany was almost inevitable. This tendency was greatly enhanced by two factors.

Jews were numerous among the leaders of extremist movements. Of the three most prominent figures among the German Spartacists, Karl Liebknecht, Rosa Luxemburg and Leo Jogisches, the two latter were Jews, as was the chief foreign participant in the movement, the cosmopolitan Karl Radek. Kurt Eisner, the Bavarian Socialist whose murder provoked the Bavarian Soviet revolt, and several leaders of this revolt were Jews. So the conviction became stronger among conservative Germans that the Jews were an antinational, subversive group.

A second and perhaps stronger reason for the growth of anti-Semitism was the considerable number of Jews among the *Schieber,* or profiteers, who became rich out of the general misery of the inflation. Immediately after the war, at a very bad time psychologically, there was a large influx of Jews from Eastern Europe into hungry, defeated Germany. These Jews were fugitives from social upheaval in Russia, from pogroms in Ukraina, from similar occasional outbreaks of mob hostility in Poland. Many of them had little to live on but their wits. Long experience of semilegal conditions under the harassment of the corrupt Tsarist officials gave them an aptitude for speculation. And the chaotic currency and general economic conditions furnished them many opportunities.

A reasonable, just estimate of the situation would have pointed out that profiteering should be curbed, regardless of the race of the profiteer, and that some of the biggest beneficiaries of the inflation were not refugee Jews, who did a small business in hawking marks on street corners, but the fully Aryan German industrialists of the Ruhr and Rhineland, including that great organizer of trusts and combines Hugo Stinnes. These industrialists were able to pay off their corporate debts at nominal figures and to pay wages in constantly depreciating marks, while they could sell their exported products for valuable foreign currency.

But people in an agony of national humiliation and impoverishment are seldom just and reasonable. The caricature of the Jew as profiteer took its place alongside the caricature of the Jew as Bolshevik.

The large proportion of Jews in such professions as law and medicine, in journalism and in the theater excited a growing hostile reaction because opportunity for the average German was sharply contracted. Jealousy and racial antagonism were stimulated because the careers in the army, in the navy, in the colonial service, to which many young Germans of the upper and middle classes formerly looked forward, were largely or entirely closed. Anti-Semitism was at once a more familiar and a more compelling slogan of hatred than anti-capitalism.

Despite all the elements of weakness in the Republican regime the revolt against liberal civilization in Germany was a longer and slower process than was the case in Russia and in Italy. Practically all Germans could read and write. They had been accustomed to freedom of speech and press and election. Such a people could not be captured by the *coup d'état* of a few adventurers. The German National Socialist Revolution took place only when national socialism had become much the strongest single faith in the country, when democracy and liberalism had been fatally undermined by a ruthless, efficient use of their own weapons, unlimited freedom of speech and writing and agitation.

The Republic survived the numerous shocks of the turbulent period from 1919 until 1923, the many riots and occasional insurrections, the inflation, the occupation of the Ruhr. And between 1924 and 1929 its position even seemed to grow stronger. A new stable currency was put into circulation. Reparations payments were stabilized under the Dawes Plan. An influx of foreign capital, mostly from America, offset the outward drain of reparations payments. In the venerable Field Marshal von Hindenburg, elected President in 1925, the country had acquired a generally respected figure as head of the state and the old soldier showed no inclination to disregard the Constitution or to exceed the prerogatives of his office. In Gustav Stresemann the Republic found a statesman who was a good European as well as a German nationalist and patriot. Such developments as the conclusion of the Locarno Treaty and Germany's entrance into the League of Nations, with their implied recognition of Germany's equality among the great powers, and Stresemann's conversations with a like-minded French statesman, Aristide Briand, seemed to offer some promise of a new peaceful era in Europe.

But the hurricane of the world economic crisis swept away all such hopes. Stresemann died, symbolically enough, in 1929, just when the storm signals were commencing to fly. The National Socialist vote mounted in direct ratio to the rising curve of unemployment. The new democratic institutions proved unequal to the test. The first blow fell when it proved impossible to obtain a majority in the Reichstag for the sternly deflationary budget which was demanded by the conservative Catholic Chancellor, Heinrich Bruening, with its severe new taxes and salary cuts for state employees. But no alternative Cabinet could be formed. In this impasse Bruening, with the cooperation of Hindenburg, commenced to promulgate the distasteful financial measures as decrees. This he did by stretching to the limit a clause in the Weimar Constitution which conferred this right on the Chancellor in special emergencies—a clause which was inserted with a view to possible civil disturbances. The Reichstag began to accept passively what it could not bring itself to approve actively. Responsible democracy had abdicated.

The liquidation of parliamentary democracy went much farther in the spring of 1932. Up to that time Bruening had been governing with the acquiescence of a small majority in the Reichstag. But Hindenburg, whose mental powers were beginning to fail with his advanced years, fell more and more under the influence of reactionary advisers. Soon after his re-election as President in the spring of 1932 he dismissed Bruening and started the dangerous experiment of ruling the country with Presidential Cabinets whose members were drawn entirely from the aristocracy and the old conservative bureaucracy.

It was an attempt to restore the prewar German system of government, without a Kaiser, and it was a resounding fiasco. Von Papen and others who persuaded the President to take this course did not understand that a conservative regime can exist on a basis of tradition but cannot be imposed on a people visibly against its will, at least not without military violence and arbitrary terrorism.

But there was no bloodshed in this Hindenburg dictatorship and freedom of speech and press was still respected. Only freedom of election was made farcical. As soon as the Reichstag would pass an overwhelming vote of lack of confidence in one of these so-called "Barons' Cabinets" it would be dissolved, a new election would be held and a new Cabinet of similar composition would be appointed. Another blow to the crumbling fabric of democratic government was the arbitrary ousting of the coalition government of Social Democrats,

Democrats and Center party in Prussia and its replacement by an appointed conservative regime. For almost a year before Hitler came into power Germany was being ruled by a regime which, by the test of elections, represented no more than 10 per cent of the population.

Such a situation could not endure indefinitely. In the modern industrial age of general literacy and newspaper reading and radio communication a dictatorship can only exist if it creates at least the outer show of being based on popular consent. It cannot continue in the face of the expressed lack of confidence of nine tenths of the people.

Of all the postwar revolutions Hitler's rise to power is perhaps the most amazing. Lenin and Mussolini had both displayed capacity for leadership in revolutionary movements. But nothing in his past had marked out for distinction the young Austrian corporal who had served through the war as a volunteer in a Bavarian regiment and who wept bitter tears of shame and rage at the news of the Armistice in the hospital where he was lying gassed. He had formerly earned a meager and precarious living at odd jobs of manual labor after having failed to realize his ambition to become an architect because of inadequate preparation. His war record was neither better nor worse than that of millions of other gray-uniformed German soldiers. Behind him was nothing, neither birth, nor wealth, nor military distinction, nor a party following.

If an imaginative writer like H. G. Wells some twenty years ago had described the precise course of events to come in Germany the story would have been dismissed as an incredible fantasy. An obscure Austrian, to become the dictator of crushed and defeated Germany, to undo everything that Lloyd George and Clemenceau and Wilson had accomplished, to achieve a Napoleonic domination of the European continent, to become a conqueror comparable with Alexander the Great or Tamerlane the Earthshaker! The whole idea would have seemed an absurd nightmare.

But Hitler's rise to power was neither a miracle nor an accident. He possessed certain qualities which were especially well calculated to win a wide popular following in Germany after the war. He was impressive as an orator, rapt, passionate, almost hypnotic. And the gift of effective public speaking is just the one in which the average German statesman is most likely to be lacking. He possessed unbounded self-confidence at a time when the German people as a whole felt helplessly uprooted; torn away from old moorings, moral, political and economic. His speeches were suffused with a cloudy mysticism, with a tragic emphasis on self which a more rationalistic people might have found banal, irritating or merely ridiculous but which struck a responsive chord in the sentimental Germans.

Hitler's mass appeal was enhanced because he was a man of the people, not a member of the sharply defined German upper class. When he exalted national pride and the German warrior spirit he won more applause because he had fought through the war as a private soldier and not as an officer. To many in the audiences which he inflamed he seemed a figure out of one of Wagner's music dramas, a savior from another sphere, a Lohengrin or a Parsifal. This impression was heightened by the simplicity of his personal life, the austere abstinence from women and drink and tobacco and meat.

Hitler possessed other qualities of the mass leader in an age of industry and technique. He was a master showman and he was keenly conscious of the value and importance of constantly iterated propaganda in slogans simple enough and crude enough to strike a low common denominator of receptive intelligence.

But the supreme secret of Hitler's triumph was that he voiced the subconscious feelings of great numbers of Germans after the end of the war. Most Germans had always prized national prestige and order above individual liberty. Hitler promised a Third Reich greater and more glorious than the Holy Roman Empire or the realm of the Hohenzollerns. The average German felt frustrated and bitter after the lost war. Hitler canalized this frustration and bitterness into a passionate rejection of all humanitarian and pacifist ideas, an exaltation of power politics in its crudest and most cynical terms. Anti-Semitism was rife in Germany. Hitler screamed his hatred of the Jew as the source of all Germany's ills from the housetops in such ecstatic frenzies as the following amazing passage from "Mein Kampf."

"If, with the help of the Marxian creed, the Jew conquers the nations of the world, his crown will become the funeral wreath of humanity, and once again this planet, empty of mankind, will move through the ether as it did thousands of years ago."

The German shopkeeper, handicraftsman, small businessman, employee, peasant—the classes which were most responsive to Hitler in the beginning—hated Marxism and were antagonistic to "big business." Both these sentiments had been embittered by the experiences of the postwar years, with the radical riots and disturbances and the growth of big trusts and chain stores which were putting the little man out of business.

Hitler told this impoverished, sometimes pauperized, middle class just what it wanted to hear. He denounced capitalism, without defining it very closely, as a source of evil degeneration. Marxism, he said, destroyed the very foundations of human culture by rejecting both personality and the conception of the nation. And he achieved a masterpiece of popular propaganda by identifying both capitalism and Marxism with the hated Jew. He offered the following parable:

"While Moses Cohen, stockholder, stiffens the back of his company until it becomes as stern and uncompromising as possible toward the demands of the workers, Isaac Cohen, labor leader, is in the courtyard of the factory rousing the workers. 'Look at them!' he cries. 'They seek only to crush you. Throw your chains away.' And up above his brother makes it possible that the chains are forged at all."

The Germans have been more attracted than any other people by historical interpretations in terms of race. As far back as the eighteenth century Herder had declared that the whole meaning of the history of civilization would be lost without the triumph of the German people. One can find traces of a similar strain of thought in Schiller. And the philosopher-patriot Fichte, whose appeals helped to arouse the German people against Napoleon, conceived the Germans as an *Urvolk* (primitive people) which had kept itself pure of Roman elements and was destined to manifest its genius as part of a divine plan.

One of the most elaborate and most emphatic assertions of the proposition that the Teutonic race is a primary force in human progress and civilization is to be found in Houston Stewart Chamberlain's "The Foundations of the Nineteenth Century." Hitler was evidently strongly influenced by this scholarly work, written by a Germanized Englishman who married a daughter of the composer Richard Wagner and became more German than the Germans in his world outlook. Many passages in "Mein Kampf" are popularized and vulgarized borrowings from the ideas of Chamberlain.

The Teuton, according to Chamberlain, is the Master Builder. The less Teutonic a land is the more uncivilized it is. Man cannot fulfill his destiny as an individual, but only as a member of a specific race.

"Race lifts a man above himself; it endows him with extraordinary, I might almost say supernatural powers, so entirely does it distinguish him from the individual who springs from the chaotic jumble of peoples drawn from all parts of the world." [3]

This British exponent of the superior qualities of the Teu-

[3] Houston Stewart Chamberlain, "The Foundations of the Nineteenth Century," Vol. I, p. 269.

tonic race was convinced that a mixture of Jewish with Teutonic blood would mean degeneration. The character of the Jew is too alien, firm and strong to be ennobled by Teutonic blood, while the European, in Chamberlain's words, "can naturally only lose by crossing with an inferior type, or, as I should prefer to say, with so different a type."

Chamberlain did not paint an unduly soft picture of the methods of the race which he admires. "From the earliest times down to the present time," he writes, "we see the Teutons, to make room for themselves, slaughtering whole tribes or races, or slowly killing them by systematic demoralization."

He believes that France, once predominantly Teutonic, at least in its ruling class, suffered a fatal racial decline as a result of the expulsion of the Huguenots and the French Revolution, with its destruction of many of the aristocracy. As for the Slavs, whom he classified originally with the "superior" Teutonic race, they have hopelessly deteriorated because of racial mixture. Chamberlain takes a very unfavorable view of the Latin peoples and hails the Protestant Reformation as an uprising of Germanism against Rome.

It would be difficult to exaggerate the explosive implications of Chamberlain's idea that the Germans are inherently racially superior to any people on the European continent. Fanatics of various religious faiths have fought with incomparable courage when they believed in the support of a supernatural power. Communists were vastly strengthened by their conviction that an infallible law of economic predestination was working for their cause. In the same way those Germans who absorbed Chamberlain's intoxicating theory felt assured of victory against what they regarded as lesser breeds of people.

If Chamberlain's original work was read by a limited audience of intellectuals and affected the thinking of a comparatively small number of extreme Pan-Germans before the first World War, its ideas, in popular and exaggerated form, have now been dinned into the consciousness of a vastly wider audience of Germans by the master propagandist, Adolf Hitler. Among the many examples of Chamberlain's influence on Hitler one may cite the following excerpts from " Mein Kampf":

"All really important symptoms of decay of the pre-War time ultimately go back to racial causes. . . . All great cultures of the past perished only because the original creative race died off through bloodpoisoning. . . . Only the loss of the purity of the blood destroys the inner happiness forever; it eternally lowers man and never again can its consequences be removed from body and mind."

This armed doctrine of racial superiority has marched with the Nazi Panzer divisions into most of the capitals of Europe.

Another influence in Hitler's theoretical thinking was that of Alfred Rosenberg, a Baltic German who became a high priest of Nazi dogma. The supreme importance of blood and race is emphasized in his work. "Mythus des 20 Jahrhundertes" ("The Myth of the Twentieth Century"). Rosenberg insists on that pragmatism, that denial of all absolute moral values, which is so characteristic of the entire revolt against civilization. The only vital thing, in his opinion, is the myth for which men are prepared to die. All forms of art and thought are valuable only in so far as they enhance racial consciousness. Rosenberg interprets various forms of activity as expressions of the same German racial soul:

"A Nordic saga, a Prussian march, a composition of Bach, a sermon of Eckehard, a Faust soliloquy, are only different expressions of one and the same soul, creations of the same will, eternal forces which at first united themselves under the name Odin, in modern times found shape in Frederick the Great and Bismarck."

An idea which found a ready response in a Germany that was embittered, impoverished and humiliated was that of national claustrophobia, of a sense of confinement within territorial bounds that were too narrow for the numbers and capacity of the German people. Hans Grimm's novel "Volk ohne Raum," the sentimental tale of a German who is driven by want to emigrate to Africa and there suffers one misfortune after another at the hands of the British, sold hundreds of thousands of copies. Its title, "People without Space," became a popular slogan.

A more intellectual sponsorship of the same idea is to be found in Moeller van den Bruck's "The Third Reich." Germany's supposed excess population of twenty millions is an obsession with him and finds expression in bitter, passionate passages like the following:

"There is no prospect of prosperity for us to-day. We are a country with a surplus population of twenty millions. Emigration is forbidden to the proletariat; it is forbidden to the nation. There is nothing for us but forcibly to break forth. . . . After a peace which robs the German workingman of the right to work there can exist only one foreign policy for us: one which shall secure us freedom of movement, one which shall burst the gates of the prison-house in which otherwise we are doomed to perish."

Moeller van den Bruck anticipated Hitler's contemptuous rejection of parliamentarism. The day of parliaments, he declared, is over, and Germany has proved too good for parliaments. Van den Bruck advocated what was to be one of Hitler's most signal achievements: the inclusion of the proletariat in a united German national front. In fact, he imagines the German proletariat as leading a war of liberation which would be both national and social, a war against "the bourgeoisie of the world." Here is a suggestion of Hitler's subsequent hymns of hate against the "plutodemocracies."

Hitler maintained that parliamentarism was not true democracy, that it was both irresponsible and incompetent. "A majority," he declared, "can never replace the Man," and he opposes to parliamentarism "the true German democracy." This is based on the free choice of a leader who is to be fully responsible for whatever he does or fails to do. Just how this leader is to be called to account, to be sure, is never made clear. Under the system of complete political repression which Hitler has established the only practical means of criticism would seem to be assassination.

Friedrich Nietzsche and Heinrich von Treitschke were two figures of the nineteenth century who contributed their share to the formation of the Nazi mind. Nietzsche, most poetic and most paradoxical of philosophers, exalted instinct above reason, spoke of "the terrible consequences of equality," denounced Christianity as a slave religion and saw as a goal for humanity the creation of the superman, who would create new standards and values.

Nietzsche was neither a German chauvinist nor an anti-Semite. Some of his ideas would be heretical by Nazi standards. And much of what he wrote (he was a profound classical scholar and a sophisticated product of the high European culture of the nineteenth century) would be beyond the mental appreciative faculty of what is in Germany an iron age, culturally as well as politically and morally. But he was an eloquent rebel against rationalism and liberalism and by this token he was one of those who unconsciously prepared the way for the coming of the Third Reich.

Von Treitschke was a historian beloved of Pan-German officers and state officials. To him there was no glory like that of the Prussian state. He repudiated international law and dismissed the hope of banishing war as not only meaningless but immoral, since the disappearance of war and its manly virtues would turn the earth into a great temple of selfishness.

There was much in the hard core of Prussianism, the steel band that always supported the German state, which Hitler took over and exalted. So he declared:

"In everlasting battles mankind has achieved greatness,—in everlasting peace it would be doomed to destruction."

This is only one of many passages in his writings and speeches which glorify war as desirable in itself. But Von Treitschke was the voice of the military caste in Imperial Germany, not of the Third Reich. His nationalism was of the old-fashioned conservative type, without the prodigious emphasis on race, the mystical "Blood and Soil" consecration, of the Nazi creed.

A modern thinker who held up for Germany and for the whole world the stern mirror of an iron age to come was Oswald Spengler, author of "The Decline of the West." This massive study, thorough, prolix and typically German in form, of the cyclical declines of former civilizations, with its prophecy of a similar doom for our own, had a prophetic ring for Germany after Versailles.

A dominant note in Spengler is austere acceptance of a hard destiny. "We, human beings of the twentieth century, go downhill seeing." Man is not naturally good and stupid, but a beast of prey, brave, crafty and cruel. Our world can no longer produce another Goethe, but it may produce another Caesar. World history is a world tribunal of judgment. It has always passed the doom of death upon men and peoples "in whom truth was more than deeds and justice than power."

Spengler foresaw the Caesarism, the personal dictatorship, that is one of the many common features of national socialism, fascism and communism. The coming of Caesarism, he predicts, will break the dictatorship of money and its political weapon, democracy. In this identification of democracy with money power he is in agreement both with Hitler and with Lenin.

Not all the thinkers whose ideas have been briefly summarized exerted a direct influence upon Hitler. But it was against the background of these ideas that national socialism, the doctrine of an iron age, was formulated. Of this doctrine Hitler was the sole author.

The conquest of a large, highly educated nation by an obscure house painter armed only with fanatical faith in his mission and dogma did not come about overnight. During the first years after the war Hitler was only one of a number of leaders of small competing groups which were united by ideas of extreme nationalism and anti-Semitism, desire for revenge and contempt for placid, unexciting bourgeois existence. These groups often quarreled among themselves and did not attract a large enough following to threaten the Republic very seriously.

Hitler first became internationally known when he launched a Putsch (the German name for an attempt to overthrow the legal order by violence) in Munich in November, 1923. This was when Germany was at a very low ebb, when the despair and financial chaos caused by the occupation of the Ruhr were at their height. With Hitler was associated General von Ludendorff, the most capable German commander of the World War. Ludendorff had gone a little soft in the head after the defeat and had become interested in reviving the worship of the primitive Norse god Wotan.

The Premier of Bavaria, Von Kahr, was a strong conservative, but he was not willing to go to the length of rebellion against the Republic. The Reichswehr under its local commander, Von Lossow, also remained loyal to the established order. So, despite the sympathy of a considerable part of the Munich population, the Putsch was a fiasco. A number of Hitler's followers, the first martyrs of his movement, were shot. The Fuehrer himself, as he came to be called, was arrested and sentenced to a short term of imprisonment in a fortress, which he utilized to write his autobiography and personal statement of faith, "Mein Kampf."

The experience of this unsuccessful revolt was useful to Hitler. He recognized that the German instinct for formal legality was too strong to be overcome by the conspiracies of a handful of enthusiasts. And he set about building up a mass party, with the idea that the German democratic regime could be overthrown by means of an adroit use of its own weapons, freedom of speech, press and propaganda.

During the years of false prosperity, or *Scheinblut* as the Germans called it, which were marked by the huge inflow of American money into Germany, Hitler achieved little progress. There were only about a dozen Nazi deputies in the Reichstag in 1928. But the crisis which began in 1929 gave to the new movement the impetus of an avalanche, sweeping away everything that stood in its path. The Nazis first emerged as one of the large political parties in the Reichstag election of 1930, when they polled 6,401,000 votes, as against 810,000 in 1928. A detailed analysis of the vote indicated that the Nazis had won their new following mostly among the middle classes and among the politically apathetic, who had formerly not taken the trouble to vote.

Even after this election some German radicals and liberals were blind to the shape of things to come. One left-wing journal contemptuously brushed aside what it called the imaginary danger of a Hitler dictatorship and saw the real threat to democracy in Chancellor Bruening and his stretching of Article 48 of the Constitution. Among German moderates there was much wishful thinking to the effect that Hitlerism was merely a transitory freak, an expression of popular resentment against economic difficulties, high taxes and unemployment.

But economic conditions became worse, not better, and the Nazis went from one election success to another and struck firmer root as an organized force. Apart from the negative side of arousing discontent over a crisis that seemed not only prolonged but insoluble there were positive elements of attraction in Hitler's crusade. The bands, the uniforms, the songs, the marching, that were part of its stock in trade appealed to a people that felt starved for color and action under a regime that was singularly lacking in ceremonial pomp. The average German perhaps missed this pomp even more keenly than he missed some material things.

Hitler pressed home his offensive against a weak opposition that was hopelessly divided politically and that was more and more demoralized by an economic crisis, reflected in a growth of unemployment from 540,000 in 1927 to over six million in 1932. Of course other industrial countries, such as the United States and Great Britain, experienced deep distress as a result of the same cause. But unemployment was less generously relieved by doles in Germany because of the greater poverty of the country. Moreover, if Germany had not lost the war it might well have endured a period of business depression without such serious political repercussions. It was the combination of the sting of military defeat with the greatest economic crisis in half a century that proved fatal to the struggling Republic.

The Nazis enjoyed and exploited the advantage of complete political irresponsibility. They denounced the Weimar "system," the Treaty of Versailles, the Jews, for all Germany's woes. At the same time they refused to enter into any combinations or coalitions with other political parties which would give them a share of power and of responsibility. Hitler, like his fellow revolutionaries Lenin and Mussolini, was bent on obtaining all power or nothing. He knew that his remedies could only be applied under a dictatorship.

The political divisions between the other parties were a noteworthy help to Hitler. Socialists and Communists were so busy fighting each other that they had little energy left with which to combat the Nazis. And there was no basic unity of purpose between these two hostile parties of the Left, the middle class Catholic Centrum and the comparatively few conservative Nationalists who were inclined to oppose the Nazis.

In the Reichstag election of 1932 Hitler obtained 37 per cent of the vote, more than the Social Democrats and Communists put together. By this time the National Socialists were much the strongest single party in the country. A ridiculous and paradoxical situation arose. The parties which were opposed in principle to parliamentary democracy, the Nazis, the Communists and the Nationalists, under a system of free election, numbered more followers than the parties which were loyal to the Republic. Democracy could almost be said to have voted itself out of existence.

Hitler made a semialliance with Hugenberg, leader of the German Nationalists, in 1930 and began to obtain useful financial subsidies from the big industrialists. At the same time his lieutenants, especially the indefatigable writer and speaker Dr. Goebbels, the future Minister of Propaganda, went into the poorer sections of the towns to try to break the hold of the Marxist parties on the industrial proletariat. Early in 1932 Goebbels was describing in his diary a visit to a crowded meeting in working class East Berlin:

"Nearly all those present were workmen whom we have wrested from 'Red' Berlin after many a hard struggle. He who has the workmen has the people. He who has the people has the Reich."

When a transportation strike broke out in Berlin in the latter part of 1932 Goebbels, despite the misgivings of some of the middle class Nazi sympathizers, insisted on supporting the strikers. His practical reckoning was that it would be easier to regain middle class followers who temporarily fell off than to win back workers if the party should oppose the strike. So the Nazis worked hand in hand with the Communists in promoting the strike and Goebbels put out the slogan:

"The scab is no patriot."

During the last years of the Weimar Republic democracy, in an effective sense, had ceased to exist, although a rule of law was still maintained and the brutalities of the concentration camps were still unknown. The old-fashioned conservative regime which was congenial to Hindenburg could not have been a permanent solution for Germany's problems. It is not known with certainty what intrigues hastened the downfall of General von Schleicher, the last Chancellor before Hitler. Nor is the question very important. For an open undisguised rule of an aristocracy of birth and wealth is impossible in a modern society where there is general literacy. The only feasible alternatives, except in backward and primitive countries, are political democracy and the modern-style dictatorship, with its mass organization and propaganda and the sham democracy of its elections and plebiscites, where the government always receives between 90 and 100 per cent of the votes cast.

So there was something predetermined about Hitler's appointment as Chancellor in 1933. The machinery of propaganda and terrorism immediately began to work, although not with the speed and efficiency of later years. Members of the Nazi and Nationalist organizations were incorporated in the police. Arbitrary arrests and suppressions of newspapers multiplied. Every art of showmanship was developed in the election campaign, which reached its climax in a speech by Hitler at Koenigsberg, broadcast throughout the nation to an accompaniment of the clanging bells of the old East Prussian cathedral.

Even so, the voting strength of the anti-Nazi parties remained formidable. It required an uncommonly daring piece of imposture, comparable on the ethical plane with the Soviet sabotage trials, to obtain a majority in this last relatively free German election. This was the burning of the Reichstag, which was attributed, most unconvincingly, to the Communists and served as an excuse for intensified terror and for subsequent expulsion of elected Communist deputies from the new Reichstag.

When the votes were counted after the election of March 5, 1933, it was found that the Nazi-Nationalist bloc had obtained about 52 per cent. A rapidly adopted series of measures made it certain that no such embarrassingly close vote would occur again. Adhering to his method of formal legality, Hitler obtained from the Reichstag a law for its own abdication, permitting the Cabinet to rule by decree for four years. There was naturally not the slightest question of resumption of independent activity after the expiration of the four-year period. Within four months the dictatorship had advanced so far that a law could be promulgated outlawing all political organizations except the National Socialist party.

Hitler's broken promises in the international field have become a byword. But one cannot reasonably accuse him of obtaining power in Germany under false pretenses. The program which he outlined in "Mein Kampf" has been carried out with extraordinary, indeed with appalling, fidelity. One can find some discrepancies and inconsistencies of detail in his pronouncements about foreign policy and economics. But in the main he has done just about what he told the German people, in "Mein Kampf," that he proposed to do.

Parliamentarism has been swept away. The leadership principle has been installed in politics, in economics, in every branch of national life. The emphasis in education has shifted from intellectual training to indoctrination with Nazi ideas and physical toughening. Purity of race has been made a primary consideration. The Jews have been persecuted with a systematic mercilessness unequaled since the Middle Ages. Labor and capital have both been placed under the control of an omnipotent state.

Dissident theories have been suppressed by every means at the disposal of a terrorist secret police. This is in line with Hitler's expressed belief that a new idea, by a systematic use of force, can crush and destroy old ones. The masses have been at once cajoled, bamboozled and dominated. Hitler declares in "Mein Kampf" that the masses are like a woman who wishes to be possessed by a strong man. Organization of the masses is necessary for the existence of a powerful modern state. But the general interest is served "not by the rule of the masses who are either unable to think or are inefficient, in any case not inspired, but solely by the leadership of those whom nature has endowed with special gifts." And he has inaugurated the struggle for world domination which he foreshadowed when he proclaimed that Germany would be either a world power or nothing at all.

From the beginning there was notably little open opposition to the dictatorship. There were about seven million Germans who voted as Social Democrats and almost five million who voted as Communists in the March election. But the Nazi seizure of power did not provoke a single protest strike, much less a riot or an insurrection. There was no duplication in Germany of the heroic last stand of the Austrian Social Democrats in Vienna a year later. All the blood that was shed in this German revolution was of the victims of Nazi terrorism, some of whom were murdered during punitive expeditions of the SA (*Sturmabteilungen*) while others were shot or maltreated to death in the concentration camps which were set up in various parts of the country.

Opposition outside the Nazi party was cowed, crushed, obsessed with an inner consciousness of futility. There was more reason to anticipate difficulties with the Nazi rank-and-file, and especially with the brown-shirted party militia. Among their members there was discontent with the slow progress of the revolution and with the failure to provide more jobs for deserving Nazis. Some of the SA leaders, such as the Chief of Staff Captain Roehm, were personally ambitious and wished to incorporate the SA formations bodily in the new national army.

But the purge of June 30, 1934, in which Roehm and a number of other SA leaders were shot, checked these rumbles of discontent and was accompanied by a shift of power within the party from the more unruly and turbulent SA to a smaller organization, the carefully selected and trained SS (*Schutzstaffel*).[4] The purge of June 30, in which seventy-seven persons were put to death according to Hitler's statement (unofficial estimates give a much higher figure), was

---

[4] Members of the *Schutzstaffel* were originally supposed to protect Nazi meetings against outside interference.

unique in its sweeping character. Party discipline afterward pretty much took care of itself. There were no more mass purges.

For the dissolved trade unions Hitler substituted the Labor Front, an organization in which employers and workers were both included. As in Italy, strikes and lockouts were forbidden. The "leadership principle" was applied in the factories. The employer was considered the Fuehrer; the workers and employees received local representation of their interests through Councils of Confidence (*Vertrauensraete*), which were supposed to meet under the chairmanship of the employer. Differences about hours, wages and labor conditions which cannot be settled locally are referred to state appointed arbiters, the so-called *Treuhaender der Arbeit,* or Labor Trustees. There has been a systematic effort to make the new order more palatable to the workers by means of recreation facilities which are provided by the *Kraft durch Freude* (Strength through Joy) organization, which arranges cheap vacation trips, excursions, sports, concerts and theatrical performances.

Under the Nazi regime Germany has experienced a remarkable transformation from an economy of overproduction (or underconsumption) to an economy where supply falls short of demand, from a condition of mass unemployment to a labor shortage. Intensive preparation for war has been partly responsible for this change. But there has also been an important factor in the new system of broader state control over every branch of economic life and every class engaged in production. The credit expansion which has helped to make possible the growth of industrial output has been kept in hand by means of rigorous controls, such as perhaps only a dictatorial state could exercise, over both prices and wages.

All classes have been required to accept sacrifices and restrictions. Wage rates have been frozen at the low depression levels. Profits have been severely limited through such methods as heavy taxation, price controls and compulsory investment of profits above a fixed maximum in state obligations. The peasant must accept fixed prices for his goods and deliver his produce to specified market agencies.

Yet in this rigorous system there have been compensations in the form of security. There has been full employment of available labor and plant capacity. If the worker's earnings are low he is free from the fear of being unemployed. If the employer cannot pocket the profits which he might obtain under a system of free enterprise, he is also insured to some extent against the risk of business failure. The peasant, whose complaint in the years of depression was lack of a market for his produce, can sell whatever he produces. In short, the net economic result of Hitler's national socialism (leaving out of account the special sacrifices and deprivations of the war) has been greater all-round economic security at the price of a more restricted and supervised individual standard of living.

The index of industrial production rose from 54 in 1932 to 137 in 1939. The value of agricultural production during the same period rose by 40 per cent and the national income more than doubled. The Nazi system was pointed toward war. Whether the same economic technique, directed toward peaceful ends, could eliminate such unfavorable sides of the capitalist economic system as periodic business slumps and mass unemployment is a very interesting question which cannot be answered until and unless the experiment is made without the element of preparation for war.

The Nazi dictatorship in Germany was a revolt against and a challenge to the whole liberal conception of civilization. For the liberal doctrine of free will it substituted an iron code of necessity and compulsion. Against liberal cosmopolitanism it invoked a racial nationalism of the most fanatical type. It was equally scornful of free trade and of free thought. It completely rejected the parliamentary model of popular self-government toward which the world had been moving. It stridently proclaimed the inequality of men and of races.

Liberalism had already sustained two severe defeats in the success of Russian bolshevism and Italian fascism. But these two dictatorships had not expanded beyond their national frontiers. Germany, located in the heart of Europe, possessed of vast potential military strength which was released by its intoxicating new doctrine of racial superiority, moved inexorably forward toward the realization of its goals, even at the risk of new world ordeal by battle.

Goethe felt prophetically that a new age in European history had begun when he saw the French revolutionary forces at Valmy beat off the halfhearted feudal levies which were invading France. The shadow of a new iron age for the old European continent, already implicit in the triumphs of Lenin and of Mussolini, deepened into the darkness of certainty when Hitler turned pivotal Germany from a force of stability into a spearhead of aggressive revolt.

Chapter Seven

THE NEW LEVIATHAN — *Vast monster of unlimited power.*

THE SHREWD, cynical and pessimistic British thinker Thomas Hobbes conceived the state as a leviathan, a vast monster of unlimited power. He justified this leviathan and its absolute power on the ground that without it there would be a war of "every man against every man"; "no account of time, no arts, no letters, no society and, which is worst of all, continual fear and danger of violent death, and the life of man solitary, poor, nasty, brutish and short."

Even Hobbes, with his lively appreciation of the evils of anarchy, might have hesitated to bestow his sanction upon the leviathan-state of the modern dictatorship. In its control of every detail of the lives of its subjects this new leviathan goes beyond any absolutist state known in the past. And between the three leviathans of our time Soviet Russia, Nazi Germany and Fascist Italy there is a large common denominator of psychology and administrative practice.

Soon after Hitler came into power in Germany a story was being circulated in Moscow that Soviet diplomats in Berlin were saying to each other:

"Now we begin to feel at home here."

Whether or not this story was true, Germany under Hitler was far more similar to Russia under Stalin than either of these regimes would have been to the Weimar Republic. There was the same atmosphere of repression, of fear, of furtive antagonisms that were settled behind closed doors, not in the open. There was the same conspicuous absence of news in the newspapers.

The distinction between the adulatory tributes which are heaped on Hitler and on Stalin lies mainly in the fact that the former are written in German, the latter in Russian. The spokesmen for the two regimes employ strikingly similar arguments against "capitalist democracy." Freedom of the press is a fiction, a mere screen for irresponsible selfish interests. Freedom of election is humbug; the money power controls everything.

Two fundamental mistakes have been made in appraising communism and fascism. The first is to regard them as political antipodes, to consider one as the sum of all evil and the other either as a progressive form of Social Democracy or as a hopeful method of maintaining law and order and social peace. There are, of course, important distinctions of theory and much less important distinctions of practice between communism, on the one hand, and fascism and national socialism on the other. But it has been a general historical experience that practice, in the long run, outweighs theory.

There are also special national characteristics of the three systems. The antecedents of bolshevism are Russian, as the antecedents of fascism are Italian and the origins of national socialism are German. As often happens in disorderly epochs of war and revolution, old national interests and ambitions are crisscrossed with the patterns of the revolutionary dictatorships.

But when full allowance has been made for the elements of difference, the likenesses between the three regimes are more numerous and more significant. And this is especially true as regards the young man or young woman who has passed through the propaganda mill, whose personality and ideas have been formed under the new regime.

A second misconception is to interpret fascism and communism as a wave of the past, a mere reversion to the despotism which was prevalent before the French Revolution. Now it is quite true that Stalin and Hitler have exceeded the cruelties of many absolute former rulers in Russia and in Germany. But only the naïve, unhistorical view that humanity is in a perpetual state of moral progress would afford any warrant for regarding fascism and communism as a reversion to the past merely because they are cruel and arbitrary.

On the contrary, these totalitarian regimes are preeminently suited to the requirements of an industrial, urbanized epoch. The impulse of the old-fashioned autocrat was to keep the people ignorant, to discourage the spread of education. The Communist or Fascist dictator wants his supporters to read and write, so that they may be more easily molded by propaganda. There was almost universal literacy in Germany before Hitler came into power, but both the Soviet Union and Fascist Italy made considerable efforts to extend elementary education.

The collectivist systems depend for half their support on such modern instruments of communication as the newspaper and the radio. The absolute ruler of the predemocratic period wished to keep his subjects passively submissive. Submission is also the objective of the modern dictator. But he achieves his aim by a diametrically opposed method. He keeps his followers so busy with an incessant round of activity, of perpetual motion, that they have no time in which to think or reflect.

The old-fashioned despotism based itself on tradition, on the disposition of people to accept without questioning institutions which had been handed down from past generations. There is not the slightest element of tradition about a Lenin, a Stalin, a Hitler, a Mussolini. All try to create new pomps, ceremonies, loyalties; create new orders; strike new medals. Their appeal lies in the very novelty of their regimes. The youth, in Russia, in Italy, in Germany, is given a sense of breaking new trails, of getting away from old and supposedly outworn ideas and traditions.

What is the area of common ground between the three totalitarian systems? The first obvious likeness is the absolute dictator who stands at the head of the system, who is irremovable except by assassination. Just because they are revolutionaries, architects of a new system, obliged to guard their power every moment without any protecting shield of inherited prestige, the modern dictators wield more actual power, take a more active part in governing, than all but the most forceful personalities among the absolute rulers of the past.

No despot can rule in a complete vacuum. He is always influenced by favorites and advisers. In Russia and in Italy the men who stand highest in the dictator's confidence belong to special high committees, the Political Bureau of the Soviet Communist party, the Fascist Grand Council. There is no corresponding institution in Germany. But Hitler has his intimate party associates, Goering, Hess, Goebbels, Frick, Ley, along with technical experts like the famous financier Dr. Schacht and the engineer Fritz Todt, whom he consults as he may choose. All the groups which stand close to the dictator are advisory in character and temporary in composition. Their membership shifts as individuals rise and fall in favor. Neither the sham parliaments which exist in the dictatorships and which are practically nominated by the ruling party nor any agency of the ruling party itself imposes any check on the dictator. His authority is uncontrolled and uncontrollable.

There is no hereditary element in these modern dictatorships. Hitler has no children, and few people in Russia know how many children Stalin has or what they are doing. Mussolini has tried to designate his son-in-law, Count Ciano, as his successor. But most Italian Fascists with whom I have talked are doubtful as to Ciano's ability to fulfill this role. Hitler at the beginning of the war appointed Goering as his first, Hess as his second, successor.

The order of succession in a dictatorship depends on force of personality and skill in intrigue among the few men who are close to the seat of power. The idea that a dictatorial regime must fall when an individual dictator dies has not been confirmed by experience. When Lenin died supreme power passed first to a triumvirate, consisting of Stalin, Zinoviev and Kamenev. Triumvirates have a tendency to prove transitory and Stalin's rise to the position of sole dictator was emphasized by the executions of Zinoviev and Kamenev and of many other old Bolsheviks. But these executions, like the purge of the leading generals of the Red Army, proceeded in an atmosphere of outward calm and indifference. There was no civil war, no street fighting, no use of the army by one faction against another.

The same principle, that a dictatorial system can survive its founder, was confirmed by the experience of Poland after the death of Pilsudski and of Turkey after the passing of Mustapha Kemal. In both cases the transfer of power to other hands was effected quite smoothly.

When I was accompanying one of the numerous mourning processions which marched through the streets of Moscow at the time of Lenin's death I asked a bearded peasant Communist from one of the Volga provinces whom the people of his district would know, now that Lenin was dead. "They know the party," was his reply.

And there was a good deal of instinctive political science in this observation. The single ruling party in the modern dictatorship gives the system an element of cohesion and continuity which is lacking in the familiar Latin–American type of personal rule by a military adventurer.

A party in a democratic country is a voluntary association

of citizens of similar political views which competes with
other parties in elections. Obviously no such definition fits
the Communist party in Russia, the Fascist party in Italy,
the National Socialist party in Germany. These are ruling
castes, utterly intolerant of opposition or free discussion either
without or within their own ranks. Lenin laid down a universal principle of modern dictatorships when he said that there
might be any number of parties in Russia, but on one condition. The Communist party must be in power, the other parties in prison.

These ruling parties control the administration of the state.
Party and state are fused to a considerable degree, although
parallel party and state organizations exist in the Soviet Union,
in Italy and in Germany. There is a purely party sphere of
organization and propaganda which is not directly connected
with the state administration.

The membership of the Communist party in the Soviet
Union has varied between a million and a half and two million
for the last decade. There is approximately one candidate, or
applicant for admission on probation, to every two members.
The size of the Fascist party in Italy is about the same; but
the population of the Soviet Union is three or four times larger
than that of Italy.

These figures of party membership convey no reliable indication as to the popularity of the regime. For the element of
voluntary spontaneity is lacking. A dictatorial ruling party
would lose its meaning and its reason for existence if everyone should join it. The aim of all these parties, therefore, is
to create a governing elite; to place devotion above numbers;
to make admission a privilege, carrying with it certain duties
and obligations.

In achieving this aim all have been compelled to reckon
with a phenomenon as old as recorded history. This is the
tendency of movements that were originally animated by
qualities of fanaticism, devotion, self-sacrifice, idealism, dur-

ing their early phase, to become morally soft and corrupt after power has been attained. Christianity certainly lost much of its original purity when it was metamorphosed from the creed of a humble, persecuted sect into the official religion of a vast empire.

And throughout the Middle Ages, when religion dominated men's imaginations so strongly, there was a constant repetition of the same significant process. A new monastic order would win a reputation for sanctity, asceticism and good works. Land and wealth would be heaped upon it. The primitive austerity would soften and deteriorate. And in time a new stricter reforming order would arise and go through the same sequence.

The ruling party in a dictatorship is exposed to a similar danger. Great numbers of people interested in getting on in the world, careerists and self-seekers who would never think of joining a revolutionary movement at a risk of personal danger, clamor for admission to the ranks of a party which has "arrived," which controls all political jobs and, in Russia, economic jobs as well.

The secular absolutisms of our time have been no more successful in preserving their original idealism than have been the religious movements of the past. It would be dramatically instructive to publish in sequence photographs of Bolshevik party congresses from the first secret illegal convention of the Russian Social Democratic party in 1898 until the present time. In the photographs of the early congresses one would see, along with some crackpots, neurotics and frustrated mediocrities, men and women of the highest intelligence and idealism.

A process of coarsening would set in after the Revolution and would proceed much more rapidly after Stalin commenced his extermination of the Bolshevik Old Guard. And the photograph of the latest Communist party congress would reveal a gathering of hard-faced bureaucrats, of men who had done extremely well out of the Revolution, who have been trained in complete obedience to the "boss," as Stalin is called, in whom there is no trace of the idealism of the pioneer Russian revolutionaries.

There has been a similar evolution in Germany and in Italy. It is interesting and revealing to read in juxtaposition two such works as Moeller van den Bruck's "The Third Reich" and Paul Joseph Goebbels' diary, translated under the title "My Part in Germany's Fight." In the work of Moeller van den Bruck, written eleven years before national socialism became a "success," there is passion, sincerity, originality, personality. However much one may disagree with the author's world outlook, one cannot brush aside his arguments with the feeling that they are banal, trivial or dishonest.

The diary of Goebbels, by contrast, reeks with the obvious effort to flatter, to gain propagandist effects. On almost every page there is some repetitious cliché about the unique greatness of the Fuehrer or about what scoundrels the Jews are. To compare these two books, as to compare the faces of the early Russian revolutionaries with those of Stalin's bureaucrats, is to sense one of the deepest and most permanent of human tragedies: the eternal vast gulf between aspiration and fulfillment.

It is remarkable how often the three dictatorships, originating under differing circumstances and working with very different human material (for there are great differences in the national characters of Russia, Germany and Italy), arrive at a similar method of solving a similar administrative problem. Sometimes this may well be a matter of conscious imitation. There was always contact and ideological sympathy between German Nazis and Italian Fascists. A witty Italian émigré once observed that Mussolini's feelings in regard to Hitler were those of a cat which had given birth to a tiger.

And neither Mussolini nor Hitler would have hesitated to borrow any serviceable ideas from Moscow. Indeed the list of things which the Fascists and Nazis could have learned and may have learned from the Communists against whom they proclaimed so many holy wars is long and impressive.

There is the whole method of government by a single party and by a combination of unlimited propaganda with unlimited terrorism. There is the practice of holding relatives as hostages for the good behavior of relatives who may be abroad. There is the organization of a network of centers of subversive agitation, espionage and sabotage in foreign countries. There is the cold-blooded commercialization of the misery which the new systems themselves have caused, the exaction of ransom from emigrants for whom life has been made impossible inside the country. There is the repudiation of any universally valid moral and legal norms.

In many cases, however, the regimes have perhaps obeyed an inner logic of their own being instead of resorting to conscious imitation. All three ruling parties, for instance, have worked out virtually identical methods of regimenting their members, based on a hierarchy of party officials and a system of constant supervision of the lower party organizations by representatives of the party leadership.

The dictatorships also display a common tendency to shed their original ideological content, to become mere power machines, revolving for the sake of movement, without any clearly defined goal. One of the most brilliant and thoughtful books inspired by the Nazi regime in Germany is Hermann Rauschning's "The Revolution of Nihilism." The author, a disillusioned former National Socialist, interprets Hitler's movement as "a revolution without a doctrine . . . dynamics *in vacuo*, revolution at a variable tempo, ready to be changed at any moment."

This tendency to turn into an opportunist power machine is equally visible in the Soviet Union. Lenin twisted Marx to suit the objective needs of the Russian revolutionary situation, just as a believer often unconsciously does violence to a dogma which he worships. But, under Stalin, Marxism, the fundamental creed of Soviet communism, has become little more than an obsolete relic.

It was a conviction of Marx and Engels, a conviction which Lenin made the cornerstone of his philosophy of violent revolution, that the state is an engine of class oppression and exploitation. The consequence of the socialist revolution would be the "withering away" of the state, because there would no longer be any class to be suppressed.

This idea was Lenin's justification for the "dictatorship of the proletariat." This dictatorship, according to Lenin, was not only more democratic than "capitalist democracy"; it was also a transitory stage, paving the way for the complete freedom that would come after the state had disappeared. Lenin did not conceive this process of "withering away" as something distant and millennial. On the contrary, it was to begin immediately "because in a society free from class contradictions the state is both unnecessary and impossible." Lenin laid down specific conditions for the withering away of the state. These conditions were the replacement of the professional army by a militia and the disappearance of the bureaucracy.

More than two decades have passed since the Bolshevik Revolution. "Class contradictions" have long been completely abolished, at least in theory, since private property in means of production has been destroyed. But the Soviet state has shown no signs of "withering away." The army has become steadily larger and more professional. All the democratic features of the early revolutionary Red Army, such as the soldiers' councils, the elimination of the salute off duty, the abrogation of special titles of rank for the officers, have been done away with. The Soviet bureaucracy is the most numerous and the most powerful in the world.

And the whole trend of Soviet life, since 1933, has been toward greater inequality. The spread in salaries, in wages and in standards of living as between the Communist ruling caste and the masses of the people and as between skilled and unskilled workers has been steadily widening. The former "party maximum," the limitation on the amount of money which a Communist might earn, has been eliminated. The difference in remuneration between a Communist factory manager or engineer and an ordinary worker is as great as it would be in any other country, although both the manager and the worker would live more poorly than their opposite numbers in other countries because of the general shortages and poverty. The wage differential between skilled and unskilled workers is greater than it would be elsewhere; the ratio in Russia is about six to one, as against two or three to one in other industrial countries.

Stalin recently endeavored to explain the conspicuous failure of the Soviet state to wither away by what he called the "capitalist environment" of the Soviet Union. The whole tremendous apparatus of the Soviet military, police and civilian bureaucracy was represented as merely a means "to catch and punish the spies, assassins and wreckers sent into our country by foreign intelligence services." This theory of Stalin's flatly repudiates the Marxist economic interpretation of history and is, moreover, extremely naïve and unconvincing in itself. For if the Soviet Union could be imagined as existing in complete isolation, in an international vacuum, there is no reason to suppose that the vested interests of its ruling caste would be given up without a struggle.

Perhaps the most unmistakable lesson of the Soviet experience has been its demonstration of Marx's one-sided narrowness in regarding the capitalist system, with its unequal distribution of wealth, as the sole cause of oppression in modern society. Inequality of power under a Communist or Fascist system automatically brings with it inequality of wealth, at least so far as personal consumption is concerned. And, what is more important, inequality of power leads to cruder and more brutal forms of exploitation (sometimes almost indistinguishable from personal slavery) than has ever been associated with inequality of wealth, especially in the later and more humane stages of capitalism.

So the power machine, a new leviathan greater and more crushing than the one which Hobbes imagined, functioning as an end in itself rather than for the realization of any ideal, is the predestined outcome of a totalitarian revolution. It is of little consequence whether this revolution in the beginning assumes a Communist or a Fascist form.

To be sure, all these power machines derive some momentum from the myths which helped to bring them into being. The Soviet Myth was Class, the supposed right of the proletariat to be the ruling class. The German Myth has been Race, the supposed superiority of a Nordic, or Aryan, race, of which the Germans are the highest embodiment. The Italian Myth has been Nation, the conception of modern Italy as the heir of ancient Rome.

All these myths are demonstrably false when they are examined in the light of objective fact. The dictatorship of the proletariat is a positive contradiction in terms. If it were feasible it would be undesirable. But it is not feasible. Supreme political power, where there is no democratic control from below, may rest in the hands of a single man, of a group, of a limited privileged class. It can never be exercised by a large mass of industrial workers.

In Russia, as in other countries, men who have once been workers have risen to high administrative office. But they ceased to be workers and they usually lost the psychology of workers after they became high officials. In the first years of the Revolution one might have spoken accurately of a dictatorship of the Communist party, or rather of the small group at the top which directed the party's policy. More recently there has been a purely personal dictatorship of Stalin. At no time except during the anarchical turmoil of the early months of the Revolution did workers, as workers, enjoy sovereign power.

There has never been a dictatorship of the proletariat in Russia. There has been a very ruthless dictatorship over the proletariat, as over the whole population. The manual working class, as a class, has a limited share of influence in shaping governmental policy in any country. But this influence is far greater in a democratic country where there is freedom of election, speech, press and trade union organization than it is under any form of dictatorship.

Equally mythical is the German racial idea. An elementary knowledge of history and anthropology is sufficient to dispose of the idea of a "pure" race. Germany during its period of weakness and division and especialy during the Thirty Years' War was swept over by mercenary armies of all nationalities. There was a strong admixture of Slav blood in Prussia, stronghold of the hard, uncompromising German nationalist spirit. Many of the apostles of the new gospel of "Blood and Soil," notably the Fuehrer himself and his Chief of Propaganda, Dr. Goebbels, are anything but Nordic types in personal appearance.

The effort to implant a strong racial and national consciousness in Italy was based on equally flimsy foundations. The Italians probably contain a greater mixture of racial strains than any other European people. The peninsula has been the scene of wave after wave of invasion, of ancient Goths, Huns and Lombards; of more modern Germans, Frenchmen and Spaniards. Saracens have left traces in Sicily and southern Italy. And, as recent military events have shown, it takes more than a black shirt to make a Roman legionary out of a present-day Italian.

But myths are valuable not for their objective truth but for their stimulus to human passions. There are few men of any race now who would be greatly moved by the vision of the voluptuous paradise which was promised to the followers of

Mohammed or by the less sensual theological intoxication that possessed Cromwell's Ironsides. Yet one of these myths carried the tribesmen of Arabia from the Indian Ocean to the Atlantic and the other enabled the plain men of seventeenth century England, the yeomen and traders and apprentices, to trample in the dust the Cavalier armies of their social superiors. So there is a powerful sustaining influence in these modern myths, although with the passing of time the myth becomes more and more subordinated to the practical needs of the power machine.

Communism in Russia started with the most complete destruction of private property ever witnessed in any modern society. There was no means by which a Russian who remained in his country could have saved any considerable amount of his property from the storm.

Fascism and national socialism, on the other hand, appealed at first to the instinct for preserving private property. Mussolini represented himself as the restorer of law and order, the enemy of bolshevism. Hitler also played strongly on the anti-Bolshevik note and promised relief from a profound economic depression. The act under which the German Reichstag virtually abdicated was significantly called a law to combat the misery of the people and the Reich.

The contrasted origins of communism and of national socialism had a considerable influence upon the relative efficiency of the Soviet and Nazi power machines. One sanctioned and drove to its uttermost limit a process of social dissolution. The other, in the beginning, preserved the existing social and economic framework more or less intact.

The Russian method was immensely more destructive and more wasteful of the human and material resources of the country. It unloosed a prolonged civil war. It decimated the trained managerial class and the technical intelligentsia. It permanently undermined popular confidence in money as a symbol of value and as an incentive to productivity. Yet the

Soviet economic system in recent years has been placing more and more reliance on the money stimulus. Experience has shown that the bestowal of such titles as "Heroes of Labor" and moral exhortations to work for the greater benefit of the "socialist fatherland" are of little permanent worth as aids to production.

One finds in high administrative and technical posts in Russia many more incompetents, many more men who could not pass a reasonable civil service examination, than one would find in Germany and Italy, where the technical knowledge and organizing ability of the middle class (apart from the Jews) has been conserved. The German power machine, in its military and economic aspects, works with far less grit and sand in its wheels than the Russian. And this is a fact of no small importance when all political and social systems are exposed to an ordeal of battle that often assumes swift and terrible forms.

After discounting the greater element of inefficiency in communism, because of its extremely destructive beginning, one must recognize that the economic techniques of communism and of fascism tend to run in parallel lines. In both systems there is the important common denominator of Caesarism, of predominance of politics over economics.

After ruthlessly smashing an old executive and managerial class the Soviet Union has found itself obliged to create a new one, and to separate this new class from the masses of workers and peasants by the usual methods of granting superior social privileges and higher monetary rewards. At the same time the Fascist systems have profoundly changed the content of the classical capitalist economic system, while preserving its outward forms and institutions. The employer's initiative is curbed in many directions. He is told by government agencies what wages he must pay, what prices he may charge, what he may and may not import from abroad, what he must do with surplus profits. There are so many and such powerful controls at the disposal of the Fascist state (ranging from the concentration camp to the milder but equally effective weapons of credit and taxation) that the former independence of the businessman has been pretty effectively destroyed, even while he remains the nominal owner of his enterprise. The Communist and Fascist leviathans, starting from very distant points of departure, tend to approach similar destinations.

All these systems profess to be far more than forms of political and economic organization. They represent themselves as integral ways of life and they demand from their followers the unconditional spiritual obedience which has hitherto been reserved for religions of the authoritarian type. It is not without psychological significance that Hitler praises the Roman Catholic Church for refusing to sacrifice "one syllable of its dogmas" and that Stalin, in one of his few interviews, referred with admiration to the severer type of ecclesiastical discipline.

Every totalitarian revolution leads logically to a secular religion. In Russia, where Lenin's atheism has acquired the force of compulsory faith, a mixture of persecution and propaganda has greatly diminished the public practice of religion. The majority of the churches, mosques and synagogues have been destroyed or are being used for nonreligious purposes. Great numbers of priests and ministers of religion have been imprisoned and exiled. Antireligious museums have been established in some of the stateliest of the surviving cathedrals. Here gaping peasant visitors can see highly colored stories of the religiosity and the crimes against the working class of John D. Rockefeller, displayed side by side with the rent rolls of medieval monasteries and cartoons presenting the Pope in a most unfavorable light.[1]

Fascism and national socialism profess religious neutrality; Catholicism has been recognized as the Italian state

[1] The engine which pulled the first train over the newly built Turkestan-Siberia Railway was labeled: "Our Reply to the Pope." The psychological idea seemed to be that Russians would work harder if they thought their labor was causing pain and displeasure to someone.

religion. But the claims of the secular absolutisms on the devotion of their subjects are jealous and exclusive. While there has been no such repression of the practice of religion in Germany and in Italy as in Russia, no closing of churches, any attempt to draw from the teachings of Christianity conclusions which would be adverse to the ideas of the secular cults would be promptly and mercilessly suppressed.

Peoples who live under modern dictatorships display a marked and interesting tendency to develop a dual personality. Except in the case of a few fanatics, the normal interests of the individual are not entirely eliminated. But a secondary collective psychology comes into existence, a psychology of complete submergence of the individual in the community. Patriotism is a familiar emotion in all countries.

But the will-less subjugation of the whole personality to the demands of the leviathan-state is something at once new and formidable. It contains an element of mass hysteria, almost of hypnotism. This psychology is produced by a constantly directed machinery of propaganda that dictates from a central source how every newspaper headline is to be written, how every radio announcement is to be made; that is quick to delete an unfortunate or suspicious phrase from a new book or play. It is amazing how weak the faculty of individual judgment becomes after a long barrage of indoctrination with a point of view that cannot be openly adversely criticized. Man is a weak reed, after all. Even in countries where there are no Gestapos, GPU and concentration camps, men often fail to speak their honest convictions under much milder pressure: fear of becoming socially unpopular, of missing a chance for advancement, etc. Small wonder that only the strongest personalities stand up under the crushing double weight of fear of very terrible punishment and fear of being isolated from the national community.

There is a saying that if one talks with one German, two Germans, three Germans, the result is grumbling and complaints. But if one hundred Germans come together the mood is summed up in the familiar cry: "Heil Hitler!" There is much psychological truth in this anecdote. I often felt in Russia that there was more genuine enthusiasm for communism in a large mass of workers than in any of the isolated individuals who would make up this mass.

So it is natural and logical, from the standpoint of its own self-preservation, that the new leviathan should do everything to prevent the human being from thinking, feeling and acting as an individual. In so far as this human being is under the control of a party organization he is kept busy with a constant round of prescribed duties. He is stuffed with synthetic slogans. He is pressed to work, to cheer, to march, always in unison with masses of other people. By every means he is conditioned to believe that individual freedom is a meaningless, even a mischievous, idea; that the individual can be free only as part of a greater unit, a class, a party, a nation.

As the individual is thus collectivized he is also atomized. His family, group, professional, corporate, loyalties are pulverized. As is often the case, the most extreme instance of this tendency is to be found in Russia. Here there is deliberate exaltation of the youth who denounces his father or mother to the authorities for a capital offense. To call for the death of one's father, if he is indicted in a Soviet state trial, is almost obligatory for the young man or woman with a career to make in the Soviet Union.

While such extremes are typically Russian, all the dictatorships place loyalty to the regime above the claims of affection, of friendship, of honor, as that term is commonly understood. The leviathan-state exalts itself into a god, and a very jealous and merciless god.

With so much in common between the dictatorships, are they likely to conclude between themselves a permanent fusion? The war has already brought Italy into the German orbit. A union of Germany with Russia would create a gigantic land empire, stretching from the Atlantic to the Pacific, a formidable counterpoise to the maritime Anglo–American empire which is sometimes foreseen as a product of the war. Whether such an enforced union is possible is now being decided on the Russian battlefields.

National Socialists dream of subjugating Russia by force. Soviet Communists look forward to the inclusion of Germany in an ever expanding Union of Soviet Socialist Republics if and when the Third Reich collapses. But there is a strong barrier to any voluntary union of the Communist and National Socialist leviathans.

This obstacle is nationalism, one of the few ideas of the past that has survived with even greater intensity under the dictatorships. Here again fascism and communism arrived at the same goal from differing points of departure. Nationalism of an overweening and exclusive type was one of the passions to which Mussolini and Hitler appealed.

Russian communism was first conceived as an international movement, with world revolution as its aim. During the first years of the Soviet regime the official tendency was to repudiate, deny and depreciate in the most extravagant and uncritical fashion all Russian prerevolutionary achievements. It was a serviceable propagandist argument with naïve and credulous foreign visitors to depict prewar Russia as a cultural and economic howling wilderness, to represent all constructive accomplishments as the work of the Soviets and all shortcomings as the inheritance of an evil past.

But more recently Stalin has been cultivating Russian nationalism, considering it a useful support of his regime. The historical images of Peter the Great and Ivan the Terrible have been dusted off and restored to places of honor. The victory of an earlier Russian Prince, Alexander Nevsky, over the Teutonic Knights was glorified in a film, although this was withdrawn in deference to German feelings after the conclusion of the Soviet–German Pact. Chauvinistic boasting about national achievements is now as characteristic of the Soviet Union as of Germany and Italy.

Very typical of the mentality which is created by propagandist indoctrination, combined with isolation from the outside world, were the remarks of two young Communists whom the French novelist André Gide met in the Soviet Union. One remarked that it was useless to learn foreign languages, because one could learn everything worth knowing in the Soviet Union. The other modestly observed that all the paper in the world could not record the great and glorious things that were being done in the Soviet Union.

This nationalism is a serious, probably an insuperable, obstacle to voluntary union between the Third Reich and the Union of Soviet Socialist Republics. And all the dictatorships are pursuing ambitions of nationalist expansion. This is true of Stalin when he regains access to the Baltic Sea and employs force and intrigue to extend the Russian sphere of influence in Inner Asia. It is true of Hitler when he uses his Panzer divisions to realize the Pan-German dream of *Mitteleuropa* and revives the idea of German hegemony over the lands along the route, Berlin to Bagdad. It is true of Mussolini when he seeks new lands along the shores of the Adriatic and the Mediterranean.

Yet the revolutionary dictatorships cannot be considered merely national governments behind new masks. The dynamic revolutionary element in the Soviet Union, in Nazi Germany, in Fascist Italy, makes all these governments impossible as partners or allies. Every attempt to reach an understanding with any one of them which would possess even the relative stability of the pre-1914 alliance or entente has ended in disaster. It remains to be seen whether the British–Soviet treaty of July, 1941, will have any happier fate.

The one-party method of government has become as characteristic of the twentieth century as parliamentarism was of the nineteenth. Revolution and war have wiped out parliamentary government on the continent of Europe, except in

two or three small countries. And even before the Second
World War extended so formidably a process which was in-
itiated by the first, the one-party system had struck roots in
countries as far removed from each other and as different in
background as China, Turkey and Mexico.

The world-wide revolt against liberal civilization has excited the most diverse reactions. Communists and Fascists
look on their states as the models of the future. Anti-
Communist and anti-Fascist refugees and crusading-minded
people in democratic countries look on the totalitarian regimes
as throwbacks to the past which can and must be crushed.
Some foreign observers, without sympathizing with the new
systems, consider them part of a process that is historically
predestined, that cannot be successfully resisted.

It is very difficult to write of the present in terms that will
be acceptable to the future. This is especially true in an age
of fluid turmoil and in the midst of a gigantic war, the outcome of which will profoundly affect the character of future
human society.

But it seems probable that certain elements in communism
and fascism, the increased emphasis on social services, the
strengthening of the state as against private economic interests, the effort to control production instead of leaving it to
the play of supposedly natural economic forces, are in the
line of inevitable historical development. Changes in these
directions were foreshadowed in all the leading industrial
countries and would have almost certainly taken place, in a
gradualistic rather than a revolutionary way, if humanity had
escaped the tragedy of the First World War.

Nineteenth century liberalism was the most favorable philosophy for the development of creative thought. At no time
in history, before or since, was the individual writer, thinker,
novelist, artist, subjected to so few external curbs. And the
rich cultural fruits of the liberal age afforded convincing
proof of the pragmatic value of liberty.

Economic liberalism, on the other hand, while it certainly

promoted a vast development of productive forces, was beginning to reveal cracks and fissures before 1914. It was being
undermined on all sides, by the growing combinations of
capital and labor and by tariffs, subsidies and other violations
of the principles of free trade and free competition. The beneficial results, even the practicability, of granting unlimited
free play to everyone's economic self-interest were becoming
more questionable. Some increased powers for the state in
the economic field were necessary, if society was not to collapse under the competing pressures of special interests.

Not the least element in the tragedy of the World War
was that it imposed an irrational stamp upon changes which
might well have come about otherwise in orderly, reasonable
fashion. This war is historically damned not only, not even
so much for the millions who were killed, for the inestimable
miseries which it inflicted, as for the dark spirit of ferocious
hatred and revenge which it imparted to the major postwar
revolutions. If one should compile a symposium of Communist and National Socialist political literature one would be
impressed by the predominance of the strident appeal to two
of the most sterile and destructive passions: hatred and envy.

No one can reckon how much of the ferocity of Russian
bolshevism was the direct outgrowth of dragging Russian
peasants from their homes, thrusting rifles into their hands
and then compelling them to fight against hopeless technical
odds. This was certainly no school of the humane virtues.

Much of the obscene brutality of Nazi concentration
camps, of the sheer delight in destruction from the air, is a
result not only of the First World War itself but of certain
effects of this war on the life of the German people: the slow
starvation from the blockade, the breakdown of normal
family life, the ruin from inflation. The war marked the
transition from an age of gold to an age of iron. It started a
cycle of hatred, violence and destruction that has now reached
a high peak, the end of which no one can foresee.

Chapter Eight

THE PEACE THAT WAS NO PEACE

THE PEACE CONFERENCE that met at Paris after the end of the first World War was the most important gathering of its kind since the Congress of Vienna, which reshaped the map of Europe after the Napoleonic storm. On the participants in this conference, and especially on the representatives of the three strongest victorious powers, Great Britain, France and the United States, rested an almost incalculable responsibility to their own and to future generations. The question whether European liberal civilization was to enjoy a prospect of revival after the shock of the World War depended very largely upon their decisions.

They failed, and the fruits of their failure were bitter—for their own countries and for the world. The ideal of the Versailles Treaty, as stated in its preamble, was to replace the state of war by "a firm, just and durable peace." But the Treaty of Versailles with Germany, like the associated treaties of Trianon, Neuilly and Sèvres with Hungary, Bulgaria and Turkey, was neither firm nor just nor durable. The failure to bring about general peace and the continuation of the declining cycle in civilization were emphasized in the prevalence of international violence on an unheard-of scale, in the wiping out of many traces of Western civilization in Russia, in the rolling of Nazi Panzer divisions through the capitals of Europe, in the crash of bombs over the House of Commons and Westminster Abbey.

One should not attribute too large a share of personal blame for the peace that was no peace to Wilson, Lloyd George and Clemenceau, the three most powerful statesmen at the conference. All three hoped that some stable world order would come out of their deliberations. All worked for what they conceived to be the best interests of their countries.

But they were in the grip of sinister forces which could not be overcome. One such force was a war-inflamed and war-intoxicated public opinion. Propaganda among the masses at the time of the Napoleonic Wars was almost nonexistent. The statesmen at Vienna enjoyed an immense advantage over the peacemakers of Paris in being able to discuss the treatment to be accorded France, the vanquished aggressor, without being constantly exposed to the pressure of popular demand for a vindictive peace, reflected in parliaments and in influential newspapers.

So, while many decisions of the Congress of Vienna are open to criticism, it achieved one very important purpose in which Versailles most conspicuously failed. It pacified the country which had done much to keep Europe in turmoil. And this pacification was due to the moderation which was shown toward defeated France. No Frenchmen were placed under foreign rule. France was not required to pay a crushing and economically impossible indemnity.

Mass propaganda, developed with special efficiency in Great Britain and the United States,[1] was an important practical aid

---

[1] Hitler, as is evident from "Mein Kampf," was profoundly impressed by the skill of British war propaganda and by the ineptness of the German effort in this field. He has more than made up for the deficiencies of Imperial Germany and has made efficient, unscrupulous propaganda a major instrument both of the maintenance of his internal regime and of his wars and bloodless conquests.

in winning the war. But its after-effects were those of Frankenstein's monster when it became a question of making a just and durable peace. For every sympathizer with the enlightened peace aims of President Wilson and the British Labor party there were a dozen Britons who had been aroused by Northcliffe's atrocity tales and had been captivated by such slogans as "Hang the Kaiser" and "Make Germany Pay." And there were a dozen Americans who had been convinced by four-minute orators that "Huns" as a species were rather lower in the moral scale than reptiles. By a tragic paradox the means that were useful in winning the war were almost predestined to lose the peace.

On the surface the victory of democracy might have seemed complete at the end of 1918. Of the three conservative empires which had existed at the beginning of the war the Russian had gone into the dissolution of a gigantic social upheaval. The Austro–Hungarian had broken up into its component national parts. The Kaiser had fled and Germany was a republic. Monarchism, except of the constitutional type, had vanished from the European political horizon. The many new states in Europe—Finland, Latvia, Esthonia, Lithuania, Poland, Czechoslovakia, Austria, Hungary—dispensed with kings.

To the superficial type of mind which believes in the regenerative value of a paper democratic constitution for all peoples, regardless of their history, background and temperament, it might seem that the world had really been made safe for democracy. But it would soon become clear that the wounds which war had inflicted on the body of European civilization were of far deeper and more lasting consequence than the apparent spread of a democracy which was seldom more than skin-deep.

The Versailles settlement would have stood a much better chance of survival if it had been either much more immoral or much more idealistic. It fell between the two stools of a vague unrealized aspiration for a new order where national sovereignty would be restrained for the common good and the retention, in most respects, of the old methods of power politics and selfish national aggrandizement. Add to this fundamental contradiction an economic unrealism that approached positive illiteracy, and it is easy to understand why the "Peace" of Versailles was no real peace, but only an armistice.

There were two clear-cut alternatives before the diplomats at Paris. They might have proceeded to a total dismemberment of Germany, on the theory that the Germans were a people of incurable aggressors, too numerous and too strong for the peace and security of Europe. The left bank of the Rhine, under such a policy, would have been assigned to France, either through direct annexation or through the creation of a puppet state under French military control. Poland would have received more German territory, including East Prussia and the whole of Upper Silesia. Finally the truncated remnant of Germany might have been divided on a confessional basis, with Catholic Bavaria uniting with Austria in a South German state—separated from Prussia.

Such a program would have appealed to a large section of opinion in France, the country most directly threatened by German military power. The French Foreign Minister, Pichon, declared that Poland must be "forte, très forte," and it was the general policy of France to support undiscriminatingly the territorial claims of the new and enlarged states, Poland, Czechoslovakia, Rumania, Yugoslavia, in which it hoped to find an Eastern counterpoise to Germany. Marshal Foch pleaded for the Rhine frontier up to the end. When Premier Clemenceau angrily asked him why he persisted in raising a question which had already been settled in the negative, the old soldier dramatically replied:

"Pour faire aise à ma conscience."

But the total breakup of Germany was inconsistent with the Fourteen Points of President Wilson, which had been accepted by Germany as the basis of the Armistice agreement.

American and British public opinion shrank from the turbu-lent and chaotic future which might have been the result of placing masses of Germans under alien rule. There was the possibility that Germany, already hungry, might go Bolshevik if driven to desperation. Then the Allied governments, already troubled by quivers of postwar unrest in their own lands, would have faced the formidable prospect of a revolutionary land bloc from the Rhine to the Pacific. There was also the consideration, especially important for England, with its dependence on foreign trade, that the destruction of the larg-est economic unit, apart from Russia, on the continent would hold back indefinitely a normal resumption of trade and industry.

So the verdict "Germania delenda est" was not imposed. The intrigues of French military authorities with the few disreputable Rhineland separatists ended in futility. Germany was diminished and weakened, but not destroyed as a great power. The victorious coalition had not been strong enough, or brutal enough, to dictate a Carthaginian peace, to obliterate Germany as a great power.

But it was also not strong enough, or not humane enough, to adopt the opposite alternative, to write the peace of reason, justice, mercy and enlightened self-interest of which Wilson dreamed in his more inspired moments. Such a peace would have started from the proposition that the war was a gigan-tic common catastrophe of European civilization, for which no power except Belgium was free from some share of re-sponsibility.

Territorial adjustments would have been made with the most scrupulous regard for the will of the populations affected. Reparations would have been limited to integral restoration of damage inflicted, so far as possible with the labor and material of the country responsible. This would have avoided both the injustice of exacting war tribute from German generations which were still unborn and the futility of trying to extract vast sums from Germany while at the same time erecting tariff barriers against German goods.

The ideal peace that might have changed for the better the whole course of European history, that might have reversed the downward cycle of European civilization, that might have made Hitler's dictatorship impossible, would have looked to the future, not to the past. It would have been based on the assumption that it was more important to prevent future wars than to exact the last ounce of flesh in retribution for the last one. It would have endeavored to strike at the root causes of war by providing for general limitation of armaments, with all-round mutual stringent control; by establishing some form of economic federation as a cure for the excessive fragmentation of Europe in small states; by recognizing that freer movement of men, goods and capital across national frontiers was the only means of alleviating the explosive effects of the unequal distribution of natural resources.

A peace conceived in such a spirit and along such lines would have meant a reprieve, perhaps a renaissance, for the perishing liberal civilization. It would have discredited and discouraged aggressive militarism everywhere. It would have softened the shock of the world economic crisis.

It was to Wilson's credit that he thought in terms of such a world settlement. But the American President was a true prophet when he foresaw, in a remarkable speech of January, 1917, that only a "peace without victory" would be the prelude to a rational world order. It was a disastrous illusion to believe that the necessary elements of reason and understanding and all-round readiness to sacrifice would be found in a dictated peace where one side could work its will with little restriction and dark forces of bitterness and revenge would be generated in the other. The sterile, negative character of the Versailles Treaty found a suitable characterization at the time it was drawn up from John Maynard Keynes, brilliant writer and economic expert attached to the British delegation:

"The Treaty includes no provisions for the economic rehabilitation of Europe, nothing to make the defeated Central Empires into good neighbors, nothing to stabilize the new states of Europe, nothing to reclaim Russia, nor does it promote in any way a compact of economic solidarity among the Allies themselves."

Defenders of the Versailles settlement emphasize the point that it freed more people than it placed under alien sovereignty. As against the six million Germans and three million Hungarians who were included in foreign states there was a grant of independent national existence to Poles and Czechs and an absorption into their own national states of Italians, Rumanians and Southern Slavs who had formerly been Austrian and Hungarian subjects. Four new national states, Finland, Esthonia, Latvia, Lithuania, arose on the shores of the Baltic. Most of the American historians, economists and geographers who were attached to the Peace Delegation worked honestly to obtain fair boundary lines as against the opposition of Europeans who were more interested in strategy than in the claims of nationality and economics.

But man does not live by nationality alone. With every new state there was a new economic frontier. Old racial and national hates stimulated the wildest excesses of economic nationalism and thwarted the feeble efforts to organize at least some kind of regional economic federalism. As Keynes, the farsighted Cassandra of Versailles, predicted:

"Economic frontiers were tolerable so long as an immense territory was included in a few great empires; but they will not be tolerable when the empires of Germany, Austria–Hungary, Russia and Turkey have been partitioned between some twenty economic authorities."

Moreover, Central and Eastern Europe represented such a complicated mosaic of races that no state with viable frontiers could be organized on a basis of common language and nationality. Of all the new states Czechoslovakia was the most liberal and humane in its administrative record. Indeed the Czechs are the only Slavs who have displayed a capacity to govern themselves without a formidable amount of police brutality.

But Czechoslovakia was a smaller Austria–Hungary, a polyglot state. Among its fourteen million inhabitants there were six distinct races, Czechs, Slovaks, Germans, Hungarians, Ukrainians and Poles. The four latter groups were all more or less discontented with the idea of being ruled by Czechs. And even between the progressive, freethinking Czechs and the conservative, strongly Catholic Slovaks there were not infrequent misunderstandings.

Germans, Jews, Ukrainians and White Russians [2] were all treated as second-class citizens in a Poland where they made up almost half of the population. The new state of Jugoslavia was undermined by the antagonism between the dominant Orthodox Serbs, with their background of Turkish rule, and the Catholic Croats, who had long been subjects of Austria–Hungary. The latter sometimes discovered that Serb police methods were more brutal than the Austrian. Rumania, perhaps the most corrupt of the enlarged countries, acquired German, Hungarian, Bulgarian and Russian minorities. Racial tolerance was not an East European virtue. When one considers the mixed racial composition of the new states and their industrial backwardness (except for Czechoslovakia), which made it impossible for them to maintain large independent war industries, their swift fall before the Nazi onslaught is more understandable.

The Treaty of Versailles did not take away from Germany much territory that was indisputably German in character, although the principle of self-determination was violated in the arbitrary handing over of the Eupen and Malmédy districts to Belgium and some features of the German–Polish frontier set-

[2] The White Russians who are referred to here are a small distinct nationality living in the regions of Minsk, Baranovici and Bialystok, not the Russian opponents of bolshevism who are sometimes called Whites.

tlement could have been more fairly adjusted. The treaties with Austria and Hungary were much more open to criticism for disregard of the principle of nationality which was always invoked when it would work to the disadvantage of the vanquished. Over three million Sudeten Germans were included, against their protest, in Czechoslovakia. Truncated Austria, with its huge head, Vienna, supported on the small body of mostly mountainous peasant regions, was refused its desire to seek improvement of its desperate economic difficulties by forming a union with Germany. The solidly German South Tyrol was assigned to Italy. Far too many Hungarians were placed under Czechoslovak and Rumanian rule.

But the worst feature of the Treaty of Versailles was its economic and financial clauses. Indemnities were no novelty. Germany had imposed a levy of five billion francs (one billion dollars) on France after the Franco–Prussian War. But indemnities in the past had been fixed as to amount and the collection involved no interference with the sovereignty of the defeated country.

Germany at Versailles was not given any figure of total liability. It was required to pay twenty billion marks (almost five billion dollars) on account. A Reparation Commission, made up of representatives of the principal Allied powers, was to assess the reparation figure by 1921 and was also given wide, almost dictatorial powers over German internal administration.

There was a clear breach of faith in the reckoning of Germany's liability. The pre-Armistice agreement stipulated that Germany was to compensate "all damage done to the civilian population of the Allies and to their property by the aggression of Germany by land, by sea and from the air." But French desire to cripple Germany and rash election promises by Premier Lloyd George led to a decision to swell the reparation figure, despite American opposition, by including the cost of pensions and separation allowances.

The Reparation Commission finally fixed Germany's liability at 132,000,000,000 marks (about 32,000,000,000 dollars). The sum was so huge that German annual remittances could not even cover the interest requirements. Germany's normal capacity to pay had been severely reduced by the loss of its colonies and its merchant marine, by the confiscation of German state and private property in Alsace–Lorraine and other regions which were separated from Germany and by the loss of about one third of its coal and three fourths of its iron ore.

Bickerings over alleged defaults in reparation deliveries led to the French occupation of the Ruhr district, the industrial and mining heart of Germany, in 1923. Mass passive resistance and noncooperation prevented the French from obtaining as much coal as they were formerly obtaining in voluntary deliveries. In the end the passive resistance collapsed under the pressure of the growing inflation and the widespread economic suffering and political unrest which ensued.

But the French victory in the Ruhr yielded no solid fruits. Great Britain expressed open criticism and disapproval of the French action. This rift in policy between Great Britain and France appeared on other occasions besides the occupation of the Ruhr and was of great importance in sapping the post-Versailles European political order. England felt safe after the destruction of the Germany Navy and the parceling out of the German colonies. France always felt itself oppressed and threatened by the potentially superior German military strength.

The suspension of the reparation deliveries caused a fall in the value of the franc. France felt too weak to pursue the type of policy symbolized by the Ruhr occupation. When the intransigent Raymond Poincaré gave way to Edouard Herriot as Premier of France the way was paved for a more business-like handling of the reparation question. A committee of experts, headed by Charles G. Dawes, fixed a schedule of payments which was to rise to a figure of about six hundred million dollars a year. France consented to forego the right to apply one-sided military sanctions as a means of collection. Simultaneously a new stabilized German currency was established.

German capacity to pay and general economic recovery were facilitated by an inflow of American investment capital. The years between 1924 and 1929 were the most pacific and hopeful which Europe experienced between the two great wars. The Locarno Treaty of 1925, in which Great Britain and Italy guaranteed the frontier between Germany and France, gave France some assurance of international support against attack and gave Germany the satisfaction of concluding a negotiated, as contrasted with a dictated, treaty. This was followed by Germany's entrance into the League of Nations. Currencies were stabilized; trade was brisk; the ravages of war were rapidly being repaired.

But this European prosperity could not endure because it rested on an economic basis which was fundamentally unsound. Never before had the delicate mechanism of the world financial system been subjected to the impossible strain of huge uncompensated transfers of money from one country to another over a long period of time. Schemes like the Dawes Plan and its successor, the Young Plan, named after its originator, the American businessman Owen Young, merely evaded questions which could not be answered and postponed a day of reckoning that could not be averted.

The economic heritage of the World War, the German reparations and the Allied war debts to America, were like the fateful Rheingold of Wagner's cycle. They were an unmitigated curse, in the end, to payers and recipients alike. Both these forms of tribute ended as they had to end, for economic reasons, in total repudiation. But the evil which they inflicted lived after them.

Abstract justice, in this case, should have been a secondary consideration. Given existing methods of trade and exchange, the question was not whether Germany should have paid this or that sum in reparations or whether Great Britain, France and other European nations should have been obliged to pay in full or in large part for the munitions and supplies which they had purchased in America. The question was rather how much the recipients of these uneconomic payments could receive without injury to themselves.

Payments at the rate of almost five hundred million dollars a year, contemplated under the Young Plan, which replaced the Dawes Plan as a supposedly permanent settlement and which was supposed to remain in operation until 1988, presupposed that Germany could somehow maintain an extra favorable balance of trade of this figure. In other words, markets had to be found annually for almost half a billion dollars' worth of German goods and services, over and above what a strongly competitive and protectionist world could absorb in the way of normal trade and exchange.

Precisely the same problem was involved in the repayment of the Allied war debts, amounting to a little over ten billion dollars, to the United States. Great Britain and France were the largest debtors. Had America been willing to adjust itself gracefully to the status of a creditor country, willing to encourage an inflow of foreign goods as a payment for its foreign investments, the problem might have been solved. But America, transformed by the war into the world's greatest creditor, retained the psychology and habits of a debtor nation. America's foreign economic policy during the outwardly prosperous twenties seems little short of mad in retrospect, although few observers were farsighted enough to point out its fallacies at the time. For this policy consisted of maintaining protective tariffs while investing money abroad from China to Peru, money which, in the last analysis, could only be repaid in terms of goods. The unavoidable aftermath was a prodigious loss of invested capital and an acute aggravation of the economic crisis of 1929–1933.

A situation in which Great Britain and France claimed per-

petual tribute from Germany while erecting tariff walls against
the entrance of German goods, in which America demanded
payment of war debts while doing everything to deny its
debtors means of making these payments, was too absurdly
unsound to last. The whole house of cards of reparations and
war debt payments collapsed under the impact of the great
depression which began in 1929. Germany had paid about
five and a half billion dollars, according to Allied estimates.[3]
America had received about three billion dollars in interest
and amortization upon its war debts.

The huge German rearmament expenditures under Hitler
are sometimes adduced as a proof of German bad faith in fail-
ing to meet reparation payments. Obviously Germany spent
far more on airplanes, tanks, ordnance and other military
preparations than it ever paid in reparations. But from an
economic standpoint the problems were of an entirely different nature. The rearmament was an internal effort, financed
and supported by an unprecedented mobilization of labor
power, capital and industrial plant. The payment of reparations involved what proved to be the insoluble problem of
transfer. Had there been any means by which Germany could
have paid in kind or by which Englishmen and Frenchmen
could have moved into Germany in large numbers and lived
off the country, the reparation payments could have been
made. But no such means were found. Great Britain is the
classical country of economic thought and Sir Josiah Stamp
(later Lord Stamp), prominent British economist and banker,
summed up the folly of the reparations experiment very
lucidly in the following sentences: [4]

"In effect we told Germany she was to produce all this
extra amount [for reparations], but that we would not take it,
except through tariff barriers, and she wasn't to produce it by

[3] The Germans estimate their payments at a much higher figure, because
they set a higher valuation on the deliveries in kind which were prescribed
during the first years after the end of the war.
[4] Compare "The Financial Aftermath of the War," p. 102.

longer hours. Also, if she paid lower wages, i. e. if she took the amount of goods required out of her people's consumption, then the tariffs were put up, particularly on the American principle, which seeks to 'equalize the cost of production' and which seeks to make good the difference between a foreign standard of wages and the home standard. So in every possible way a check was put, unconsciously no doubt, upon Germany's ability to discharge her debt."

There was a tragic footnote to Sir Josiah Stamp's analysis. With his wife he was killed in one of the innumerable air raids launched against London by a Germany which had gone berserk from a combination of causes, of which the economic chaos of the postwar years was not the least.

Throughout the depression there was a shower of measures in restraint of international trade. During a single month in 1932 Great Britain imposed a new tariff on potatoes; the Netherlands set up a quota on imports of porcelain, earthenware, bricks and bicycle tires; Switzerland raised tariffs on German leather goods, bottles, axes, cutlery; France set up quotas for imports of meat and fish presses, mercury, sheet metal, various kinds of machines and tools. These tariffs and quotas bore hardly on all exporting nations. But Germany, required to produce its surplus for reparations and faced with a tremendous drain in the flight of short-term foreign capital, began to suffer an acute sense of economic claustrophobia.

Many observers hoped that the League of Nations would prove an agency for redressing the worst injustices and blunders of the peace settlements. The South African Premier, General Jan Smuts, voiced this sentiment when he said, on signing the Treaty of Versailles:

"There are territorial settlements which will need revision. There are guaranties laid down which we all hope will soon be found out of harmony with the new peaceful temper and unarmed state of our former enemies. There are punishments foreshadowed over most of which a calmer mood may yet prefer to pass the sponge of oblivion. There are indemnities stipulated which cannot be enacted without grave danger to the industrial revival of Europe and which it will be in the interests of all to render more tolerable and moderate. . . . I am confident the League of Nations will yet prove the path of escape for Europe out of the ruin brought about by this war."

But the League started under a fatal handicap which prevented it from playing the healing and pacifying role which Smuts and others foresaw. This handicap was the unwillingness of the great powers which belonged to the League to abate a jot of their national sovereignty. It was only on the basis of such an abatement that the League could have become a parliament of man, an effective arbiter of world affairs.

Within its limitations the Geneva institution could and did perform excellent work in such fields as control of drug traffic and establishment of international labor standards through an affiliated, although independent, body, the International Labor Office. It developed an international corps of technical experts. It provided a pleasant meeting place and forum for discussion. It settled minor disputes which would scarcely have led to war in any event. But in the great crises the League was helpless because it could not exercise powers which its member states had not delegated to it.

Verbal censures were of no practical effect in checking Japan in Manchuria. Halfhearted economic sanctions were the best the League could offer when Italy attacked Abyssinia. And this best was not good enough. The British Government, under strong pressure of public opinion, might have gone further. The French Government, eager to conciliate Mussolini, was unwilling to go so far. And the sole result of the feeble effort to stop Mussolini's African adventure by keeping out Gorgonzola cheese and other Italian exports was humiliation and loss of prestige for Great Britain, for France, for the League.

By the time the Second World War began, the League was suffering from atrophy of all its vital faculties. It carefully avoided taking any stand on the conflict because all the member states, except Great Britain and France, feared to take any steps which Germany could have regarded as unneutral. The League's last significant action, and it was a worthy one, was to exclude the Soviet Union from membership after the invasion of Finland.

The League received a severe blow at the outset when America refused to join, although President Wilson had been one of the most ardent apostles of the idea. A strong tide of resurgent nationalism, of postwar psychological letdown, of distrust of involvement in European affairs, was probably the main factor in this decision. Not a few radicals and liberals who would normally have favored the League idea were profoundly disillusioned with the terms of the peace treaties and opposed American underwriting of such a postwar order. Partisan politics, aggravated by the President's untactful handling of the Republican opposition, also played its part.

Great Britain joined the League, but constantly opposed French efforts to put "teeth" into its constitution. The influence of the Dominions was isolationist and the average Briton felt a horror at becoming involved in war on some East European issue. Ironically enough it was to defend Poland that Great Britain was drawn into its second continental war. From the beginning the two leading Allied powers were at variance as to what the League should be.

England desired a cooperative association of nations, with a minimum of the coercive element and with few specific obligations for its members. France would have liked a superstate, with an international army and with the most precise and binding commitments on the part of the affiliated powers to take military action against aggression. What France really wanted was a maintenance in peace of the coalition which had won the war against Germany.

This hope was soon frustrated. America refused to enter the League, to ratify the Treaty of Versailles or to confirm the assurance which Wilson had given in Paris that America would guarantee France's frontier against attack. England used the American attitude as an excuse not to extend its guaranty to the French frontier, although it consented later to act with Italy as a coguarantor under the terms of the Locarno Treaty.

Lord Balfour, as spokesman for the British Government in 1925, cited American abstention as a reason why the League could not prevent wars arising from what he called "deeply-lying causes of hostility between great and powerful states." He made this statement in connection with the decision of the Conservative Government to reject the Geneva Protocol which the representatives of the previous Labor Government had accepted and which went far to meet the French demand for swift, automatic, concerted action against an aggressor.

The conflict between the French and British viewpoints was very largely a question of geography. It was France that would have to bear the brunt of a new German attack. Germany had been defeated, disarmed, humiliated and impoverished. But its unity remained; its superiority in man power remained; its industrial advantage over semiagricultural France remained. The French mind was naturally preoccupied with the problem of security. True, there were the alliances with Poland, Czechoslovakia, Rumania, Yugoslavia. But realistic Frenchmen knew that these Eastern European states were weak reeds on which to lean. The alliances might become a liability rather than an asset, especially in the event of an alliance between Germany and Russia.

Great Britain, on the other hand, instinctively reverted to its historic position as an aloof although interested spectator of continental affairs, prepared to intervene actively only when its vital interests were threatened. While security was the first consideration of French leaders of almost all parties,

British statesmen were inclined to stress the importance of disarmament, both as a means of relieving international tension and as an aid to economy.

So the interplay of diplomacy, both within and without the League, often centered around the attempt to strike a bargain, under which Great Britain would give satisfaction to the French demand for security in return for French concessions on disarmament. But the problem proved too complex for solution, with the result that neither security nor disarmament was ever attained.

The failure to reach any plan of agreed limitation of armaments during the twenties, when Germany was still a republic and the international atmosphere was reasonably favorable, was an ominous indication that the terrible lessons of the First World War had been in vain, that the shaken fabric of civilization would be exposed to a new shock. Germany had been compulsorily disarmed by the Treaty of Versailles. Conscription was abolished; the German Army was limited to 100,000 men; the manufacture of aircraft and heavy artillery was forbidden. Part V of the Versailles Treaty, prescribing German disarmament, began with the clause:

"In order to render possible the initiation of a general limitation of the armaments of all nations."

So there was an implied pledge to follow up the compulsory disarmament of Germany and its allies with a general agreed scheme of limitation of armaments. A complete absence of mutual confidence and national hatreds and suspicions which had been embittered, not assuaged, by the First World War presented insuperable obstacles to the realization of any such scheme. Every country looked at the problem merely from the standpoint of its own national interests, urged the abolition or restriction of the weapons in which it was weakest and the retention of those in which it was strongest.

It was only in 1932, almost thirteen years after the signature of the Treaty of Versailles, that a disarmament conference under the auspices of the League of Nations opened its sessions. The preparatory commission for this conference had held numerous sessions and listened to innumerable projects and resolutions without coming to any preliminary agreement.

And the conference began under the most unfavorable political conditions. The Weimar Republic was already tottering to its fall. During the relatively calm and prosperous years, from 1925 until 1929, when Stresemann was directing German foreign relations, it would have been much easier to have negotiated an arms limitation convention with Germany. By 1932, with Hitler looming on the horizon and nationalist influence in Germany growing, the conference was almost foredoomed to shipwreck on the irreconcilable clash between the French demand for security and the German demand for equality of treatment in the matter of armament.

To the peoples concerned, each of these demands seemed vital to national honor and safety. The deadlock in the Disarmament Conference was abruptly broken when Germany walked out in October, 1933, simultaneously serving notice of its intention to quit the League. Great Britain and France pursued the sterile policy of rejecting German proposals while reacting with nothing stronger than words to German acts of rearmament. In 1932 England and France were unwilling to accept a German army of 200,000. In 1934, after Germany had left the Disarmament Conference, Hitler proposed a plan under which Germany would have a short-service army of 300,000 and "defensive armaments," accompanied by pacts of nonaggression. He professed willingness to accept a ten-year period of control of armaments.

While there is no reason to suppose that Hitler would have felt bound by any paper pledges, it is perhaps unfortunate that an experiment in mutual control of armaments was not tried out during this early phase of the Nazi regime. Certainly this experiment, even if it had failed, could have led to nothing worse than what actually occurred. This was an unlimited, all-out armament race which began with the German repudiation of the Versailles limitations in 1935 and ended with the crushing of France in 1940.

The League failed in disarmament, as it failed in every big problem, for lack of essential material power and moral prestige. Its constitution was at once too feeble and too rigid. There were convenient loopholes in the wording of the obligations which its members assumed. Even Article 10, the strongest in the Covenant, with its pledge by members of the League "to undertake to respect and preserve as against external aggression the territorial integrity and existing political independence of all members of the League," possessed its qualification. This was the provision that "the Council [of the League] shall advise upon the means by which this obligation shall be fulfilled." Here was a large loophole, especially in the event of division of opinion in the Council. Article 10 was a poor shield in an age of *Blitzkrieg* and undeclared war.

At the same time the League in practice was always on the side of the *status quo*. There was just one feature of the Covenant, Article 19, which envisaged, in the following terms, the possible revision of existing conditions by negotiation and consent:

"The Assembly may from time to time advise the reconsideration by members of the League of treaties which have become inapplicable and the consideration of international conditions whose continuance might endanger the peace of the world."

But Article 19 was never invoked. The League lacked both the power to prevent change by violence and the flexibility to serve as a forum where possibilities of peaceful change could be weighed and discussed.

Every large power which took part in the establishment of the League offered its own suggestions as to the proper draft of the Covenant. These suggestions naturally reflected the individual national interests and aspirations of the powers. It is interesting to recall that the Italian project, which was given no serious consideration, provided that certain questions might be decided according to the principles not of international law but of equity and political expediency. Every member of the League was to be assured "the necessary conditions of its independent and autonomous development." More specifically, "the international distribution of the foodstuffs and raw materials required to sustain healthy conditions of life and industry must be controlled in such a way as to secure to every country what is indispensable to it in this respect."

This Italian draft project, of course, antedates Mussolini. Its character is interesting because it shows that, to an expanding people in an overcrowded territory, justice is not synonymous with the maintenance of the *status quo*, as it often seems to be to inhabitants of lands where population pressure is not a problem.

Ardent advocates of the League idea in America, in Great Britain, in France, all of which were sated countries—America because of its vast territory and unrivaled natural resources, Great Britain and France because of their huge empires—are often inclined to take too narrowly a legalistic conception of the conditions of world peace. If one looks back at the course of history, it seems doubtful whether a permanent freezing of frontiers, enforced by the will of a mighty superstate, would have always served the best interests of human progress. Such a superstate, for instance, would have been obligated to defend Mexico against the American invasion in 1846. But it is certainly improbable that the development of Texas and California would have been paralleled if these states had remained under Mexican rule.

This is only one of many possible illustrations of the complicated ethical problem involved when a vigorous growing people asserts its claim to take over land belonging to a country which is unable to develop it adequately. An ideal world society would have to work out an extremely delicate balance between cases of flagrant and unjustified aggression and cases which would fall under the more euphemistic category of growth and change. It would have to combine security with flexibility. The League failed to achieve either.

A notably futile gesture in the cause of peace was the Pact of Paris, concluded in 1928 after an exchange of notes between the French Foreign Minister, Aristide Briand, and the United States Secretary of State, Frank B. Kellogg. This mere declaration of intention not to resort to war as an instrument of national policy, without provision for compulsory arbitration or for sanctions in the event of violation of the pledge, was of no practical value. The chief effect of the Kellogg Pact was to render declarations of war obsolete.

What kept Europe free from major conflicts during the twenties and the early thirties was France's preponderance of armed strength over Germany. There were some German evasions of the stringent disarmament clauses of the Treaty. The Soviet Union, friendly to Germany until the temporary change of Stalin's policy after Hitler's rise to power, granted training facilities to German aviators. Some features of military training were provided by the various organizations which sprang up in Germany as militant champions of political causes. The most important of these were the conservative nationalist *Stahlhelm*, largely composed of ex-service men, the Nazi *Sturmabteilungen*, the Republican *Reichsbanner* and the Communist *Rotfront*. Means were found to evade the treaty restrictions along the eastern border with Poland.

But French superiority in artillery, in aircraft and in the general military training of its conscripts was indisputable until 1933. One cannot say with certainty at what moment between 1933 and 1939 Germany caught up with and overtook France. But, while the French rout in 1940 speaks for itself, a Franco–German war before 1933, probably before 1936, could have had only one end: a crushing military defeat of the Reich.

The German Government knew this and refused to countenance any overt military action, even when nationalist passion was aroused to its highest point by the occupation of the Ruhr. The most important gage of this French superiority was the demilitarization of the Rhineland. On the left bank of the Rhine and on a strip of territory fifty kilometers to the east of that river Germany was forbidden to maintain troops or to erect fortifications. So, in the event of hostilities, France would be assured of a running start, of being able to penetrate deeply into undefended German territory. This advantage was all the more pronounced because many of Germany's war industries were located in the industrialized valleys of the Rhine and the Ruhr.

If one were to select the single link in the amazing chain of events between 1933 and 1939 which led to a complete reversal of the balance of military strength between France and Germany without the firing of a shot, it would be the march of the German troops into the Rhineland on March 7, 1936. It is scarcely an exaggeration to say that on that date France lost the Second World War.

Given French military preponderance, plus the French alliances in Eastern and Southeastern Europe, plus the certainty that British sea power would be thrown into the scale if France should be attacked—and the chances of a German military resurgence might have seemed negligible. But what happened after 1933 showed the vast importance of psychology in international affairs, the immense possibilities of purposeful unity when pitted against irresolution, division and indecision. The Versailles structure could not have been successfully challenged and overthrown by means of a single blow. It could be and was destroyed in piecemeal fashion, by a process of sapping and undermining.

One circumstance that played into Hitler's hands was the absence of a complete cordial understanding between Great Britain and France. After the emotional orgy of the "Hang the Kaiser" election had passed, Great Britain quickly reverted to its traditional role of the calm spectator and occasional arbiter of continental affairs. Public opinion in England, a commercial nation where economics has always been widely studied, was quick to realize the harmfulness to world trade of the reparation and war debt levies and of the rampant economic nationalism which was generally practiced by the small countries which multiplied in number after the peace.

England also underestimated German recuperative military power. It sometimes made the mistake of confounding what was a genuine French desire for security with a revival of the ambitions of Louis XIV and Napoleon. There was some truth in the French reproach that England, after the destruction of the German fleet, the confiscation of the German merchant marine and the seizure of the German colonies, was inclined to sit back in its fancied island security and listen with indifference or even with hostility to French representations of the potential danger from a Germany which was the most populous country in Europe, after Russia, and much the most advanced in an industrial technique that could easily be set to military uses.

The final German defeat obscured for England, and no doubt for the whole world, the formidable and impressive character of the German military accomplishment. France was remembered only as the heroic victor of the Marne and of Verdun. The mistakes of strategy, the disastrous defeats at the beginning of the war, the despairing mutinies of 1917, were forgotten.

Great Britain and France could never agree as to how far Germany could safely be conciliated or as to what England should do to underwrite French security. A few friendly gestures were made toward the Weimar Republic. The military occupation of the Rhineland, for instance, was terminated in 1930, five years before the prescribed time. The effect of this move, however, was unfortunately lost in the growing storm of the world economic crisis, which strengthened so much the influence in Germany of the prophets of violence and catastrophe.

In general, Great Britain and France applied the wrong policies at the wrong times. The methods of uncompromising, ruthless force which would have been suitable in dealing with Hitler were reserved for the unfortunate German Republic in the first years of its existence. Equally unfortunate, Hitler's unilateral actions, backed by the threat or bluff of the use of force, invariably obtained the concessions which had been denied to the peaceful and reasonable diplomatic methods of the Republic. The natural result was an enhancement of Nazi prestige, an object lesson for the German people of Hitler's thesis that violence does "pay."

Not until 1939 was there solid agreement between Great Britain and France as to what steps should be taken to check German aggression. On the surface the Treaty of Locarno seemed to afford France a pretty solid guaranty of British support not only against German attack but against a remilitarization of the Rhineland. But on close examination this guaranty falls far short of Aristide Briand's optimistic interpretation:[5]

"Henceforward the violation by the Reich of the Rhineland demilitarized zone ought to suffice to unloose British and Italian action."

For the Locarno Treaty stipulated immediate action only in the event of a "flagrant" breach of the clause which established the demilitarized zone. A "nonflagrant" violation was to be referred to the Council of the League, a move which would be singularly unlikely to produce prompt and effective action.

[5] For a thorough treatment of this question see the excellent book by Professor Arnold Wolfers, "Britain and France between Two Wars," pp. 49 ff.

When Germany put the issue to the test in March, 1936, the Italian guaranty was already null and void. Italy was in the midst of the Abyssinian campaign and was on terms of semihostility with the sanctionist powers, among which England was the leader, with France a very unwilling follower. The British Foreign Minister, Anthony Eden, clearly indicated that he did not regard the German march into the Rhineland as a "flagrant" breach of treaty obligations when he said there was no reason to suppose that the German action "implies a threat of hostilities."

Not all the blame for the relinquishment of this priceless pledge of security, the demilitarized Rhineland, rests with England. France was also irresolute, uncertain of itself. Strong independent French action would certainly not have aroused positive British opposition and would have possessed ample legal justification, since Hitler's action was a violation not only of the dictated Treaty of Versailles but of the freely negotiated Treaty of Locarno.

It is only on the basis of a joint British and French failure to understand the tremendous issues at stake, to look facts squarely in the face, that one can explain the success of Hitler's coup on March 7, 1936. And it was piling folly on folly for England and France, after refusing to fight when there was every prospect of victory, in 1936, to declare war, with every prospect of defeat, in 1939. The two powers were weak when they should have been strong, adventurous when they should have been cautious.

Hitler's assault on the bastions of Versailles began with the German withdrawal from the League of Nations and from the Disarmament Conference in the fall of 1933. He then moved toward the realization of his plans of revenge and conquest with an uncanny sureness of psychological touch, striking first at the points of least resistance, representing each new step as final, utilizing each new acquisition as a steppingstone to further advance.

An uprising of National Socialists in Austria in the summer of 1934, accompanied by the murder of the Premier, Engelbert Dollfuss, who had set up a conservative Catholic authoritarian regime, threatened to involve the Third Reich in complications which were beyond its strength at that time. Mussolini mobilized troops on the Austrian frontier. Hitler avoided the showdown for which he was not prepared. The Austrian Nazis were disavowed, to be honored as heroes and martyrs four years later.

Then the German dictator set out on his methodical course of undoing the Treaty of Versailles, a process that was to reach its climax when a new armistice of Compiègne would be dictated to the defeated French in the same railway car where Foch had announced his terms in 1918. The first success was the Saar plebiscite of 1935. This coal mining and industrial region had been detached from Germany and placed under the administration of the League, with the understanding that a plebiscite, to be held after fifteen years, would determine its final disposition. The Nazis developed their familiar methods of mass propaganda, not unaccompanied by intimidation, and 90 per cent of the Saarlanders voted in favor of reincorporation of the territory in Germany.

Soon after the Saar plebiscite Hitler, in March, 1935, denounced the Versailles Treaty restrictions on Germany's armaments. The reaction, as he foresaw, did not go beyond empty protests. The Disarmament Conference had proved a fiasco and public opinion in Great Britain and France was not keyed up to the point of fighting to prevent Germany from rearming. Hitler still professed to respect the engagements of Locarno. And he took the sting out of his rearmament for Great Britain and drove a wedge between that country and France by concluding a separate naval agreement with England, under which the German Navy was fixed at 35 per cent of the British.

A year later came the successful coup of reoccupying the

Rhineland. Its effects were far-reaching. The faith of the smaller powers in collective security, already shaken by Manchuria and Ethiopia, began to crumble completely. The countries of Eastern and Southeastern Europe realized that France could no longer give them sure and swift protection by marching into Germany's vital industrial centers. A general atmosphere of *sauve qui peut* began to prevail, except in Czechoslovakia, which clung to what proved to be the delusive hope of help from France and the Soviet Union in its hour of need.

Poland had already concluded a ten-year pact of nonaggression with Germany. Marshal Pilsudski, the Polish dictator, decided on this step after he had become convinced that France would not fight a preventive war against the Third Reich. Poland was relatively far down on the list of Hitler's prospective victims. It required all his personal authority to make this pact outwardly palatable, because many Germans hated and despised the Poles and were eager for a quick revision of the eastern frontiers which had been drawn at Versailles. But with Poland immobilized Hitler had a freer hand in regard to the two countries which he had marked for disintegration and conquest. These were Austria and Czechoslovakia.

Austria fell very easily. By 1938 any prospect of foreign intervention to maintain the existing regime had disappeared. German military power had become too formidable. Italy was already allied with Germany in supporting the Spanish General Francisco Franco in his struggle against the radical Republican Government. Great Britain and France were in no position to act.

Moreover, Austria was a solidly German country, with a strong Nazi movement. The Austrian people were divided, in what proportion no one can say with certainty, into three main political groupings. There were the supporters of the existing Catholic conservative regime of Dr. Kurt Schuschnigg, successor of the murdered Dollfuss. There were the Nazis and there were the outlawed Austrian Social Democrats. The taking over of power in Austria was easy. Not a shot was fired. For the first time since the World War, German troops marched into the capital of another country, although this occupation of Austria was represented as an act of brotherly solidarity.

The Allies had vetoed the desire of the great majority of the Austrian people to unite with Germany immediately after the World War, when the inclusion of Austria might have strengthened the moderate and democratic forces in Germany. They condemned the truncated country to an "independence" that was a long economic agony. For Vienna, the former capital of an empire of fifty million inhabitants, was an impossible capital for a shrunken state of some seven millions. Austria was forbidden in 1931 to seek an alleviation of its economic difficulties by forming a voluntary customs union with Germany. Finally Hitler's violence solved a problem for which democracy had found no solution.

Czechoslovakia was a harder nut to crack. Here Hitler's Trojan Horse consisted of the three and a quarter million Germans who lived in that polyglot republic, mostly in regions adjacent to Germany. Austria was taken in March, 1938. By September, Hitler was threatening war if these Sudeten Germans were not permitted to secede. By annexing Austria, Hitler had encircled Czechoslovakia on three sides. Hungary and Poland also put forward claims to territorial revision at Czechoslovakia's expense.

There was a treaty of alliance between France and Czechoslovakia. But after the remilitarization of the Rhineland the French will to fight for countries in Eastern Europe had sunk to a low ebb. The deputy Jean Montigny was by no means speaking only for himself when, as early as 1936, he recommended a policy of "relaxing engagements which are too heavy, of committing France to a realistic policy in which it would be certain to face war only for the defense of its vital interests."

Both France and England were deeply divided as to the wisdom of fighting on the Czech issue. So Hitler's sweeping diplomatic victory at Munich, which gave him, along with the Sudeten Germans and a minority of Czechs, the strong Czech military defense line, built in the mountainous country near the frontier, was comparatively easy.

After another of the brief intervals which regularly intervene between Hitler's springs, he fell upon the rump state of Czechoslovakia and it collapsed without resistance. Bohemia and Moravia became a German protectorate. Slovakia became nominally independent and Hungary annexed the eastern regions of the country.

This was the German leader's last victory without war. There was a revulsion in England against the so-called policy of appeasement and Premier Chamberlain, perhaps against his own judgment, was forced into a more bellicose attitude. If Hitler was to be stopped in Eastern Europe the awakening of British public opinion had come about at least three years too late. The key to the defense of Poland and Czechoslovakia had been thrown away on the Rhine.

During the last months before the beginning of the Second World War there was a curious reversal of roles as between England and France. It was France that had conceived and supported the idea of holding Germany in check by means of the new and enlarged states in Eastern Europe. England was conspicuously disinterested in this part of the world and always refused to assume specific obligations to defend the frontiers of the new states.

But after the sharp change in British policy which followed the German march into Prague, Great Britain took the lead in a belated and unsuccessful attempt to build up an Eastern front against Hitler. France, where the ideas of isolation, of security behind the Maginot Line, of concentration on the development of the overseas empire, had made much progress, followed the British lead, but passively and unenthusiastically.

Hitler's tactics were always to defeat his enemies in detail. Each conquest was preceded by a similar process of political and military encirclement. Czechoslovakia was enveloped after the occupation of Austria. After the seizure of Czechoslovakia, Poland was caught between two extended German military pincers, one represented by East Prussia, the other by Slovakia. The Poles were traditionally ready to fight for a lost cause. Strengthened by assurances of British and French support, they adopted an intransigent attitude toward Hitler's proposals for the reincorporation of Danzig in Germany and a change in the status of the Corridor, the wedge of Polish territory which separated East Prussia from the remainder of Germany.

But Poland's chances of successful resistance were negligible, especially after the Soviet Union, the huge neighbor to the east, concluded with Germany a pact of nonaggression that soon proved to be a pact of mutual aggression against the unfortunate Poles. The frontiers of the country were singularly difficult to defend because of their irregular configuration, their length and the lack of natural barriers.

Hitler would not stop in his attempt to reshape the map of Europe. After Great Britain and France resolved in the spring of 1939 that the next German aggressive move would be a *casus belli*, war became merely a question of time and circumstance. On September 1, when the Germans invaded Poland, on September 3, when Great Britain and France pronounced their declarations of war, the peace settlement that failed came definitely to an end. The destinies of many peoples were again thrown into the melting pot of war, with its infinite destructive possibilities and its unpredictable revolutionary implications.

The justice of the Treaty of Versailles and the minor treaties which were associated with it has been hotly debated. But the supreme pragmatic test of the worth of a peace settlement is its durability. By this test the failure of Versailles is final and indisputable. It gave Europe no true peace, only a precarious and uncertain armistice.

There is, of course, room for argument as to whether Versailles failed because it was too severe or because it was not severe enough. A fair verdict might be that it failed on both counts, that it was too severe in conception and too feeble in execution. Wilson's Fourteen Points, the supposed charter of the new European order, were violated both in the spirit and in the letter. But when the whole new European structure was challenged by the angry violence of a resurgent Germany there was not enough resolution or even instinct of self-preservation to apply measures of prevention and resistance when these would still have been effective.

The effort, as impossible as the squaring of the circle, to reconcile the imperialist ambitions of the victorious powers with the requirements of a cooperative world order imparted a quality of exasperating hypocrisy to some features of the settlement. It would have probably created less bitterness if the Allies had annexed the German colonies on the old-fashioned basis that the victors are entitled to the spoils instead of trying to moralize their acquisitions by one-sided propagandist disquisitions on Germany's unfitness for colonial administration. Forcing Germany, under Article 231 of the Treaty, to admit sole responsibility for the war injected a note of unnecessary humiliation and recrimination into the postwar international atmosphere. Almost no Germans and few objective students of history in other countries would have subscribed to this thesis. Again it would have been more sensible to base frontier changes and reparation demands on the indisputable fact that Germany lost the war, not on the unprovable thesis of Germany's sole responsibility.

Could Versailles have been maintained by the stern uncompromising use of force which statesmen like Poincaré always advocated? The answer is both Yes and No. A firm stand on the remilitarization of the Rhineland by Great Britain and France would have either postponed the Second World War or insured that it would be fought under far more favorable circumstances than those of 1939.

But no amount of physical force could have upheld some features of the peace treaties. All the cannon and bayonets in the world would not have made sense out of the dreary economic nonsense of war debts and reparations. Mere physical force could not have averted the unhappy economic results that were certain to follow the Balkanization of Eastern and Central Europe; the emergence of so many new small and medium states, with their competing armies and bureaucracies and their frontiers bristling with barbed wire and trade restrictions.

Historically the European order which was set up after the First World War must be considered reactionary and out of harmony with the trend of the age. This was not the least of the reasons why it broke down so soon. Economic boundaries were multiplied at a time when the rise of the mass-production technique imperiously demanded larger, not smaller, economic units. The full demands of nineteenth century nationalism were granted, except in the case of the defeated peoples. But there was no provision for the economic cooperation which the conditions of the twentieth century made essential to general well-being.

One unmistakable cause of the swift decline and fall of Europe's peace was the singular poverty of the victorious powers in creative leadership. After Hitler came into power it was probably already too late to bring Germany into a voluntary partnership of European powers. But for more than a decade after 1918 England and France had the destinies of the continent in their hands. The two countries were often at cross-purposes and there was a striking and tragic failure to launch any big imaginative international ideas or enterprises which might have averted the crumbling of all bases of order in the thirties.

Much could have been achieved, especially in the economic sphere, by a free federation of European peoples. Yet this idea never advanced beyond the debating stage. There was no constructive approach to agreed disarmament and there was no attempt to strike at the economic roots of war, to take practical steps toward remedying the explosive effects of unequal distribution of natural resources in a world where restrictions on the free movement of men, goods and capital were constantly increasing.

During the most promising period of the twenties the attitude of the victorious powers was defensive, conservative, cautious to the point of sterility. Most unfortunately it proved impossible to mobilize for good causes a fraction of the fierce energy which the totalitarian dictatorships mustered for bad ones, or to make for enduring peace a small fraction of the sacrifices which peoples impose on themselves to win a war.

The causes of the failure of the peace were psychological, as much as political and economic. The effect of the war on France and England, on one side, and on Germany, on the other, was curiously dissimilar. In Germany defeat unloosed a demonic energy for revenge and conquest of which Hitler became the symbol. In France and England the aftermath of the war was a paralysis of the capacity for positive action.

Europe's sources of creative and fruitful energy had dried up as a result of four years of exhausting and destructive struggle. Instead of trying to anticipate and prevent disaster there was a widespread mood to wait passively until catastrophe had become reality. And so the twenty-one years of nominal peace between the European great powers after Germany surrendered in 1918 were only a short-lived, deceptive respite. The infernal cycle of war and violent revolution had not been broken.

Chapter Nine

THE CLASH OF REVOLUTIONS IN THE ORIENT

IN THE EAST, as in the West, the last two decades have been an era of turmoil, of war and revolution. The direct influence of the World War was much slighter in the Far East than it was in Europe. Japan took a minor part in the hostilities. China did not fight at all. There were none of the dislocations, political, economic and psychological, that are the inevitable sequence of huge casualty lists, widespread devastation, wrecked currency systems.

Japan, indeed, enriched itself out of the war. Japanese businessmen enjoyed unprecedented opportunities to sell their goods in all the markets of the world, especially in Asia and in South America. For the great industrial nations, the United States, Great Britain, Germany, were all too busy turning out munitions and war supplies to produce their normal export quotas.

So the Orient escaped the more shattering impacts of the war. But the European conflict accelerated certain processes of change that had long been at work in the East. The familiar adjective "unchanging" had become thoroughly inapplicable to the two leading peoples of the Far East, the Japanese and the Chinese. Neither China nor Japan had ever lived in a completely static society.

China had lived through prolonged cycles of war and social upheaval. The Taiping Rebellion alone, in the nineteenth century, may have taken more lives than the First World War.

Under the Tokugawa Shogunate, Japan, after the beginning of the seventeenth century, did everything in its power to freeze its social order and to isolate itself from the outside world. Death was the penalty for leaving the country or for building a boat large enough to leave Japan's home waters. Communication with foreign countries was restricted to the one Dutch ship that was permitted to call at the port of Nagasaki for purposes of trade every year. Every precaution was taken to see that these foreigners should have no intercourse with the Japanese. But even this shut-in system experienced its changes and its crises. The Shogunate was already tottering from internal weaknesses when the famous "black ships" of Commodore Perry appeared off the coast of Japan and made the first breach in the wall of self-imposed isolation. Contact with the West, both friendly and hostile, was an immense force for transforming the East. Largely under this impact Japan and China have undergone more fundamental change during the last few decades than during the preceding few centuries.

The missionary who went to these Eastern lands after they had been opened up to foreign trade and travel was more of a revolutionary than he suspected. The pioneer missionaries were all concerned primarily, and often exclusively, with saving the souls of the heathen. It was for this purpose that they were prepared to undergo all hardships and dangers, including martyrdom.

But the foreign missionary, by his racial origin, by the clothes he wore, the house in which he lived, the books which he read, was an unconscious challenge not only to the old patron gods of the district where he worked but to the entire Eastern way of life.

Education went hand in hand with evangelical activity. And the mission school naturally reflected the politics, the economics, the ethics, the psychology, of the missionary's native land. Such ideas as political democracy, freedom of inquiry, the value of individual personality, worked as a ferment of dissolution, or at least of modifications, in old societies where governmental authority had never been controlled from below and where the individual's tastes and preferences were subordinated to the interests of the family.

The hospital, like the school, was a frequent accompaniment of the missionary endeavor. And here a whole new world of natural science, a subject which had long been dormant in the Orient, was revealed. The mission schools and the other growing contacts with the West were a stimulus to study abroad. And, as opportunities for such study were largely restricted to members of the governing and well-to-do classes, the influence on public affairs of the Western-educated Chinese and Japanese was out of all proportion to their numbers.

The three most powerful women in China, Mme. Chiang Kai-shek. Mme. H. H. Kung and Mme. Sun Yat-sen, are all graduates of American colleges and speak fluent English, which sometimes becomes eloquent in the mouths of Mme. Chiang Kai-shek and Mme. Sun Yat-sen. One is often impressed in Japan by the prevalence of liberal ideas among some older men who spent impressionable years in foreign countries during the latter part of the liberal age.

Apart from the cultural ferment that was let loose in the Orient by the penetration of Western ideas there was the constant political and military pressure of the Occident during the expansive nineteenth century. Trade and imperialism, backed by warships and troops, forced the gates of all but the most remote and secluded Asiatic countries.

Here the experience of Japan and of China was profoundly different. The history of the turbulent last decade in East Asia, with the steady progression of Japanese conquest from the rolling steppes of North Manchuria to the hot ricelands of Indo–China was largely predetermined by the head start which Japan had gained in successfully assimilating the industrial and military secrets of the West.

One of the motives that prompted Japan to shut itself off from the outside world was fear of foreign conquest. The Spanish, the Portuguese and the Dutch were already establishing themselves as traders and conquerors in the Orient. The early Tokugawa Shoguns realized that infiltration of foreigners, and especially of missionaries, was a frequent prelude to invasion. (The tactics of the "Trojan Horse" did not originate with Hitler.) This, rather than theological intolerance, which is not characteristic of Far Eastern peoples, was the reason for the fierce persecution which practically extinguished the practice of Christianity in Japan in the seventeenth century.

The policy of seclusion that had seemed hopeful as a means of preserving national independence in the seventeenth century was no longer effective in the nineteenth. The foreigners were imperiously knocking at the door. One could not fight warships and cannon with spears and bows and arrows.

So Japan went from one extreme to the other. A new policy of intercourse with the outside world was inaugurated in 1868. From the most isolated of the larger Oriental peoples it became the most modernized. Japan's leaders recognized that the West could be resisted only with its own weapons, only by learning the magic that enabled these "hairy barbarians" to journey over thousands of miles of ocean and hurl death-dealing missiles into the towns of peoples who did not want to accept them and deal with them on their own terms.

There was no Japanese Peter the Great. It is the Japanese way to work through anonymous groups, not through outstanding personalities. But within a generation a remarkable transformation was achieved. Commissions scoured the countries of the West, seeking blueprints for everything from battleships to universities, asking questions about everything from scientific agriculture to constitutional law.

Starting late, Japan was able to absorb quickly, if superficially, some of the knowledge which it had taken the West a long time to acquire. Impressed by the victory of Germany in the Franco–Prussian War, Japan modeled its army and its system of conscription on the German. The navy took its lessons from Great Britain as the leading sea power. Universal primary education was introduced, something that had never been known in an Oriental country. Parliaments were the fashion in the outside world and Japan in due course obtained a parliament and a constitution, both so well supplied with checks and balances as to impose little real restraint on the executive authority. Railways, factories, shipping, gradually developed. The time would come when Japan, where it had been a capital offense to construct a ship of any size, would possess the third largest navy and the third largest merchant marine in the world.

While it was providing itself with this protective armor of Westernization an inner Japanese core was carefully preserved. The theory of the divinity of the Emperor, of his unique role as at once the tutelary deity and the patriarchal ruler of the Japanese people, was cultivated by every means. It was brought home to every child in Japan by the solemn reading of the Imperial Rescript on Education in the schools; by the cherishing of the Emperor's portrait as the most precious possession of the school, to be saved ahead of human lives in the event of fire or other disaster.

The supposedly divine Emperor was a force for national unity and stability in a period of rapid, bewildering change. Another such element was the family system, where the authority vested in the head of the family over his relatives was associated with an obligation to look after their welfare. To the Western mind this family system, so strongly entrenched both in Japan and in China, involves a great restriction of individual liberty. It seems to sacrifice the young to the old, the woman to the man. It bears hardly on the infrequent individualist. But as a source of inner cohesion its value was considerable.

The setting up of Western-influenced codes and courts and the still more convincing argument of a successful war against China in 1894–95 freed Japan from the obligation to give preferential legal status to foreigners who resided in the country. And after its victory over Russia in 1904–05 Japan had "arrived" as a great power. It had escaped the colonial or semicolonial status which had been imposed upon almost all other Asiatic peoples. Instead of becoming a victim of imperialism it had become, in a small way, an imperialist power itself. The semitropical island of Formosa was its first foreign conquest. Then came Korea, a country over which China had formerly possessed a vague claim to suzerainty. After the Russo–Japanese War, Japan took over Russian privileges and concessions in South Manchuria.

China's reaction to the impact of the West was very different from Japan's. Inequality in the pace of historical development is a frequent cause of war. It was China's national tragedy to be two generations later than Japan in setting out on the road of purposeful modernization.

There were strong natural and geographical causes both for Japan's swift advance and for China's retarded development. Japan is a small compact group of islands with an extremely homogeneous population, bred to discipline in the stern school of Japanese medieval feudalism. The area of Japan proper is only about equal to that of the state of California. Once the course had been set toward Westernization the knitting together of the country by means of roads, railways and shipping connections was comparatively simple.

A uniform system of elementary education and military conscription helped to break down the walls of separation that had formerly existed between the realms of the great nobles.

China was a huge empire, twenty times the size of Japan. Even if there had been the will to make it over along modern lines, the task would have been long, difficult and complicated. But under the Manchu Imperial dynasty which ruled China until 1911 there was no such will. The atmosphere of the Imperial court was petrified and decadent.

The response to forceful Western methods of trade promotion was one of resentment. There were several wars between China and Great Britain and France, the most active powers in breaking down the opposition of the old empire to foreign commercial penetration. But China was without modern industry, modern weapons and modern military organization. Its resistance was bound to be and was ineffective. The Chinese submitted and hated and sabotaged. But their government gave them no lead in learning how to resist the West with its own weapons.

All the key approaches to China passed into foreign hands. Industrial development, as a general rule, took place only in areas which were largely or wholly under foreign control. China possessed no navy. Its towns were at the mercy of any squadron of foreign gunboats which might threaten to bombard them. Its soldiers were mercenaries without any sense of national loyalty.

China was too huge to be swallowed whole by any acquisitive power. But it was helpless against foreign aggressive demands. A kind of joint imperialism, now cooperative, now competitive, grew up and the more accessible regions were parceled out in spheres of influence. This system spared the costs of conquest and administration while it assured the beneficiaries the advantages of profitable trade and investment.

Great Britain took the lead in developing Far Eastern

trade. English became the *lingua franca* of the Orient, the foreign tongue most generally understood by educated Chinese and Japanese. From its Crown Colony of Hong Kong, a lofty island with a splendid natural harbor, acquired after the "Opium War" with China in 1840,[1] Great Britain dominated the approach to the Pearl River, the chief water artery of South China, and controlled the transshipment trade of this region.

British political influence and vested interests prevailed in the International Settlement of Shanghai. What had originally been an unhealthy mud flat developed into the cosmopolitan commercial and industrial metropolis of China, a metropolis under foreign administration. Located near the mouth of the mighty Yangtze River, Shanghai became the inlet and outlet for a large part of China's trade. At Tientsin, the chief port of North China, and at Hankow, the largest town in Central China, six hundred miles up the Yangtze, the larger European powers established their concessions, self-administering areas for the residence of their nationals. Many Chinese moved into these foreign concessions and settlements because of the greater security of life and property which prevailed there.

Russia, the only great power which possessed a long land frontier with China, did not overlook its possibilities of pressure and expansion. Russian intrigue was active in such remote outlying parts of the Chinese Empire as Outer Mongolia and Sinkiang, or Chinese Turkestan. Two of the favorite devices of imperialist powers to promote their trade and political influence were the construction of a railway and the seizure of a convenient port. The Chinese Eastern Railway, built with Russian capital and bisecting North Manchuria, with a spur

[1] The attribution of the term "Opium War" to this conflict was perhaps a victory of Chinese over British propaganda. The immediate cause of hostilities was the disregard by British merchants of a government prohibition against bringing opium into China. But British historians are inclined to emphasize the other issues which entered into the quarrel.

running to Dalny (later Dairen), the chief port of South Manchuria, gave Russia a predominant stake in this northeastern region of China. This stake later had to be shared with Japan, which took over the railway and its subsidiary enterprises as far north as Changchun (the later Hsinking) after the war with Russia.

Germany carved out its sphere of influence in Shantung Province, with the flourishing port of Tsingtao as its center. France built a mountain railway from its colony of Indo-China into Yunnan Province, in the far interior of China. This railway, together with a concession and naval base at Kwangchouwan, in Kwangtung Province, gave France valuable advance posts in Southwestern China.

So China occupied an anomalous international status. Theoretically it was an independent sovereign state. But foreign armed guards were posted on some of its railways, foreign warships patrolled its rivers and coastal waters, foreigners governed and policed some of its largest cities, and foreigners lived and carried on business in China without being subject to Chinese laws and taxation. It is often argued on behalf of this system of foreign penetration that the Chinese, on their own initiative, would not have built up such relatively sanitary and well-administered cities or practiced such efficient methods in trade and finance. In all probability this is true.

But it is also true that this extensive foreign tutelage exercised a retarding and stultifying effect on the development of Chinese national consciousness and Chinese economic initiative. Chinese business and finance were overshadowed by the towering structure of imported foreign capitalism. And the entire situation, where some foreign rights rested on tradition, others on disputed treaty interpretations, was prolific in causes of friction.

The prerequisite for China's national awakening was the overthrow of the Imperial regime which was a dead hand on the advance of the people and which had proved itself incapable of reforming from within. Secret revolutionary societies, such as the Kuomintang, or National People's party, aiming at the overthrow of the dynasty, were fairly active, especially in Canton, where the lively volatile character of the people made them especially receptive to revolutionary ideas. A nationalist element was intermingled with the progressive desire to get rid of a reactionary form of government. For the Imperial dynasty was foreign in origin, the result of the Manchu conquest of China in the seventeenth century.

The overthrow of the Manchu Empire, already rotten-ripe for fall, occurred with little fighting in 1911. But the disappearance of the old regime created a vacuum which no political forces in China at the time were able to fill. A Western model constitution, promulgated after the proclamation of a republic, lacked both vitality and reality. With its mass illiteracy and its absence of experience in self-government China was quite unsuited for democratic institutions on the American or British pattern.

So the renovation of China along modern progressive lines did not begin on any large scale until the late twenties. The interval between the fall of the dynasty and the rise to national political power of the Kuomintang was filled with an aimless series of struggles for pelf among politicians and of civil wars between the military chieftains who possessed the actual administrative power in various parts of the country. These wars, fought by half-hearted soldiers with antiquated weapons, were not very sanguinary and did not cause any great destruction of property. They resembled somewhat the comparatively bloodless struggles of the *condottieri*, or professional mercenary chiefs, of the Italian Middle Ages.

But the achievement of China's unity seemed to be an insoluble problem. No local war lord possessed enough power or prestige to bring the country under his sway. An atmosphere of continual civil strife, actual or threatened, of jockeying for power among corrupt politicians in Peking, was not conducive to Chinese strength.

All this time Japan was systematically gaining ground in all the elements of national power. It was learning how to manufacture textiles and other goods cheaply, thanks to its combination of an Oriental standard of living with a near-Occidental standard of efficiency. The quality of the Japanese products was seldom high. But for many people in the poorer regions of the world the choice was between Japanese goods and no goods at all. In a country so military-minded as Japan, where the army and navy absorbed a large share of the budget, any increase in wealth from trade or other sources meant an increase in military and naval power.

China's true revolution took place in the twenties. It was a curious compound of Chinese backgrounds with foreign influences, American, Russian, in its later phase German—since Chiang Kai-shek adopted many ideas about the building up of a Chinese nationalist army from a German advisory military mission which remained for some years in Nanking.

China could not be united by the campaigns and plots of the war lords. The momentum of a mass movement, animated by definite political and social ideals, was required in order to attain this objective. And this mass movement, led by the Kuomintang, swept up from its base at Canton in a northward campaign in 1926 and reached Peking in 1928.

The founder of Chinese nationalism was Dr. Sun Yat-sen. His program was summarized in his so-called Three People's Principles. One of these was democracy; a second was nationalism—both ideas of the nineteenth century. The third principle, which is probably inadequately rendered as People's Livelihood, conveys suggestions of the twentieth century, of socialism and planned economy.

Like almost all leaders of revolutionary movements, Dr. Sun was a dreamer. Not all his blueprints for the reconstruc-

tion of China would pass the test of engineering and financial feasibility. But he clearly grasped some basic facts. If
China's unity was to be real, there must be a great expansion
of transportation facilities. There were enormous provinces
in the interior of the country without a mile of railway. And
if the Chinese masses were to rise above the border line of
starvation on which great numbers of them lived, new opportunities for employment must be created through industrial
development. If China was to determine its own economic
and social destiny the incubus of foreign imperialism must be
shaken off.

In the early part of his career Dr. Sun was influenced by
the example of American democracy and was an admirer of
Abraham Lincoln. One of his most intimate associates, Hu
Han-min, during a visit to Moscow repeated to me Lincoln's
formula "government of the people, by the people, for the
people" as the ideal of the Kuomintang. In his later years
Sun Yat-sen became acquainted with the theories of Russian
communism, largely through the medium of interviews with
the brilliant, neurotic Soviet envoy to China, A. A. Joffe.[2]
While Joffe and Sun Yat-sen agreed that China was not economically ripe for communism, the Chinese nationalist leader
welcomed the Russian military, political and technical advisers whom Moscow sent him. Chief among these was Michael
Borodin, whose strong personality and swift appreciation of
Chinese conditions made him for a time almost an uncrowned
dictator of the Chinese nationalist movement.

It was the Russians who supplied the technique of mass
propaganda, hitherto unknown in China, that paved the way
for the sweeping victories of the nationalist armies when they
moved northward. For the first time in history Chinese soldiers were told why they were fighting. Secret revolutionary
agents slipped into the territory held by the war lords of

[2] A. A. Joffe, a devoted follower of Leon Trotsky, committed suicide in
1927.

Northern and Central China and undermined the will to resist. The Kuomintang advance swept up to the Yangtze River and led to the capture of Shanghai and Nanking in the spring of 1927. There was a fierce antiforeign outbreak when Nanking was taken, a number of foreigners being murdered, assaulted and raped, while the lives of the majority were probably saved by the intervention of American and British warships.

At this point a rift developed in the revolutionary movement. Workers' unions, peasant unions, student unions, had sprung up all over the country in the wake of the advancing nationalists. There was an incessant wave of strikes in the towns and of agrarian disorders in the villages, some incited by the Communists, while others were spontaneous.

Middle class and well-to-do sympathizers with the nationalist movement were shocked and alienated. The revolution had gone far beyond the social and economic bounds which they would have liked to mark out for it. Chiang Kai-shek, the commander in chief of the nationalist armies, carried out a countermovement in the Nanking–Shanghai area, breaking off with the Russian advisers and outlawing the Communists.

For a time Borodin sustained an anti-Chiang government at Hankow. But the balance of force was against the radicals. Like all Chinese troops the Kuomintang soldiers were mercenaries, willing to obey their officers so long as they were paid. The majority of these officers belonged to the class of rural gentry whose property was threatened with confiscation by the spread of the agrarian movement.

The radical wing of the Kuomintang gradually melted away and some of its members, with rather typically Chinese flexibility, were quick to change sides when they recognized that there had been a turn in the political tide. A few convinced Communists among the military leaders carried some of the troops with them, retired into the hilly country of South Central China and launched a long and embittered civil and social war, rallying the poorer peasants to their side. But the main towns remained in the hands of Chiang Kai-shek and the greater part of the country acknowledged the authority of the new nationalist government.

On the surface the Chinese national revolution had been completed. But the split with the Communists and with the Leftist members of the Kuomintang, who more or less sympathized with the Communists, was a devitalizing influence. The swing, the rush, the spontaneity, of the time when the nationalist movement enjoyed the ardent support of large masses of the people were gone. The civil war which had begun with the Communists was a drain on the energy and finances of the new government. Chiang Kai-shek, who emerged as the supreme leader of the nationalist regime, had to contend with other familiar Chinese problems, with the independent attitude of local war lords, with corruption in the administration, with the poverty and chronic disorganization of the country.

And the regime which came out of the Chinese nationalist revolution was only beginning to deal with these problems when it was confronted by a threat to China's independence that was both closer and more imminent than the imperialist privileges which were still maintained by the Western powers. For Japan in 1931 experienced the beginning of its postwar revolution, a revolution that was not immediate or spectacular but that gradually led to the transfer of effective power from the men of diplomacy and finance to the men of the sword.

The first outward expression of this revolution was the seizure of Manchuria by the Japanese Army, acting in defiance of or at least with complete disregard for the civilian government in Tokyo. The division of authority in South Manchuria, where Japan possessed extensive rights not only of economic development but of public administration and policing within the zone of the South Manchurian Railway, while China theoretically possessed sovereignty over the country, was charged with possibilities of controversy.

There had been disputes over projected new Chinese railways which would have competed with the South Manchuria Railway. A Japanese officer, Captain Nakamura, had been murdered while engaged in a mission to Inner Mongolia. And there was fear in Japanese military circles that the resurgent Chinese nationalism would lead to a demand for the surrender of the Japanese privileges in South Manchuria.

The Japanese Army, employing as an excuse a very doubtful case of alleged sabotage on the railway line, opened up hostilities and seized Mukden, the capital of the Manchurian local government,[3] on September 18, 1931. The Japanese occupation was extended to the whole country, which is about three times the size of Japan proper. Japanese troops took over the northern part of Manchuria, where the Soviet Government had resumed joint operation of the Chinese Eastern Railway with the Chinese, and the Soviet share of interest in this railway was later sold to Manchoukuo.

The Manchurian "Incident," as the Japanese called it, might have come to a more satisfactory conclusion if there had been either strong intervention or no intervention on the part of outside powers. Japan might have backed down before a strong show of naval force by Great Britain and the United States. And, if the League of Nations had not taken up the question and given China deceptive hope of effective support, Japan and China might have composed the dispute on some basis less sweeping than the complete annexation of Manchuria.

But Great Britain was entirely indisposed to fight or even to resort to economic sanctions in a part of the world where its direct interests were small. The American Secretary of State, Mr. Henry L. Stimson, was personally in favor of

---

[3] Manchuria was never under the direct administrative control of the Chinese central government.

strong action to restrain Japan. But it is doubtful whether the President or the Congress would have sanctioned war.

With Great Britain lukewarm and other powers both unable and unwilling to oppose Japan with anything stronger than words, the League intervention was a fiasco. Japan left the League and kept Manchuria. The theory of collective security had received a shattering blow.

World attention was naturally focused upon the international aspects of the seizure of Manchuria. But the effects of this annexation upon Japan itself were perhaps still more important. For Manchoukuo, where the Japanese Army ruled without any of the checks which the political parties and business interests represented in Japan itself, became both an experimental station for military state socialism and a steppingstone toward the conquest by the army of a more dominant position in Japan itself. From the beginning the Manchoukuo economy was a war economy and the army often tried out first in this conquered territory measures which were applied in Japan itself later on. The occupation of Manchuria was the beginning of a road that has led Japan a long way toward military state socialism. It signified the beginning of a Japanese revolt against the liberal ideas and institutions which had been imported from the West during the Liberal Age.

The Japanese are quick to respond to what seems to be the prevalent political and economic trend abroad. The victory of the democratic powers and the downfall of Imperial Germany, which some German-trained Japanese officers considered invincible, made a deep impression and helped to make the twenties one of the most moderate periods in Japanese history.

During the World War, Japanese foreign policy had been thoroughly and logically selfish. The Island Empire entered the war ostensibly as an ally of Great Britain. But its deeper motive was to take advantage of the opportunity to round out Japan's possessions by seizing the German possessions in the Orient: the Caroline, Marshall and Mariana Islands in the South Seas; and Tsingtao, Germany's port in China. Japan took the occasion of the preoccupation of all the great powers, except the United States, with the war to serve on China its far-reaching "Twenty-one Demands" in 1915. And for some years the Japanese Army tried to establish a permanent foothold in Eastern Siberia, after the joint Allied intervention in that region.

After the end of the war, however, Japan gave way all along the line, partly because it was impressed by the speed and success of American intervention in the European war, partly because the army's continental ventures were costly and the protests of businessmen and financiers were still heeded by the Japanese Government. Siberia was evacuated and Japan gave up the idea of dominating the Chinese province of Shantung and contented itself with commercial advantages at Tsingtao. Japan accepted the Washington Naval Treaty, with its limitation of the British, American and Japanese navies in the proportion 5:5:3. It signed the Nine Power Treaty, with its pledge to respect the sovereignty and territorial integrity of China.

And the hostility of the aroused Chinese nationalism was first directed against England, rather than against Japan. Nearly all the Chinese strikes, boycotts and riots during the turbulent years from 1925 until 1927 were directed against Great Britain. Japan was well content to stand by and to push the sales of its own textiles in China whenever there was an anti-British boycott.

The seizure of Manchuria, however, shifted the emphasis and made Japan *the* enemy, in the eyes of Chinese nationalists. Administratively Manchuria had never been really a part of China. Chang Tso-lin and his son, Chang Hsueh-liang, had ruled the territory as virtually independent sovereigns. But racially Manchuria was overwhelmingly Chinese. Its sparsely settled northern plains had been filling up with colonists from the North Chinese provinces of Hopei and Shantung. To consent formally to the alienation of this territory from China was something that no Chinese nationalist government, however anxious to placate Japan, could venture to do.

And the Japanese Army could no more stop within the confines of Manchuria than the Chinese Government could acknowledge the loss of this land. There were always new frontiers to be safeguarded, new border regions to penetrate. It was only a question of time until the supreme test of strength between revolutionary Japanese imperialism and revolutionary Chinese nationalism would take place.

Japan's shift from the moderation of the twenties to the violent expansion of the thirties was an Oriental aspect of the world-wide revolt against liberalism. Westernization, although probably a necessity, was by no means an unmixed blessing for Japan. Along with material advantages it brought psychological stresses and strains and baffling new economic problems.

Unemployment, for instance, scarcely existed in the shut-in feudal economy of pre-Restoration Japan. But once Japan took over capitalist methods of production and trade, sent its ships to the seven seas and became linked with the international system of commerce and finance it had to take its share of slumps as well as of booms. An indirect consequence of overspeculation in the United States might be a new load of poverty for the debt-burdened farmers on the little rice farms of Japan.

A visible result of the introduction of Western medicine and hygiene, enforced with typically Japanese bureaucratic thoroughness, was a sharp upward trend of the population curve. A primary consideration for any Japanese Government was to provide food and work for the additional million people who were coming of working age every year. And this was far from an easy problem to solve.

Japan's agriculture had long sustained what is probably the maximum number of people who could live on the land. Emigration was ruled out because countries with a white population, such as the United States, Canada and Australia, barred out Japanese. And other Asiatic lands, except for the Philippines, were even more thickly peopled than was Japan. Birth control ran counter to the conservative character of the Japanese family system, to the instinct for producing many sons. It has never been widely practiced in any Oriental country.

There remained industrial development. And the growth of trade and industry was the chief means of supporting an increasing population that lived more and more in towns. But here again there were difficulties in a world of protectionism, of tariffs and quotas. In the competitive world which it had entered, Japan had some advantages. One of the most important was the existence of a large reservoir of labor that was cheap, by Western standards, and that could be trained to a fairly high level of efficiency.

But there were also disadvantages. Japan is a country poor in natural resources, without iron, without cotton, without rubber, with very little oil, to mention a few of the more conspicuous deficiencies. And it lacked accumulated wealth. It could easily undersell the Western powers in the Asiatic markets, where purchasing power is very limited. But it was at a great disadvantage in financing enterprises which required large initial investments.

Like the rest of the world, Japan suffered acutely from the great economic crisis of 1929. This crisis was an important, perhaps a decisive, factor in the victory of Hitler. And its effects helped to shift the balance of power from moderates to militarists in Japan.

Japan's career of expansion is usually thought of as simply an attempt to dominate other peoples. It is that, of course. But it is more than that. It is an attempt, partly conscious, partly unconscious, to cut the knot of contradictions in which Japan became involved through its adoption of the Western economic system, to make the sword more powerful than gold, to assure a livelihood for the Japanese people by the double means of conquering foreign markets and peoples and establishing in Japan itself a rigidly controlled economic system.

Japan could be fairly described as a dictatorship without a dictator. And during the last decade it has taken on many features of fascism without formally changing either its constitution or its form of government. The Constitution, after all, was a gift of the Emperor Meiji. To discard it, even to modify it, would carry a suggestion of sacrilege.

But many of the ideas of the younger military officers, who, with their sympathizers in the civilian bureaucracy, have been pushing the moderates into the background, are akin to those of European fascism. Always impressionable, Japan has imitatively succumbed to the latest political vogue.

Exaltation of the soldierly qualities, indoctrination with nationalist ideas, suspicion of foreign influences, antipathy to individualism, desire to control both economic processes and human thought—on all these points there is much in common between Japan's military extremists and the German Nazis and Italian Fascists. So there is some ideological cement for the tripartite pact of September, 1940, although national interests primarily dictated the conclusion of this agreement.

There has been some direct imitation of Fascist models. Since the conclusion of the anti-Comintern Pact of 1936 between Japan and Germany there has been a marked growth of German influence in Japan. There have been exchange visits of professors and students, of publicists and artists, between the two countries. German films have been prominently displayed in Japan and Japanese in Germany. A German book has been translated into Japanese for the purpose of spreading the idea of anti-Semitism—practically unknown in Japan, a country where there are no indigenous Jews. The German Embassy has maintained close contact with Japanese military officers. The old prestige of Imperial Germany in Japanese Army circles, dimmed by defeat, has been revived by Hitler's succession of diplomatic and military victories.

There is also some truth in the claim of Toshio Shiratori, one of the extreme nationalists in the Japanese diplomatic corps, that Japan possessed many features of fascism hundreds of years before this system ever appeared in Europe. Bureaucratic control of daily life, police espionage, sacrifice of the individual to the community—these are not new ideas in Japan. And there is a very old tradition of anticapitalism, of contempt for trade. In the Japanese Middle Ages the impoverished samurai, or man of the sword, felt the same superiority to the trader that the European knight would have felt to the Jew. The samurai was not supposed to handle money or to know anything about its value—a circumstance which explains the swift bankruptcy of many members of this class when they were thrown on their own resources after the Restoration.

There was no real possibility for peaceful coexistence between a Japan that was setting its course on imperialist expansion and a China that was animated by the ideals of a genuine, if incomplete, national revolution. The years between the conquest of Manchuria and the beginning of the larger war between Japan and China represented a period of uneasy armistice.

The ultimate trial of strength began in 1937 and became the greatest war Asia had known for centuries, fought with weapons that would have amazed such mighty conquerors as Tamerlane and Genghiz Khan. Japan chose a moment for initiating hostilities on a large scale when there was little prospect of foreign intervention. Great Britain and France were checkmated by the growing threat of German aggression in Europe. Isolationism was at a high point in the United States and it has always been a feature of American Far Eastern policy not to act without the British cooperation which would certainly not be forthcoming if it were a question of naval action or even of economic sanctions.

So Japan, taking advantage of every new aggravation of the European crisis, went far beyond the limits of its Manchurian adventure in 1931. It carried war by land, air and sea to all but the most remote parts of China, showing scant regard for foreign vested interests and trading rights in the process. And it encountered from the Western powers no resistance beyond notes of protest. America and Great Britain gave some material support to China, but did not cut off trade with Japan.

The Soviet Union might have caused some concern to Japan if it had not been for the purge of the leading generals of the Red Army which took place shortly before the beginning of hostilities in China. The Japanese military leaders reckoned correctly that Stalin would not choose to become involved in a major war after decimating the directing staff of the army. The Soviet Union gave some support to China with airplanes and tanks, but took no steps toward active military intervention.

So the war, at least during its first four years, was mainly a trial of strength between Japan and China. The Island Empire enjoyed the advantages of its long start over China in adopting Western industrial methods and western weapons. Its army, gradually overcoming a Chinese resistance that was weak and fumbling in some places, courageous and well organized in others, occupied the seven largest cities of China: Peking, Tientsin, Shanghai, Nanking, Hankow, Canton and Tsingtao.

But the Japanese victories were less decisive than they would have been if China had been a more highly developed country, dependent for its economic life on the smooth functioning of means of communication and on contact with the outside world. The great majority of the Chinese people were peasants living on a minimum subsistence standard of homegrown products, and they were less susceptible to blockade than a richer people would have been.

And China's nationalism proved its reality in the ordeal of unequal conflict. Chiang Kai-shek, who had grown in stature as a national leader since he had first appeared on the Chinese political scene, displayed a pertinacity which is not the most characteristic Chinese quality in the face of military reverses. He held together the threads of the Chinese resistance in remote Chungking, on its high bluff above the Yangtze River, battered as it was by repeated Japanese air raids.

Contrary to the expectations of some Japanese, the war promoted unity rather than disintegration in China. The civil war with the Communists had ceased before the Japanese invasion began. The Communists, who had shifted their base of operations from South Central China to an area in the Northwest, had considerably toned down the ferocious social revolutionary character of their original regime. Instead of killing members of the well-to-do classes on sight, they contented themselves with restricting rents and curbing abuses of agrarian exploitation. Their armies cooperated with the Kuomintang troops against the Japanese, carried on effective guerrilla warfare in mountainous Shansi Province and provided leadership and organization for peasant resistance in the districts of North China where the Japanese held the main towns and railways without being able to subdue and control the hinterland.

After the autumn of 1938, when the Japanese captured Canton with negligible losses after an unopposed landing and a quick dash and entered Hankow after a hard upriver campaign, the war entered a stage of stalemate, and there were only minor shifts in the front. The Japanese High Command

was unwilling to risk campaigns in the mountainous interior
of China, where good roads are scarce, railways are nonexistent and lines of communication would become almost
impossibly long. The Chinese have lacked the artillery and
the technical preparation which would be required to drive
the Japanese out of the large towns where they have established garrisons.

The result is a deadlock, which might last for a long time
if it is not to be broken by some external force. Both countries are suffering severely from the war, but not to the breaking point. The Japanese have lost the modest comforts which
they gained as a result of the rise in their standard of living
after the first World War. To sustain the struggle in China
they must wear clothes of poor quality, submit to rationing
of some foodstuffs and commodities, shiver a little more than
usual in their picturesque but drafty homes. But they are a
stoical, disciplined people and they have no means of voicing
discontent. The situation still seems far from the stage where
riots and revolts could be expected.

China has suffered much more, because the war has been
fought on Chinese soil. Large areas, especially in the lower
Yangtze valley, have been desolated. Millions of Chinese have
fled from their homes into the interior of China where the
Japanese cannot penetrate. The Chinese currency has got out
of hand and there has been a serious inflation in the prices
of rice and other staple products, which bears hardly on the
poorer people in the towns. But the overwhelming majority
of the Chinese still look to Chungking as the center of national leadership. The Japanese can show no evidence of
popular support for the puppet governments which they have
brought into existence in the occupied territory. Manchuria
now seems more or less resigned to Japanese rule; the original
semipolitical, semibandit resistance has been crushed. But the
Japanese are obliged almost literally to sit on bayonets in
China proper.

There are two external circumstances which may affect the issue of the Sino–Japanese struggle. Japan's imperialists look longingly to the rich lands of Southeastern Asia and the adjacent seas, to Malaya, the Dutch East Indies and the Philippines. Here Japan would find almost everything necessary for the self-sufficiency which is the primary desire of every military state. The Dutch East Indies are a storehouse of oil, tin, rubber, sugar and a long list of tropical products. Malaya is rich in iron, tin and rubber. In the Philippines are large reserves of manganese, iron, hemp, copra.

During the first half of 1941 Japan was poised, yet hesitant, to strike. It was divided between the temptation of laying its hands on some or all of these glittering prizes and the fear that an aggressive southward move would lead to war with Great Britain and the United States. Its leaders hoped that a collapse of Great Britain in Europe and a diversion of American naval strength from the Pacific to the Atlantic would pave the way for a maximum of conquest with a minimum of risk.

The other circumstance is the nonaggression pact which was concluded between Japan and the Soviet Union in April, 1941. One obvious effect of this pact was to give Japan some relief from fear of a Russian attack in the event of Japanese involvement in the South Pacific. It fitted in with Hitler's purpose of utilizing Japan as a threat to British and American interests in the Orient and was probably concluded under German pressure.

The Soviet–Japanese agreement may have an unfavorable effect on China. The Soviet–German Pact of August, 1939, let loose war on Europe and soon proved to be a compact of mutual aggression against Poland. The future, perhaps not a very distant future, will show whether Stalin, in shaking hands with Matsuoka in Moscow, has contrived to incite a new war in Asia and to divide China into Soviet and Japanese spheres of influence. The outbreak of the Soviet–German

War has created another possibility: that Japan, in the event of a severe Soviet defeat, would endeavor to seize Eastern Siberia and Outer Mongolia.

The advance of invention, the improvement of communications, the growth of trade, have brought East and West much closer together during the last century. And the same forces helped to link these geographically remote parts of the world in a common tragic destiny. The institutions and ideas which forced their way from the West into the East through the most diverse channels—through exchanges of diplomatic contacts; through missionaries, intent on winning believers for the Gospel; through the Chinese and Japanese student, discovering new fields of thought; through the reverberations of such European cataclysms as the World War and the Russian Revolution—did not make for peace and stability in the East, any more than in the West. Western ideas of nationalism, Western improved weapons of destruction, the capitalist technique of production with its temptation of commercial imperialism, led to the clash and turmoil of war and revolution, in the Orient as in the Occident. All the principal developments of the last seventy-five years in the Far East, the modernization of Japan, the nationalist remolding of China, the Japanese attempt to find a remedy for political and economic dilemmas in foreign conquest, are deeply rooted in Western origins, models and examples. And no doubt the future pattern of an East that is being recast in the melting pot of war will be shaped very largely by that of a West that is undergoing an even greater upheaval.

Chapter Ten

THE WAR OF STEEL AGAINST GOLD

THE WAR WHICH BEGAN in September, 1939, was in some respects simply a resumption of the conflict that had ended with the Armistice of November 11, 1918. France and England were again arrayed against a Germany that had slipped every bond imposed by the Treaty of Versailles, that even enjoyed a more favorable starting point for hostilities than the Germany of 1914.

This was true as regards both the diplomatic and the military preparation of the Second World War. Public opinion in France and England did not realize this. So Germany gained an additional element of surprise when the full power of its war machine was brought into play.

Hitler started the war with the man power and industrial resources of Imperial Germany, except for Alsace–Lorraine and the districts which had been taken by Poland. At his command were the ten million Germans of Austria and the Sudetenland. He could utilize the great Skoda munitions plant and the other factories of Bohemia, the most industrialized part of Austria–Hungary.

His pact with Stalin eliminated the prospect of the two-front war which had always been the nightmare of German strategists. The Russian invasion of East Prussia early in the First World War caused the dispatch from France of two German divisions which might have been of decisive value at the Marne. And Russia kept pounding away at the German and Austrian lines intermittently for almost three years, until its collapse in 1917. This prevented Germany from achieving sufficient superiority in troops and matériel to break the stalemate of trench warfare in France. The pact with Russia was worth a hundred divisions to Hitler.

Italy in 1914 was a friendly neutral in relation to France and England. It was destined within a year to join the Allied coalition, to create a new front which would require the employment of large numbers of Austrians and a smaller number of German troops. Italy in 1939 was a malevolent neutral, committed to entering the war on the German side at the first convenient opportunity. This changed attitude of Russia and Italy (to say nothing of Japan) was alone enough to swing the military odds against England and France.

Germany in 1914 was superbly prepared for war. But it was prepared within the limitation of a system based on respect for private property and for individual liberty. The Imperial Government could not hold the threat of arbitrary incarceration in a concentration camp over the head of a recalcitrant employer. Nor could it, in time of peace, throw workers about from one industry to another or forbid them to quit jobs. After all, there were free trade unions in Germany under the Kaiser, and there was a strong Social Democratic party. As a witty German émigré once remarked to me:

"The Allied war propaganda represented the Kaiser's government as being very much what Hitler's regime really is today."

The Germany of Hitler could and did exercise in time of peace the most extreme powers of a wartime dictatorship. It pressed out of the people and out of the industrial machine

the very last ounce of production. With its mixture of terrorism and propaganda it forced and induced the type of supreme
effort and sacrifice which a people usually puts forward only
when there is a feeling of mortal danger.

Germany spent ninety billion marks, or about thirty-six
billion dollars, on rearmament during the six and a half years
which elapsed between Hitler's coming into power and the
beginning of hostilities. This was just about three times the
combined military expenditures of Great Britain and France
for the same period. And Germany outstripped its prospective enemies not only in the amount but in the character of
its spending.

Most French and British military leaders and experts were
strongly conditioned in their thinking by the experience of
the last war. They assumed too readily and too uncritically
that the tactics which had led to victory in one war would
be equally successful in another. The First World War, after
a prodigious competition in slaughter on a deadlocked front,
had been won mainly through a combination of two factors:
the relentless pressure of the British blockade on Germany's
supplies of food and raw materials and the throwing into the
scale of America's vast human and material resources.

What Gamelin, Gort and the other French and British
generals hoped was to repeat the victory without the slaughter. They believed that it would be possible to build up ultimate overwhelming air superiority by utilizing the resources
of the British and French empires and of the United States.
Meanwhile the German Army would be contained by the
Maginot Line and Germany's production would be limited
and crippled by the blockade.

A cartoon that was widely circulated in France (perhaps
it still hangs in tattered shreds in some places to mock the
country in its defeat) showed the wide expanse of the British
and French empires and the comparatively tiny area of Germany. It bore the cheerful caption: "We shall win, because

we are the stronger." I overheard the bitter comment of an intelligent Frenchman as he looked at this cartoon in the days of the collapse:

"Yes, we *should* have been the stronger. But Hitler's resources were all on the battlefield and ours were scattered over the seven seas, mostly unexploited and unused."

Just because they had been defeated, German officers devoted more intensive study to possible new methods of winning a war than their French and British colleagues. From the lessons of the First World War they drew several main conclusions, all of which Hitler put into practice.

There must be no two-front war. Here the answer was the pact with the Soviet Union.

There must be greater self-sufficiency. Everything from chemistry to controlled economy was pressed into service to achieve this end. German tanks rolled over the roads of Poland and Belgium and France on tires made of synthetic rubber. German airplanes poured down their explosive and incendiary bombs while flying on the output of synthetic oil plants. The production of home-grown cereals was increased and strict rationing was introduced from the first day of the war. In the previous war, rationing was only instituted as an emergency measure after the larder had already begun to run low.

Finally, and most important of all, the new war must be swift and decisive, not a prolonged agony of attrition. In the modern airplane and the modern tank, weapons which were in their infancy twenty-five years ago, German strategists recognized the means of giving offense a new advantage over defense, of restoring to war the element of mobility which had been so completely absent in the Western Front of 1914–1918. And Germany, of all European countries, was best equipped to turn out airplanes and tanks in large quantities. For Germany, after the United States, was the land of mass production. British manufacturers were proverbially slow in achieving the economies of large-scale combination, in modernizing their plants. The French instinct was for fine quality, for specialized work, not for mass and quantity.

This French instinct was part of the national art of civilized and pleasant living. But it was a handicap when it was a matter of supreme necessity to obtain the largest possible number of airplanes with the utmost possible speed. It was the French tendency to dally over designs, to experiment with time-consuming changes and improvements, instead of adopting reasonably satisfactory models and producing these in maximum quantities.

While private economic enterprise has certainly provided a far higher and more varied standard of living than either communism or fascism, the capitalist system is better adapted to peace than to war. The economic objective in war is simple: the greatest possible production of airplanes, tanks and other munitions and supplies. The manager of a wartime munitions plant never has to worry about overproduction. The profit motive, an incentive to better quality and better service in peacetime production, is often a drawback when everything must be subordinated to war needs. The efficient conduct of war demands a centralization of industrial power for which the competitive system is not a good preparation.

The best proof that modern war on a large scale demands a considerable measure of state socialism is the fact that all the great powers engaged in the First World War, irrespective of their former political and economic systems, found themselves obliged to vest more and more power in the hands of new state agencies of economic administration. Foreign trade, food distribution, munitions production, transportation, allotments of raw material—all such branches of activity were more or less nationalized.

Now Germany possessed the immense advantage of having instituted what amounted to wartime industrial mobilization several years before the war began. It took care in advance of many of the problems with which England and France began to grapple, rather feebly and ineffectively at first, after the commencement of hostilities. The Third Reich was adjusted to mass military production, to rationing, to controlled disposition of labor, to raw material priorities, long before the first tanks rumbled across the frontier into Poland.

So, while there was in 1939 a resumption of the national war between Germany on one side and Great Britain and France on the other, it was, on Germany's part, a war with revolutionary overtones. During the turbulent hungry months immediately after the end of the First World War it seemed at times as if the German social order might break down, as if the country might "go Bolshevik." This did not occur. But in 1933 Germany did experience a type of revolution far more conducive to military efficiency than a German imitation of Russian bolshevism could have been. For national socialism conserved the efficiency of capitalist methods of production and management while shedding the limitations which orthodox capitalist finance would have imposed on preparation for war. And by abolishing every semblance of political opposition and civil liberties it removed another potent check on the sacrifices which are required in total preparation for war: the freedom to voice criticisms.

The infernal cycle of war and revolution completed one full turn when the German armies invaded Poland. The lost war was a main cause of a revolution which enabled Germany, two decades after a peace that had left her economically stripped and militarily impotent, to begin a new war with reserves of strength which were greater in many respects than Germany possessed in 1914.

It is doubtful whether Germany under the Imperial regime could have regained its international power so rapidly. For Hitler owed much of his success to essentially revolutionary methods, daring, cynical, adroit, original and unscrupulous as the diplomacy of an old established regime cannot be. There was none of the heavy-footed fumbling which one is apt to associate with German diplomacy before and during the First World War. The Nazi Foreign Ministry committed no such crass blunders as the Zimmermann note of 1917, proposing to Mexico to attack the United States and annex Texas and California.

While the Nazi regime, like all the dictatorships, has brought with it a period of intellectual decline, of paralysis of creative thought, while the cultural level of the average Nazi leader is certainly far below that of the typical high official of the old regime, Hitler and his associates have shown a high measure of skill and resourcefulness in the practical fields of war, diplomacy and propaganda. Nazi agents pounced like vultures on the many elements of weakness and disintegration in the other European countries. They knew and made use of the racial feuds which weakened all the states of Eastern and Southeastern Europe. They exploited the profound cleavages in French public opinion.

They took advantage of a quite reasonable apprehension that the aftermath of a new great war would be social revolution, ending in some form of bolshevism. To credulous conservatives they posed as champions of order against communism up to and even after the conclusion of the pact with Stalin.

One reason why so much of the resistance to Hitler collapsed even before the war began, why the barriers erected against German expansion to the east and southeast proved to be only papier-mâché, was the deep wedge which communism and fascism had driven into the unity of many of the European nations. Before 1914 substantial unity within a nation could be taken for granted. But the two totalitarian revolutions aroused so much passion as to lead to a ferocious civil war in Spain and to a state of latent civil war in France.

Russia, moreover, had completely fallen out of any feasible scheme of European balance and order. Russian aid was inseparable from the extension of the Soviet system. No one could reasonably expect that Red Army troops would come into Poland or Czechoslovakia or the Baltic or Balkan states, on the pretext of protecting these countries against Germany, and depart without raising the Soviet hammer and sickle flag over the country which they had come to "help." To non-Communists this remedy might well seem worse than the disease. So the states of Eastern Europe were thrown on their own resources in resisting Hitler, and those resources were altogether insufficient.

There were intelligent and farsighted individuals in Great Britain and France who recognized the desperate nature of the crisis which the two countries faced after the declaration of war. But their voices were silenced by censorship, by the easy accusation of defeatism. The general atmosphere in London and in Paris during the first months of the war was a curious compound of apathy and complacency. France was split from top to bottom and from Left to Right on the whole issue of fighting Hitler in order to save Poland. It is doubtful whether a great country ever entered a war so unwillingly or with such a conspicuous and obvious lack of enthusiasm.

There was more unanimity in England. But the British, with their confidence in the decisive value of sea power, did not appreciate until France had collapsed the formidable menace of Germany's systematic development of modern mechanized weapons. British, as well as French, military thinkers had become attached to a cult of the defensive, to the conviction that offensive land operations when met by armies of approximately equal strength and training, would lead to nothing but huge casualty lists.

Great Britain and France committed three tragic major blunders, along with a host of lesser mistakes, in dealing with Hitler. The first was to permit him to rearm and to remilitarize the Rhineland without opposition. The second was to go to war on behalf of Poland after all possibility of aiding Poland, or any other East European country, had been thrown away.

The third was to double the blunder of declaring war by waging it halfheartedly, lackadaisically, passively.

The German method of conducting hostilities was admirably calculated to create this mood of passivity. The swift crushing of Poland and its obliteration as a state by means of partition between the Soviet Union and Germany had the disheartening effect of eliminating any tangible attainable war objective. There was an enthusiastic American diplomat who expressed the belief on more than one occasion that England and France in 1940 would achieve such mastery of the air that Germany's airplanes would be shot out of the skies and Germany would surrender unconditionally without further fighting. Then, to complete the job, the air armadas would sweep on to the East and serve notice on Stalin to get out of Poland. But few Frenchmen were as foolish as this highly placed foreign observer.

A strong local offensive against French territory, air bombings of French towns, would have aroused a sense of national peril, a conviction that here was a real war. But Germany was fighting a war of nerves, of psychological moods, as well as a war of arms. The German High Command almost ostentatiously refrained from initiating vigorous hostilities until it was prepared to deal the supreme crushing blow.

One of the smoke screens that concealed the true proportions of the German threat was the widespread circulation in France, in England, in America, of stories about alleged German military and economic weaknesses. It was said, for instance, that the German tanks and armored cars which took part in the occupation of Austria were of such poor quality that many broke down en route. Food difficulties in Germany, and their effect on national morale, were exaggerated. Up to the very end some of the French were consoling themselves by repeating stories that the German air force was so nearly exhausted that one-armed men and untrained boys were being used as pilots.

Some of these tales were circulated in good faith by German refugees who hated Hitler and let their hopes for his downfall influence their judgment. Others had the indeterminate origin of the rumors that float about so plentifully in every war and are the natural children of censorship and secrecy. But when the full history of the war can be written it will not be surprising to learn that German propaganda agencies through various channels fed these stories to eager listeners in the Allied countries. It was correctly calculated that there would be a tremendous psychological shock when the contrast between these soothing stories of German weakness and the terrific striking power of the German war machine was revealed.

The few weeks between the night of May 9, when the Germans let loose their great offensive, and June 16, when France appealed for an armistice, represent one of the swiftest periods of fateful change in history. Up to that time the Second World War had largely followed the pattern of the first. Germany had won important victories in the East; but the Anglo–French line in the West was intact and was widely believed to be impregnable. The British blockade was in force and the German submarine war had been less destructive than in 1917.

Then, as if by magic, the front in France disappeared. Germany was on the Atlantic Ocean. Its facilities for submarine attack and sea raiding were vastly multiplied by the possession of bases from the North Cape to the Pyrenees. Large-scale war on the continent, for the time being at least, was ended and Germany could augment its power with the resources of the conquered countries.

But Great Britain remained unsubdued, an island, center of a great empire, facing up to a hostile continent. The mighty German land and air power, proved irresistible in Europe by a succession of overwhelmingly victorious campaigns, stopped at the water's edge. The natural barrier of the British Channel, guarded by sea power and by air power which was dauntless in spirit and high in quality although relatively weak in numbers, was more effective as a defense against invasion than the artificial catacombs of the Maginot Line.

Science and invention and applied technique have long been advancing not in arithmetical but in geometrical progression. And the war of 1939–1941 was as different from the world conflict of 1914–1918 as that war was from the Napoleonic campaigns, fought without railways or motor transport.

A war of masses has given place to a war fought by elite groups. The members of the elite corps of modern armies, the air force and the armored units, possess over the rank-and-file infantry soldier all the superiority of the medieval knight, that human fortress in his chain-mail armor, against a mob of insurgent peasants.

The First World War was distinguished by its shock of masses; by its terrific losses in killed and wounded, incurred in struggles for small patches of ground. The Second World War has demonstrated that a mass army of the old type, however courageous, however well trained, is as helpless against superior mechanized power as a crowd of civilians would be.

France has an unbroken tradition of universal military service, dating from its Revolution one hundred and fifty years ago. Every able-bodied Frenchman was liable to conscription. Mobilization was complete; one was struck by the prominence of cripples and blind, victims of the earlier war, on the streets of Paris, after the fit had been combed out by mobilization in 1939. But the vast majority of these French soldiers never had an opportunity to fire a shot at a German.

With its lines pierced at every point by the infiltration of German mechanized units, about half of the French Army, some two million men in all, found themselves prisoners. Hundreds of thousands of Germans perished in the vain assault on

Verdun in 1916. Less than thirty thousand Germans were killed in the conquest of all France in 1941.

There has been the same experience in Poland, in Yugoslavia, in Greece. All these countries possessed armies of tough, disciplined peasant soldiers. But these armies were nothing but droves of prospective war prisoners when Germany struck with its complete mastery of the air and its endless columns of tanks. A similar result, sweeping victory achieved at the price of negligible losses for the winning side, was to be seen in the British victories over the Italians in Libya and in Ethiopia.

There is profound prophetic significance, politically as well as militarily, in this ease with which the army that is superior in high-powered modern weapons can crush resistance, regardless of difficulties of terrain. The German tanks and bombers were as effective in the mountains of Yugoslavia as in the plains of Poland and Flanders.

The obvious lesson for every great industrial power is to concentrate attention on its elite units, on its air force and its motorized divisions. There is little practical value in training masses of men in handling rifles which they will most probably never be able to fire should they encounter an army equipped for modern war.

For the peoples who are not and cannot be great industrial powers the conclusion to be drawn, while hard, seems inescapable. Modern science has robbed them of their liberty. The independence of the small state was always precarious and limited. It often depended on the rivalries of larger neighbors. But now even this limited and precarious independence belongs to the past. The small state of the future can exist only within the framework of some larger association, forced or free. Barring the advent of anarchy or total chaos, this is one of the few predictions that can be uttered confidently in the fluid and everchanging present situation.

Air power was the Great Unknown of modern war. Its destructive possibilities had already been proved in Spain and in China. That it would affect the character of warfare was obvious. But military experts did not agree as to how decisive this effect would be.

Some enthusiasts for the new arm, such as the Italian General Douhet, believed in the possibility of a lightning war, to be decided by air bombing alone. It was hotly debated whether the airplane had made old conceptions of sea power obsolete, whether the battleship could stand up to the bomber.

Air power has been enormously effective. Masses of airplanes, used in close coordination with motorized units on the ground, have made it possible for the German armies to march into so many European capitals. It has bridged or helped to bridge more than one narrow sea. The airplane has begun to rival the submarine as a menace to shipping.

But air power has not proved invincible. It has not, by itself, broken the resistance of any people—not even of Chinese and Spaniards, who were unable to hit back. Terrible as the destruction wrought in England has been, the number of persons killed after many months of the fiercest close-range attacks from the air is only about the number of Americans who lose their lives in highway accidents every year. Prolonged intensive air bombing has not made the great cities of England uninhabitable, has not crippled British industrial production and has not made British ports unusable.

With the fall of France the two strongest combatants of the first World War, Germany and Great Britain, faced each other again in what gives every indication of being a duel to the death, with slight prospect of compromise or accommodation. On one side is the greater part of a continent which Hitler has brought under his control. On the other is a world empire, with possessions in every continent and a heart and brain in the beleaguered fortress of the British Isles.

The classical land of individual liberty, of parliamentarism, of free enterprise, is pitted against the most powerful and the most efficient of the modern dictatorships. It is a war of land power against sea power, a war where great territorial changes have been accompanied by very small loss of life. If it is not decided quickly by a successful German invasion or strangulating blockade of England it may well go on for a very long time because of the difficulty which each side experiences in getting at the other.

Bismarck said that war between England and Russia would be a war between a whale and an elephant. This observation holds good for the present struggle, although aviation makes it possible to exchange more blows between a predominantly land power and a predominantly sea power than would have been possible in the time of the Iron Chancellor.

Great Britain has lost its last foothold on the continent. There is nothing in the comparative resources of the belligerents in man power and matériel to suggest that a successful large-scale British offensive on the continent could be launched in any predictable future. One of the ablest of American military commentators, Mr. Hanson W. Baldwin, estimated in the spring of 1941 that Hitler disposed of two hundred and fifty divisions, against fifty of roughly equivalent training and equipment for the whole British Empire. Certainly whenever Germans and British have clashed in Europe, the German advantage in numbers and in equipment has been overwhelming.

It is doubtful whether Hitler's continental empire can be conquered by blockade, although the stoppage of access to overseas minerals and raw materials and foodstuffs is a valuable British weapon. Economically Europe is a lopsided continent. Its remarkable growth in population and prosperity during the nineteenth century was largely based on overseas trade and investment, on an increasing exchange of its manufactured goods for the foodstuffs and raw materials of other parts of the world. Europe is top-heavy with men and industrial plants and short of many foodstuffs and of such overseas products as cotton, tin, rubber, oil, manganese and nickel.

Still the German war machine can sustain itself for a long time on the resources of a subjugated Europe, especially if it succeeds in conquering the more productive regions of the Soviet Union. The conquest of additional territory in the Near East and in North Africa which would enhance the self-sufficiency of Hitler's realm cannot be ruled out as a possibility.

If a total victory for Great Britain over Germany thus seems a dim and certainly a distant prospect, a complete victory for Hitler also seems doubtful. Much the greatest part of the British Empire is beyond the physical grasp of a Germany which still lacks naval strength. Unless the British Isles can be successfully invaded or unless the approaches to these islands can be cut off by submarines and airplanes Hitler faces the prospect of a protracted struggle, in which the resources of the American continent, and especially of the United States, will weigh heavily in the balance against him.

Hitler's career of conquest poses anew the old question whether Europe can be united either by force or by agreement. Ever since the fall of the Roman Empire there has been the dream of supranational European unity which assumed various forms in various ages. The name of Rome carried an eternal symbolism of authority.

As Saint Augustine foresaw so prophetically in "The City of God," a Roman spiritual power, the Catholic Church, succeeded the fallen Roman temporal power. Throughout the Dark Ages and the Middle Ages the Roman Church furnished the strongest bond of unity for a Europe that was almost dissolved in feudal anarchy, where central governments were weak and the sense of nationality was still struggling to be born. Latin, the language of the Church, was the common tongue of the few educated men and women. It was under the sign of the Cross that the greatest common undertakings of the Middle Ages, the Crusades and the building of the mighty cathedrals, were carried out.

With the Reformation the conception of a single indivisible church ceased to be a reality. But there was also a secular dream of a continuation of Roman law and authority. Charlemagne was crowned at Rome and a long line of German princes bore the title of Roman Emperors. But no genuine unity was created under this shadowy realm, which had ceased to be Holy, Roman or an Empire centuries before Voltaire coined the phrase.

The feudal economy and political system of the Middle Ages were not compatible with the existence of a large, centralized, well-organized empire. But when gunpowder and printing heralded the end of the medieval institutions, when a more modern type of state, headed by an absolute sovereign, came into being, the possibility of the domination of Europe by a single power emerged. The possessions of Charles V, which included Germany, Austria, Spain, the Low Countries and large parts of Italy, were of almost continental dimensions.

There was a period when France, the richest, most populous and most centralized state in Europe, seemed likely to obtain complete hegemony over the other powers. It required all the efforts of coalitions in which England played a prominent part to hold in check the armies of Louis XIV. The British tradition of opposing the appearance of any power on the continent so strong as to be dominant dates back even further than the wars against Louis XIV. It found expression in the struggle against Philip II of Spain which reached its climax in the defeat of the Armada.

Napoleon came closer than anyone before Hitler to uniting Europe under a single sovereignty. Both the parallels and the contrasts between the Corsican Little Corporal and the Unknown Soldier [1] of Berchtesgaden are sufficiently striking to be worth noting.

Like Hitler, Napoleon was an alien who came to greatness

[1] At the time of the Munich settlement a German newspaper referred to Hitler as the Unknown Soldier who never stopped fighting.

in the land of his adoption. Like Napoleon, Hitler was no respecter of boundaries or of nationalities. Both conquerors challenged many conventional ideas both of military tactics and of law, government and social and economic order.

Hitler's problems and difficulties are remarkably similar to Napoleon's. Both had to reckon with the sullen, if suppressed, hatred of the subdued peoples. Both were confronted by an England which refused to accept the mastery of a single power over the continent and which was able to blockade their land empires. Napoleon's relations with Tsar Alexander I after the Peace of Tilsit, which left France and Russia the sole European great powers, were not unlike those of Hitler with Stalin during the uneasy two years after the signing of the very brittle German–Soviet nonaggression pact. They were a compound of outward friendship with secret distrust and preparation for hostilities. Carrying the comparison between Hitler's position and Napoleon's somewhat farther, one can recognize three advantages and three disadvantages for Hitler, by comparison with his predecessor. The advantages are as follows:

(1) The advance of scientific technique, in its present stage, works for the conqueror. The airplane and the tank are more formidable weapons of suppression than any which were at Napoleon's disposal. Guerrilla warfare is infinitely more difficult to organize. In the more compact, thickly settled occupied countries one may say that guerrilla warfare is a physical impossibility.

(2) Napoleon, after the blighting of his naval hopes at Trafalgar, had no means of striking directly at England. He possessed neither airplanes nor submarines. If one may trust the testimony of Jane Austen's and Thackeray's novels, life in England went on very normally while Napoleon's power on the continent was supreme. No bombs fell on London. Except for a small number of professional officers and hired or pressed soldiers and sailors, no one took any very active part

in the hostilities. Sea power was far less liable to challenge.

(3) The same scientific progress that has so greatly reduced Great Britain's island security has made an invasion of Russia far more feasible. Napoleon was beaten by Russian distances and Russian climate, rather than by the Russian Army. He did not possess even a mile of railway, to say nothing of the thousands of motor vehicles which Hitler can draw on for his invasion of the Soviet Union.

There are three points in which Hitler's position compares unfavorably with Napoleon's. They are:

(1) Raw materials, oil, copper, nickel, rubber, cotton, tin, manganese, tungsten, to mention a few of the more important, are of greater strategic value now than they were for the simpler warfare of Napoleon's time. The United States and the British Empire, together with those regions of South America and Africa and Asia which are accessible to Great Britain and inaccessible to Hitler so long as British control of the seas is maintained, are much richer in these materials than is Hitler's land empire.

(2) The British Empire and especially the self-governing Dominions, Canada, Australia, New Zealand, South Africa, are making a much greater contribution to the British war effort than the embryonic empire of the Pitts.

(3) Napoleon had nothing to fear from the agricultural United States of that time, with its few million colonists. Hitler has much to fear as the economic weight of the United States, the most powerful industrial nation in the world, with its one hundred and thirty million inhabitants, is thrown into the scales against him.

After the fall of Napoleon there was no practical experiment in the unification of Europe until the present time. Metternich tried to establish a reactionary European federation, a league of sovereigns, in the Holy Alliance. Mazzini dreamed of a revolutionary federation of democratically governed peoples. But the Holy Alliance melted away as the fears which had been inspired by the twin specters of the French Revolution and its formidable offspring, Napoleon, subsided. And Mazzini's dream remained a dream. Nationalism was a force for division, not for unity.

Yet the Pan-European idea would not down. Leon Trotsky was a strong advocate of a socialist United States of Europe. During the Russian civil war he delivered an oration to gaping peasant soldiers in the provincial town of Balashov, in which he predicted that a Europe which had been united under socialist auspices would send forth an armada to conquer the last stronghold of capitalism, the United States.

A cosmopolitan thinker, Count Coudenhove-Kalergi, envisaged a nonrevolutionary type of united Europe as the only salvation for the old culture of the continent, so deeply divided by national lines and threatened, as Coudenhove-Kalergi believed, by the political, economic and cultural pressure of such large units as the British Empire, the United States and the Soviet Union.

Trotsky's vision was never realized. The Russian Revolution stopped at Russia's frontiers. And Count Coudenhove-Kalergi unfortunately remained a prophet without honor in his own continent. In retrospect it seems quite probable that the realization of a big new creative idea like the federation of Europe in the liberal twenties would have offered the best means of assuaging the wounds of the first World War and stemming the trend toward violent revolution and dictatorship, so certain, in the end, to produce another war.

Had there been statesmen with imagination to conceive and practical ability to execute such a scheme the course of history might have been profoundly changed. A politically and economically united Europe could have forced an earlier ending of the war debts and reparations folly. It could have launched cooperative enterprises of development in Africa and Asia where German energy and technique would have found constructive expression, instead of being left to fester in a sense

of frustration and claustrophobia and finally set to work over-
time turning out means of maniacal destruction.

But the opportunity to create a free Pan-Europe was allowed to slip. What are the prospects of Hitler's forced
Pan-Europe?

Obviously the outlook is intimately bound up with the
issue of the war. If through the attainment of air superiority
or any other means England can win a decisive victory, the
whole edifice of conquest will crumble as rapidly as Napoleon's. Germans will be fortunate to escape with their lives
from the occupied countries.

On the other hand, if England should find itself crushed
or obliged to accept a compromise peace which would leave
Germany supreme on the continent, Hitler's Pan-Europe
would become a reality for an indefinite period of time. The
outlines of this system are already fairly clear, because Germany has been organizing as it conquers, without waiting for
the end of the war.

The new administrative boundaries of Germany have
already been pretty clearly drawn. They coincide closely with
those of Imperial Germany, supplemented by Austria and the
Sudetenland and rounded out by the annexation of additional
Polish territory in the East. Around this Germany, the central planet of the European firmament, would revolve a group
of satellites, ranging in status from subordinate allies like
France and Italy to crushed helot peoples like the Poles and
the Czechs.

The new European order would rest on an overwhelming
preponderance of German armed strength. A victorious Germany, one may be sure, would not display the irresolution,
the weakness, the bad conscience, which marked the policies
of England and France during the thirties and facilitated
Germany's rapid rearmament.

How long such an order would last or what social and
economic changes it would bring about are questions which

almost defy the imagination. The mark would probably become the sole currency of any consequence and European trade and industry would be welded into a unified whole, with Germany controlling all the key positions and regulating, in one way or another, the production of the other countries. Unless there were an almost inconceivable shift in the Nazi psychology this German-dominated Pan-Europe would certainly lack the elements essential to genuine federation, equal treatment of the members and voluntariness. The absence of any cement but force would create internal stress and strain and might finally prove fatal to the whole structure.

But it has been proved a mistake to underestimate German military striking power. It may be equally fallacious to underrate the German capacity for organization, to dismiss the possibility of a prolonged *Pax Germanica* on the European continent and in adjacent regions of Asia and Africa. If any people can dominate Europe by force it is certainly the Germans. They occupy a strategic central position. They are the most numerous race, after the Russians, and are far superior to the latter in military and economic efficiency. They possess the industrial basis for a tremendous development both of land power and of air power.

It is conceivable that the rulers of a Nazi empire in Europe would be able to play off one subject people against another, to exploit those numerous racial feuds and distrusts which made the military conquests of Europe so much easier than it would otherwise have been. Peoples which fared badly after the first World War, such as the Hungarians and the Bulgarians, could be and have been favored at the expense of the Czechs and the Yugoslavs. And the rich opportunities for setting one race against another and all non-Russians against the Communist rule from Moscow may have been an important reason for Hitler's decision to break with Stalin. The Finns may be useful auxiliaries in the North, the Ukrainians in the South. And the economic results of Soviet rule in

Latvia, Lithuania and Esthonia have been so disastrous that these small Baltic states may welcome the Germans as deliverers.

In the event of a British victory it is unlikely that the pre-1939 unrestricted sovereignty of small states would be or could be restored. It is one of the hard lessons of the present war that the small nation which cannot maintain a modern war industry is deprived of the means of effectively defending its independence.

If it is to be a *Pax Britannica* in Europe, not a *Pax Germanica*, the European countries will have little alternative except to become satellites of Great Britain, which will probably assure itself a monopoly, or at least a secure preponderance, of air power. British rule, in all probability, would not be so direct or so brutal as the German. It will perhaps be disguised behind some such formula as a European federation or a revived League of Nations.

When Great Britain continued the struggle after the collapse of France it became a common saying in England: "At least we are in the finals." And, if one makes the indispensable reservations for the possibility of unforeseen revolutionary developments or all-round social collapse, the final issue of the Second World War would seem to lie between the two countries which proved strongest in Europe's previous ordeal by battle, Germany and Great Britain.

There is, of course, no certainty that the war will end in a clear-cut victory for either of the major combatants. There is reason to fear that we have by no means seen the worst that a diabolically perverted human ingenuity can achieve in destruction in all the elements, in the air, on land and on sea. I was recently talking with a famous American aviation authority, who was explaining the technique of air raids.

"It is more useful to have a short intense air raid than a longer one of less violence," he said. "It is harder to control

fifteen or twenty fires if they break out at the same time than
to check the same number if they are spaced over a longer
interval."

We paused and both expressed the same thought:

"What an age of criminal lunacy we are living in!"

It is indeed the World's Iron Age, and we must grimly face
its implications. A prolonged war, extending over a period of
several years, carries a terrible threat of a peace that will indeed be a peace without victory—except for famine, pesti-
lence, social and economic chaos.

It was the hope of being able to exploit such a state of
collapse of civilization that has certainly been one of the
strongest motivations of Stalin's policy in the present conflict.
A prerequisite for the success of such a policy, however, was
to keep the Soviet Union out of the war, and here all the
Soviet dictator's Asiatic wiles have not been successful.

But it may prove easier to smash the Red Army, so gravely
weakened by purges of its higher commanding officers before
it was put to the test of a major war, to overthrow Stalin as
a dictator, than to defeat or prevent the emergence after the
end of hostilities of that social pathology, that sinister mixture
of despair, bitterness and blind, irrational hatred and desire
for destruction which found expression in Russian bolshevism
after the last war.

A spread of anything like Russian bolshevism over Europe
at the end of the war would be the irrevocable death knell
of Europe's culture and civilization. It would be a catastrophe
comparable in scope with what would have happened if the
savage Mongols in the thirteenth century had trampled out
the flickering light of European medieval civilization.

The Second World War is too vast a cataclysm to fit easily
into any single category of explanation. It is first of all a war
of Steel against Gold, using those words in their widest symbolic significance. It is a war in which one side relies for

victory on its maximum organization of labor power and complete control of capital and industrial plant and natural resources, while the other, committed to a freer political and economic system, bases its hope of success on the gradual bringing into play of potentially greater resources, which may compensate for the losses and defeats that followed a slow start in the armament race. Inasmuch as Germany's economy of Steel involves a fundamental revision of many accepted economic laws and institutions, the war possesses a revolutionary element; one doubts whether the economy of Gold can win without making big adaptations, of which some may well prove permanent.

Both national socialism and communism have revealed themselves in the war as vampire economies, almost compelled to live on the loot of conquered and annexed countries. There were curiously similar scenes in the German occupation of France and in the Soviet occupation of the Baltic countries. Discipline was well maintained in both cases. There were apparently very few cases of outrage against the population. But there was a prodigious process of buying out the conquered countries.

German officers and soldiers who, with their families, had been compelled for many years to forego butter for guns used their military success to acquire as much "butter," literally and figuratively, in the shape of foodstuffs and manufactured goods, as they could purchase with currency of questionable value. Red Army officers and their wives did the same thing in the Baltic states and in eastern Poland. These were peasant countries with very modest standards of living. But the shops of their largest towns seemed to offer incredible luxury to Soviet Russians whose successive Five Year Plans have produced mountains of optimistic statistics, but a standard of living far lower than that which prevailed in the regions of the former Russian Empire which escaped, until recently, the Communist experience.

This second world conflict is a war of the younger, fiercer, more dynamic imperialism of peoples who are predatory, in part at least, because they arrived late on the colonial stage and found the more desirable regions already preempted, against the older, more passive, more sated imperialisms of Great Britain and France and what may become the budding imperialism of the United States. It is a war of collectivism against individualism. Here again Germany and England are the dramatically appropriate protagonists. Germany is the country where collectivism has been most successfully mated with efficiency. England is the classical land of liberalism, of tolerance, of individual judgment.

When a struggle of cosmic proportions is in progress each side refuses to think except in terms of complete victory. To accept less would seem to betray the sacrifices which have already been made. The longer the war goes on, the greater the bitterness, the less the disposition to think in terms of compromise and accommodation.

Yet, apart from the still uncertain military issue, it seems doubtful whether the war will end in a total victory of the principles for which either side professes to be fighting. Fascism and communism represent a formidable revolt against liberal civilization. But there are some regions of the world which this revolt will scarcely reach. And national socialism may be modified in character by success and by the demand of the German masses for a higher standard of living and for relaxation after the strain and hardships of the war.

And even if the totalitarian onslaught is completely crushed it will leave enduring traces. It is becoming increasingly evident that Hitler can be defeated only if his enemies take over a considerable part of his system of war socialism, of state control over all phases of national economy.

And it is by no means certain, it is scarcely even probable, that this control will be discarded as it was after the last war. In peace, as in war, there will be a totalitarian challenge. Every belligerent country will face staggering problems of mountainous debt, of demobilization of swollen war industries. In many cases there will be a vast amount of physical destruction to be repaired. There will be little disposition on the part of the masses to accept widespread unemployment.

How much of the capitalist system will survive the double shock of the war itself and of the postwar crisis is hard to anticipate. That it will be changed, and changed much more deeply than after the First World War, seems highly probable.

Chapter Eleven

THE FALL OF FRANCE

THE FALL OF FRANCE resounded through the world like that of Rome in the fifth century and Constantinople in the fifteenth. To civilized men on five continents, from Buenos Aires to Chungking, Paris was a supranational capital of arts and letters, of culture and civilization. The last cries of Prague and Warsaw sounded faintly in American ears. But when Paris fell, and the whole of France shortly afterward, even those in faraway countries with least knowledge and experience of foreign affairs must have dimly, confusedly realized that a relatively soft and civilized world could end, that a new age of iron had set in, not only for Czechoslovakia, not only for Poland, not only for France, but for the whole world.

France's disaster occurred so swiftly that the mind could scarcely grasp its magnitude. Until the middle of May, life, except for the soldiers at the front, was amazingly normal for a country that was engaged in a life-and-death struggle. Shops were full of goods and crowded. Fashion shows attracted throngs of spectators. Once the first scare about air bombings, which pretty nearly emptied Paris of children in the first days of the war, had subsided, operas, concerts and theaters went on much as usual.

I am surprised, in retrospect, to remember how well Paris
was eating up to the very eve of the German occupation.
There was talk of ration cards; but these had not been introduced, except for sugar. Such limited restrictions as existed on
the consumption of meat and pastries and alcohol were easily
evaded. Even the blackout, such an emphatic tangible re-
minder of war in England, was little more than a mild, rather
pleasant darkening in Paris, which showed off the medieval
charm of the old city to greater advantage on clear nights.

Then, in one incredibly swift, blinding month France suffered a national shipwreck such as few countries have experienced. . . . Ten million refugees, almost a quarter of the
population, fleeing wildly to unknown destinations, consum-
ing the food stocks of the unoccupied regions like a horde of
locusts. . . . German soldiers on guard at the Arc de Triomphe
and Napoleon's Tomb. . . . Paris a virtual desert, its whole
gay, busy life blotted out as if by the action of a malevolent
spell. . . . German armored divisions parading through the
countries with little more resistance than French troops might
have encountered in Indo–China or some other colonial land.
. . . The armistice that marked France's elimination, perhaps
a permanent elimination, from the ranks of the great powers.
. . . Then the ungrateful, complicated tasks of a reconstruction
that was undertaken under conditions far more unfavorable
than those which followed the debacle of 1871.

I lived through with the French people the whole tragedy
of this ill-conceived and badly prepared war. I saw at firsthand the four months of prelude to war, the eight months of
deceptively quiet war without real fighting, the six weeks of
devastating *Blitzkrieg*. I was part of the huge teeming mass of
refugees that flooded from northern into southwestern France.

I was a refugee myself, as my wife and I were obliged to
leave Paris with nothing but what we could carry in our
hands. I learned all the vicissitudes of life during a period of
national disaster: the extreme difficulty of obtaining food and

drink and shelter; the virtual impossibility, in many cases, of obtaining means of transportation; the occasional sick feeling that comes with the sense of being trapped in a town that would soon become a scene of fighting. I have gone to sleep night after night without knowing whether a bomb would leave anything of my place of refuge in the morning.

Once out of this kaleidoscopic nightmare, when every day was likely to be one of hurried personal evacuation to some place farther away from the *Panzerdivisionen*, I tried to set down, while the sights and sounds and moods of the French collapse were still fresh in my mind, some kind of plausible answer to the many-sided question: Why did France fall? When Poland collapsed after three weeks of German on-slaught there was a sense of shock. But almost everyone felt that such a thing could not happen in an advanced, militarily prepared Western country. Yet after six weeks France was knocked out just as completely as was Poland. What is the explanation?

Not the least cause of the disaster was the world of make-believe, of illusion, of misconception of the real balance of forces in which most people in France, in Great Britain and in the United States lived during the first nine months of the war. A pessimist myself ever since hostilities began, or, more accurately, since policies were adopted which made an out-break of hostilities under most unfavorable conditions for the democratic powers unavoidable, I was often surprised and dis-mayed by the unreasoned confidence in a cheap and easy vic-tory which prevailed not only in France and in Great Britain but in the United States. Public opinion was naturally doc-tored and doped by war propaganda and censorship in the belligerent countries. But a more detached, realistic viewpoint might have been expected in the United States.

America was a victim of what is perhaps a national weak-ness for wishful thinking. Shortly before the German offensive that shattered so many illusions began, I had an interesting conversation with one of the soundest, best-informed American interpreters of European affairs.

"You know," my companion said, "whenever I write an article showing how strong Germany is, but pointing out one or two weak points, I usually receive a request for a different type of article, emphasizing only the weaknesses. I am afraid American public opinion is being misled. Because the majority of the American people passionately want the Nazis to lose, they are falling too easily into the dogmatic assumption that 'Germany cannot win.'"

How many neat, logical, documented articles one could read in French and British and American newspapers and periodicals, casting up figures of the world's stocks of gold and iron and oil and copper and other strategic materials, always pointing to the comforting conclusion that the odds against Germany were overwhelming. The facts and figures were accurate enough in the main. But the conclusions were valid only on the assumption of a war like that of 1914–1918, a static war of endurance and attrition. In a short war, where the whole issue depends on one decisive campaign, it is only the man power and material available for immediate use that count.

France was a victim of the illusion that superiority in natural resources is a sure guaranty of victory. It was also a victim of exaggerated faith in two other weapons: its own Maginot Line and the British blockade.

The Maginot Line, which I visited several times after the beginning of the war, is a magnificent piece of military engineering. Its forts, built into hillsides in the rolling country of Lorraine and surrounded by enormous masses of barbed wire, commanded every bit of intervening countryside with the flanking fire of cannon and machine guns.

The forts, which varied in size but were all of one type of construction, were independent units, with facilities for storing large reserves of food and water and the most modern devices for disinfecting sections which might be subjected to gas attack. They were manned by a permanent professional body of "fortress troops," with a high proportion of electricians and other technical specialists. The officers were admirably trained and eager to show the visitor all the defensive possibilities of their posts. I could scarcely count the number of ladders, slippery with oil and grease, up which I dutifully scrambled to a precarious perch on a gun turret, meanwhile trying to pay respectful and intelligent attention to the rapid flow of technical French in which the officer in charge was expounding the range of fire and the protection which camouflage afforded to his own guns.

The Maginot Line proper, which extended from the Belgian frontier to the Rhine, certainly could not have been stormed by frontal attack without tremendous, perhaps prohibitive, losses. What most people in France and elsewhere forgot was that the Maginot Line covered only a small segment of the frontier. Once the much weaker defenses around Sedan, where the Maginot Line tapered off into much slighter fortifications along the Belgian frontier, had been pierced, it was only a question of time until the Line could be turned and taken in the rear. Its elaborate forts, with their vast communicating underground passages, had become as useless as the Great Wall of China.

The blockade can be a weapon of great, even decisive, importance in a long war between two fairly evenly matched sides. It was of no use to France in those bitter days of mid-June when the Germans were in the heart of the country. In the same way it would be small comfort to America to know that its own or an allied fleet might starve out an invading enemy after a term of years if that enemy had advanced from the Atlantic to the Mississippi and obviously required only a short time to complete the military occupation of the country as far as the Pacific Coast.

Apart from these illusions, France suffered cruelly because

the two men primarily responsible for its war preparedness, the Premier and Minister of National Defense, Daladier, and the Generalissimo, Marshal Gamelin, were unimaginative mediocrities at a time when chiefs of the stature of Napoleon or Carnot, the revolutionary "organizer of victory," were needed. Again and again, during the weary trek from Paris to the Spanish frontier, I heard from tired, beaten, soured French soldiers the bitter words:

"We were betrayed. The politicians sold us out."

Of outright treason in high places there is no proof. But there is abundant evidence that Daladier, Gamelin and their associates were guilty of something almost as harmful as treason: sheer inability to anticipate the character of modern war and to make adequate preparation for it.

Daladier, puffed abroad as the strong silent man who had unified France, was merely the average, common-or-garden, left-of-center politician of the Third Republic. An amateur in military affairs, he was inordinately vain of his fancied capacity as a specialist in this field. Actually he knew little more of the art of war than the millions of other Frenchmen who had shared his experience of having fought through the World War.

There was something pathetic, as well as inadequate, about this little man from the provinces, this former teacher and baker's son from a small town in Provence, who was called on to meet a gigantic crisis which, as he knew in his heart, he could not cope with. There was too much peasant shrewdness in Daladier to permit him to share the illusions of some of the bellicose Paris intellectuals. As he said to an American visitor a few weeks before the beginning of the war:

"Our only chance of preserving peace would be to convince the Germans that we are the stronger. But we are not the stronger; we know it, and the Germans must know it too."

Weighed down with this premonition of defeat, he went through the motions of mobilization and declaration of war. He assumed one post after another; he was supposed to be at the same time Premier, Minister of Defense and Minister of Foreign Affairs. A kind of ingrown suspicious moroseness in his personality became enhanced with the crushing responsibilities of war. He proved unable to delegate authority, and the routine work of all the three vitally important ministries which he headed suffered in consequence.

Gamelin, head of the French defense system for many years and an intimate associate of Daladier, was the worst possible type of commander in chief for the modern war in which the scientific discoveries and technical advances of the last two decades have created such a revolution. Cautious and conservative, Gamelin overrated the fortified line in the same degree as he underestimated the striking power of the airplane and the tank. The projects for the creation of special mechanized units, composed of tanks manned by professional soldiers able to operate them with maximum efficiency, put forward by a young colonel named Charles de Gaulle were coldly received, pigeonholed and not acted on. Gamelin instinctively surrounded himself, as a rule, with officers of the same type, elderly generals who had advanced by the safe, slow stages of military bureaucracy and who were inclined to be prejudiced against any innovation. There was a little of the quality of Chinese mandarins about these men in whose hands France placed its military destiny. The commander of the French field armies, General Alphonse Georges, who had been severely wounded when King Alexander of Yugoslavia and the French Foreign Minister, Barthou, were assassinated at Marseille in 1934, was of a more bulldog fighting type. But it was one of the contraband jokes of Paris salons that Gamelin and Georges were so busy fighting each other that they had no time to fight the Germans.

Extremely cautious in his general conduct of the war, Gamelin took a tremendous last-minute risk when he left the fortified positions along the Belgian frontier, which were not, of course, as strong as the forts of the Maginot Line but which had been strengthened during the winter lull, and marched into Belgium to meet the Germans there. No doubt this risk was political as much as military. The British and French governments felt that Belgium and the Netherlands could not be left to their fate. But the experiment turned out disastrously. The whole British expeditionary force and the best French armored divisions were isolated and cut off when the Germans broke through a weak spot in the French defenses around Sedan—a name which had already acquired a disastrous connotation in French minds as the scene of one of the most crushing defeats during the Franco–Prussian War.

Incidentally, among many just criticisms that could be leveled against the French preparation for and conduct of the war, one that is unjust is often heard. This is the alleged failure to extend the Maginot Line to the sea. This criticism leaves out of account the fact that a chain of massive underground forts of the Maginot Line type could be constructed only in hilly country. And the country along the Franco–Belgian frontier is generally flat and ends in billowing sand dunes near the sea. There could have been no forts of the Maginot Line type where there were no hills into which they could be built. But the defensive advantage of such simpler fortifications as had been created along the Franco–Belgian frontier was thrown away when the advance into Belgium was ordered. These border fortifications were finally taken by the Germans in reverse, by an attack from behind.

While France, like England and America, during the quiet period of the war was nursing itself in illusions of a victory to be won without supreme effort, there were certain hard facts of the situation which impressed every observer who was not obsessed by wishful thinking, but which propaganda and censorship combined to obscure. A very intelligent French publicist and politician, M. Marcel Déat, who stood almost alone, after March, 1939, in publicly opposing the policy of fighting Germany on the Polish issue (although the number of private doubters and skeptics as to the advisability of war was legion) warned his countrymen on the eve of the war that "France today is not that of Richelieu and Louis XIV." Another of M. Déat's Cassandra predictions (which became increasingly rare in the weeks immediately before the outbreak of hostilities and ceased altogether during the war) was that France, even if victorious, "would be crushed beneath its laurels." Crushed it was, but without even any laurels for consolation.

Nations' reputations often survive their real strength. In the time of Louis XIV and Napoleon, France, the most populous country in Europe, possessed ample reserves in man power and could aspire to the domination of the continent. But the collapse of 1940 merely proved again what had been conclusively demonstrated in 1870–71, what had been obscured in 1914–1918: that France alone is no match for a united Germany.

The odds against France in trained soldiers were two to one, or even greater, if one bears in mind that some French armies were immobilized in the Maritime Alps, waiting for the Italian entrance into the war which took place after the issue of the war had already been decided. Gamelin, more eminent as a wit and an intellectual (he was an enthusiastic student of Bergson) than as a soldier, remarked at the beginning of the war:

"If Italy attacks us we shall need ten divisions to crush her. If she remains neutral we will need twenty divisions to watch her. If she enters the war on our side we shall need thirty divisions to support her."

Italy at least fulfilled this middle role of the constant passive threat.

It is doubtful whether anyone has calculated Germany's advantage over France in industrial power; four or five to one would scarcely be an exaggerated guess. So it is not surprising that France entered its last desperate battle on the Somme and the Aisne with only sixty divisions, against Germany's one hundred and fifty, supplemented by eleven armored divisions.

One cannot emphasize too strongly the fact, generally unrecognized at the time, that France entered the war under vastly less favorable circumstances than was the case in 1914. Only two great powers, France and Great Britain, were obliged to bear the full burden of the struggle. In the First World War, Russia had been an active ally and Italy a friendly neutral from the beginning. If it had not been for the Russian pressure in the East the victory of the Marne might never have been won and France might have been crushed in 1914 almost as quickly as in 1940.

It often happens that the most obvious cause of a national catastrophe is the least readily recognized. The French defeat was such an unexpected shock to the outside world that there was a rush to seek out hidden, unsuspected causes in treason in high places, in fifth column activity, in defects of psychology and morale. When the history of this period can be written more soberly it is probable that the simple explanation of the German victory will also be recognized as the fundamentally correct one. Germany had more men, more airplanes, more tanks, more reserves, and used its troops and its modern weapons with far more imagination and skill than the French General Staff could muster.

There were, to be sure, some nonmilitary causes of the debacle. The war was largely lost diplomatically before it even began in a military sense. Franco–British policy in relation to the Third Reich was ghastly in its wavering, fumbling ineptness. It is difficult to say, in retrospect, which was the more tragic blunder: not to have made war on Hitler in 1936 or to have declared war in 1939.

There can be little doubt that France singlehanded could have crushed Germany when Hitler remilitarized the Rhineland in 1936. Germany's massive rearmament was then only in its first stages. The French forces could have moved quickly into Germany's industrial centers in the Rhineland and the Ruhr. It is highly probable, indeed, that Hitler would have ordered the withdrawal of his troops at this time without opposition if his daring bluff had been called.

Once this opportunity had been missed, acquiescence in German eastward expansion, motivated by the hope of an ultimate clash between the Third Reich and the Soviet Union, was the sole reasonable policy. That such a clash took place in 1941, when Hitler had the British Empire, with its American "arsenal," as his implacable enemy, is the surest proof that it would have been easy to canalize German expansion in this direction in 1939. The Pact of Munich seemed to indicate that this policy had been adopted. But there was not sufficient clearheaded realism in London and in Paris to adhere to it.

The crowning blunder was the British guaranty to Poland in March, 1939. Such a guaranty would have been justified only if the Soviet Union, like the Russia of 1914, had been a reliable ally of France and Great Britain.

But Stalin's entire record spoke loudly against any such assumption. This Asiatic despot hated everything humanistic and individualistic in Western civilization and rejoiced in the prospect of its destruction. He was, moreover, keenly conscious of the inferiority of his much purged Red Army to the Reichswehr. It was almost incredibly naïve for the French and British statesmen to believe that Stalin would willingly sustain any part of the shock of Hitler's attack, more especially after Great Britain and France had obligingly taken it on themselves to face the onslaught of Hitler's airplanes and tanks by endeavoring to bar the way to further German expansion in Eastern Europe.

In the ill-conceived British guaranty to Poland was the germ of the Soviet–German Pact, which almost predetermined the issue of the war for France, before it began, since it gave Germany full security in the East and made it possible to let loose the full force of the German arms against France. Rapprochement with the Soviet Union, which Hitler had hitherto avoided, was the obvious retort to the Anglo–French alliance with Poland. And Stalin was delighted with the prospect of the "capitalist" and "Fascist" states weakening each other in a war from which the Soviet Union, standing aloof, might hope to reap both territorial and revolutionary advantages.

On June 22, 1941, if not sooner, Stalin realized that his cunning game of winning the war by staying out of it, of speculating on a struggle up to the point of exhaustion and collapse of the other belligerents, had failed. But any regret which the Soviet dictator may have felt (he could have fought Germany with much better prospect of success when the French Army was still intact and Hitler would have faced a real "two-front war") was of little benefit to France, knocked out beyond hope of recovery, or to Great Britain, forced to go through a grim ordeal the end of which is not in sight. The responsibility of those Frenchmen—the politicians, diplomats, publicists, molders and leaders of public opinion—who shaped their country's policy so maladroitly that Hitler's blow fell on civilized France, not on the barbarous Soviet Union, is heavy almost beyond estimate. "Whom the gods wish to destroy . . ."

If, as may be argued, France and Great Britain were convinced that war with Hitler was unavoidable and wished to fight such a war in combination with the Soviet Union, they went about the realization of this objective in a singularly unpromising way. Stalin could never have been cajoled into fighting on the side of the democracies. He might have been coerced into doing this if Great Britain and France had manifested an ostentatious unconcern for the fate of Eastern

Europe; had thereby encouraged Hitler to attack the Soviet Union; and then had joined in the war, after Stalin had become involved beyond any possibility of withdrawal. But statesmen bred in the Western tradition and still more that innocent, gullible thing called public opinion in France and England were singularly poorly qualified to deal with the unfathomable duplicity of an Asiatic like Stalin on equal terms.

The swift fall of France was a stern condemnation of many features of French political life. The many parties, the short-lived Cabinets, the party bickerings and intrigues—all this was not a very edifying picture in normal times. It was an utterly intolerable waste of national energy and resources after 1933, when France's secular enemy beyond the Rhine, through means which seemed both brutal and fantastic to individualistic and democratic peoples, succeeded in preparing for war with a thoroughness and completeness unequaled in modern history.

Yet by some fatal perversity France became more deeply, ruinously divided as the energy and concentrated economic effort generated by Germany's revolution bridged more and more rapidly the margin of military advantage which the Versailles settlement had left to France and finally transformed German inferiority into superiority. With how much bitterness every Frenchman whose loyalty is to France rather than to a party or a creed must look back on the strife and division of the years from 1934 until 1938; on the Paris riots, with their Fascist overtones; on the excesses of the *Front Populaire* period, when a continuous series of strikes for a time reduced the French airplane output almost to zero.

While Hitler's spies were busy and active and his agents carried out a certain amount of corrupting influence in French "high society," Muscovite communism made a disastrous contribution to France's tragic destiny. For communism in France was not a negligible exotic cult, as in the United States and

in Great Britain. It was a mass movement, with a substantial
following among the industrial workers, especially in the
"Red belt" of factory suburbs of Paris, and a large representation in parliament.

The French Communists, following the shifting orders from
Moscow, first did everything in their power to aggravate
class differences within the country, to stir up strikes and
sabotage, to disparage and destroy any conception of French
unity and patriotism. Then, during the period when Stalin
was holding out the mirage of associating himself with a system of collective security, the Communists became the most
bellicose group in France. They did everything in their power
to push France into a war for which Communist-inspired
strikes and antimilitarism had made it materially and psychologically unprepared.

Finally the war came. But the French Reds, instead of going
into the front line trenches singing the *Internationale* in the
crusade against fascism, executed another rightabout turn in
response to Stalin's pact with Hitler. During the last months
before the outbreak of hostilities the French Communists were
the most zealous advocates of war and found themselves in
the curious company of some French conservatives who believed that war was necessary in France's national interests,
but who greatly miscalculated their country's military
strength and prospects of victory. The Communist newspaper,
rather inappropriately called "L'Humanité," foamed with
rage against anyone who suggested that a compromise solution
of the Danzig and Polish Corridor problems should not be
insoluble or who even suggested that peace, in itself, was
desirable.

But after Stalin had struck his insecure deal with Hitler,
"L'Humanité," which continued to appear illegally after it
had been officially suppressed, carried out pure defeatist propaganda. All antipathy to Hitler and to fascism miraculously
vanished. Both in this newspaper and in the little mimeographed

propaganda leaflets which were widely distributed the Communists stressed the hardships of the war, denounced the collaboration of the Socialist trade union leaders with the government, did everything in their power to stir up disaffection. So effective was the Communist underground organization, at least in Paris, that foreign correspondents periodically received information bulletins in English about alleged hardships of the arrested Communist deputies.

The French police system was unable to cope with this widespread antiwar agitation, which fell on fertile soil; for it is doubtful if any people ever went to war more unwillingly than the French in 1939. "Sullen determination," "grim resolution," these were the hack phrases with which foreign observers attempted to camouflage the real mood of France when the war broke out and to explain the total absence of cheers or demonstrations of patriotic enthusiasm. The French people were indeed sullen and grim. But their hatred was for the war, for the vaguely conceived forces which had brought it on, rather than for the Germans. French morale was just strong enough to go through the required mobilization without revolt or mutiny. But it was not strong enough to withstand the shock of the first great offensive. On one of several visits to Nancy, the town in eastern France where war correspondents were assigned as the starting point for visits to the front, I saw the words *À bas la guerre* scrawled on the wall of the local cathedral. This phrase certainly reflected a widespread mood.

The army was on the lookout for Communist agitation and it is doubtful whether many illegal Communist leaflets reached the soldiers. But Communist propaganda, carried on by means of leaflets, of secret meetings, of whispering word-of-mouth campaigns, was certainly effective in slowing down work in the munitions factories. I was impressed, during a trip through France in the quiet winter months, with the lifelessness of the trade unions in the larger industrial towns. Some of the local

Socialist trade union secretaries, who themselves supported the war, although in some cases with a rather conspicuous lack of enthusiasm, told me that many of the workers preferred to listen to the Communists and suspected the Socialists as mere agents of the government.

The Communists, of course, have pursued the same "party line" in America as in France. Militant advocates of crusading war and collective security until August 23, 1939, they promptly faced about, praised the pact which they had publicly repudiated as unthinkable and impossible until the news of its signature appeared, and went over to a policy of all-out opposition to war and preparation for war. This attitude was maintained until June 22, 1941, when they promptly became prowar, for America, as a reaction to Hitler's invasion of the Soviet Union.

A liberal democracy, for its own health, must always maintain the maximum freedom of speech and press and public expression of opinion. Witch-hunting and hounding of unpopular minority views are dangerous symptoms. By liberal principles there should not be the slightest objection to a group of citizens of America, or any other country, advocating as a desirable proposition the reorganization of society along Communist, Fascist, monarchist or any other lines by orderly and constitutional means.

But, as the sad experience of France shows, a new and sinister element is introduced into the situation when a body of citizens, an unfortunately large body in France, places itself unreservedly under the orders of a foreign power. The amount of harm which such a group can do by endeavoring to use its fellow citizens as cannon fodder to promote the interests of this foreign power is almost incalculable. So long as communism remains what it has been ever since the establishment of the Communist International, with its tightly centralized constitution—namely, a movement completely controlled from Moscow and utterly subservient to every shifting breeze of Soviet foreign policy—there is surely a strong case for depriving adherents of communism of rights of citizenship. So long as Communists practice unqualified allegiance to a foreign power they should not be permitted to abuse the rights of a citizenship which they have, in effect, themselves voluntarily renounced. They should be given the status of aliens and subjected to the restrictions of aliens, as regards voting, participation in politics and engaging in political propaganda.

While Germany derived a good deal of demonic energy from its successful revolution, France was weakened and divided by two abortive revolutionary movements. There was a strong Fascist trend among the French upper and middle classes in the early thirties and this found its most dramatic expression in the February riots of 1934, which led to firing by soldiers and police, some loss of life, the fall of the Cabinet and the temporary installation of a semidictatorial regime headed by an elderly politician named Doumergue.

Behind this Fascist trend were a number of forces. France had suffered from the world economic crisis and from the consequences of maintaining the franc at an artificially high level, in relation to the heavily devalued pound and dollar. There was general and often justified cynicism about the financial honesty of politicians and newspaper editors. This was a chronic mood with the French "man in the street"; but it reached a high pitch after sensational exposures of swindling transactions by an international adventurer named Stavisky, who had found some patrons and protectors among the Radical Socialists, an important party of the French Left. Old feuds in French politics had also been carried over into modern times. There was much distrust of political Freemasonry among conservatives. The instinctive anti-Semitism of the French Right, which had come out so dramatically at the time of the Dreyfus case, also played its part, although this passion, even in the bitterness of defeat, never reached the pathological proportions which it assumed in Germany.

But French embryonic fascism, which found rallying points in a number of groups and parties, of which the most important was the *Croix de Feu,* a conservative ex-combatants' organization headed by Colonel de la Rocque, and the French Popular party, led by an ex-Communist who completely repudiated his former faith, Jacques Doriot, lacked the drive, the mass popular support, which might have led to victory. After all, France had not experienced internal disorder comparable with what took place in Italy before the rise of Mussolini. Nor did the French feel the sense of acute bitterness and frustration which came to the Germans as a result of the lost war and the inflation.

The skeptical mood, so characteristic of the Frenchman of all classes, was against blind hero worship and untried political experiments. With all its faults and weaknesses, the Third Republic had endured for almost seventy years and was far more deeply rooted in the national consciousness than the regimes which Mussolini and Hitler overthrew and replaced.

So French fascism sputtered but failed to burst into a real flame. The appeal of a conservative ex-officer like Colonel de la Rocque was too narrowly restricted to the relatively well-to-do classes. And in 1936 there was a swing of the French political pendulum in the opposite direction.

The three large parties of the Left, the Radical Socialists, the Socialists and the Communists, formed a single political bloc, the so-called *Front Populaire,* and swept the parliamentary election of 1936. The Radical Socialists, it may be noted parenthetically, were not socialistic at all and were not very radical. They were perhaps the nearest approach to French liberals, a party which recruited its following from the French middle class and peasant proprietors, mildly anticlerical, a bit given to declamation about the principles of the Great French Revolution but quick to take alarm at any serious threat to the principle of private property. They were the most typical and politically the most powerful party of the Third Republic. About no group of Frenchmen would André Siegfried's epigram apply so well:

"The heart of France is on the Left; its pocketbook is on the Right."

Now this coalition of the Left, which supported the Cabinets which governed France for the next two years (the Communists abstained from actual participation in these Cabinets), was accompanied by enough extremism to frighten and exasperate the French bourgeoisie, which never had quite forgotten the guillotine of 1793 or the excesses of the Commune in 1871. There were sit-down strikes and there was slack work and there were several devaluations of the franc which bore hard on the large *rentier* class, because prices caught up very rapidly with the lowered gold value of the currency and there was ambitious social legislation. Some of this was overdue and thoroughly justifiable. But some of the new laws were too rigid and were adopted with too little regard for special local conditions.

But the *Front Populaire* did not achieve enough in the way of solid and permanent change to hold together its own followers. The parties which it included were inclined to distrust each other. Finally it fell apart altogether, partly because of internal differences, partly because the Communists, always obedient to Moscow, adopted a different attitude from the other parties toward the Munich settlement. Feelings within the Left coalition had already become aggravated because of the strikes, which alienated the propertied elements among the Radical Socialists, and because of varied viewpoints about France's policy during the Spanish civil war.

Neither fascism nor the vague radical laborism which characterized the Popular Front governments was strong enough to win a decisive victory and reorganize France along new lines. But both these abortive semirevolutionary movements left the French, as a people, weakened, divided, suspicious of each other. There were French workers who hated the capitalist class more than they did the Germans. There were Frenchmen of property who would rather see the Swastika flying over Paris than the red flag of a French workers' revolutionary government.

So France entered the war under great disadvantages, military, diplomatic, political and moral. Yet the situation was not entirely hopeless. The country could have made a better showing if the tremendous seriousness of the danger had been realized and if an iron directing will, such as France found during the Revolution, had half led, half driven the people to accept immense sacrifices; to turn the country into an armed camp, where everyone would have lived on a Spartan ration of bare necessities—in short, to match the effort which Germany made not only during the years before the war but during the first eight months of the conflict, so deceptively mild in outward appearance.

But this iron will was conspicuously lacking. During a trip behind the lines through France, I happened to read one of the flaming appeals of the great War Minister of the French Revolution, Lazare Carnot. The very spirit of that stern, terrible and heroic time seemed to live again in the words of the appeal, which called on the young to fight, on the older workers to make cannon and powder and bullets, on the women to go into nursing and similar work, on the old men to come out on the public squares and preach "undying hatred of kings."

But Carnot's spirit was not characteristic of France in 1939–40. There was an abundance of appeals, official and private, but the mood of the country never kindled into a flame. A banal and stupid censorship prevented the harsh facts of the situation from being dinned into the consciousness of the French people, of their British allies and of America, where a quicker realization of the peril might have stimulated swifter and more effective aid with airplanes and material.

The attitude of the government was that there was all the time in the world in which to win the war.

France refused to turn its butter into cannon. In those last disastrous weeks it had more pastries than Germany, but fewer tanks; more good clothes, but fewer airplanes. One fears that France will pay dearly, and for many years, for having maintained a relatively soft, comfortable standard of living in a life-and-death struggle for existence.

It is too soon to fix with historical certainty personal responsibilities for the fall of France. But the slowness with which the French and British orders for airplanes and other munitions were placed in America is, in retrospect, almost incredible. Here there was, no doubt, the fatal obsession with the Maginot Line and with the efficacy of the blockade, the belief that it was just as well to husband gold, since it was to be a long war and there would be plenty of time for victory.

Lenin, greater as a man of action than as a social and economic theorist, uttered a profound truth when he told his followers never to "play with revolution"—to fight with the last ounce of strength when once the order for decisive action had been given. The same principle, of course, should hold good for war. France committed one mistake in declaring war. It committed another in waging this war halfheartedly, without mobilizing the national resources of labor and material to the uttermost limit.

Military historians will someday cast up a reasonably accurate balance sheet of German and French strength as regards trained divisions and artillery and tanks and airplanes. But this will not tell the whole story of the war or explain why catastrophe overtook France so swiftly. There was a psychological and a moral defeat as well as a military defeat.

From the beginning of the war I was impressed by the absence of any sign of popular enthusiasm. To the average Frenchman the war was a misfortune—an inevitable misfortune, perhaps, but a misfortune just the same. Considerable sections of public opinion were definitely hostile—the Communists because Moscow had ordered them to take this attitude; certain propertied and conservative groups because they foresaw the crumbling of the property system and the destruction of social order as the probable consequence of a long war, even apart from its issue.

In judging the susceptibility of the French well-to-do classes to the argument that bolshevism would be a sequel to the war, regardless of how it turned out, one should remember that a very savage civil and social war had been raging across the frontier in Spain. Passionate sympathies were aroused on both sides in this connection even in a country so far removed from the scene of conflict as the United States. It is easy to imagine how a typical French Catholic country squire or officer would feel about the prospect of the establishment of a Red regime across the Pyrenees.

The opposition to the war was not sufficiently strong and organized to cause any overt opposition to the order for mobilization. But pessimism, not to say defeatism, hung over the country in a thick pall. I made a number of trips to the front and at officers' messes, in peasant homes in Alsace and Lorraine and in the long automobile trips to and from the front line positions I talked with perhaps a score of officers, ranging in rank from general to lieutenant.

Not one of these officers foresaw the military disaster that was to come. But I cannot recall one who was an optimist about the prospect after the end of the war. All looked forward gloomily to general impoverishment, social upheaval, to new and perhaps insoluble problems and difficulties. I do not believe one of these French officers was a traitor or a slacker. They did their duty, with few if any exceptions, when the last terrible test came. Some most probably lost their lives in the uneven struggle.

But the mental attitude of these officers (and soldiers are seldom more enthusiastic than the men who lead them) was that of commanders of the Roman legions when the barbarians were breaking through the frontiers of the empire. It was that of Byzantine officers leading what they felt in their hearts was a lost cause against fanatical Saracens and Turks. It was not the spirit of the young untried leaders of the ragged, enthusiastic armies of the French Revolution. It was not the spirit that could reverse what seemed to be hopeless odds, that could wrest victory from defeat.

France, in this short and catastrophic war, when, as one of the older French publicists remarked, much that had been built up in ten centuries was lost in ten months, distinctly suffered from the psychological disadvantage of being interested only in conserving, in defending. Morally as well as physically, it was no match for the dynamically aggressive Third Reich, where old-fashioned efficient German militarism was lit up and inflamed by Nazi revolutionism.

The French surrender perhaps stunned and alienated public opinion in America more than the French defeat. Only one who lived through that kaleidoscopic period, when each day seemed to contain enough misfortune for a month or even a year of ordinary war, only one who saw the chaos personified in the millions of hapless refugees and who lived through the bedlam of Bordeaux, can realize how completely hopeless the prospect of further resistance seemed to Marshal Pétain and his associates.

A certain element of *amour-propre* also entered into the situation. In those dark hours of rout and threatened social collapse and dissolution the army still remained a force for cohesion and it was to the army chiefs that the French people instinctively looked for leadership. France was at least spared the double horror of Russia in 1917, widespread mutiny among the troops and class war in its most brutal forms all over the country after the prodigious slaughter and the military defeats on the front.

It was difficult for veteran soldiers like Pétain and Generalissimo Maxime Weygand, who took over the command in a vain attempt to stem the onward rush of the Panzer divisions, to believe that England could stand when France had fallen. Both thought primarily as soldiers and both knew that France was much better prepared militarily than was England. Neither Pétain nor Weygand appreciated the importance of sea power or the possibility that England might hold out as an island fortress. Neither appraised at full value the amount of help which England might obtain from its overseas empire and from the United States.

Another psychological factor that strongly influenced the decision of the French Government to capitulate and remain in France rather than flee abroad is that the outlook of the great majority of Frenchmen begins and ends in France. France possessed a great overseas empire, the largest in the world after the British. But a negligible number of Frenchmen, soldiers, administrators, traders, lived in this empire.

The French have furnished their full share of gifted colonial administrators, intrepid explorers, devoted missionaries, scholars with a wide and sensitive understanding of the history and culture and folkways of Asia and Africa. But they have never been successful colonizers. There is no equivalent in the French Empire for those outposts of overseas Britain, Canada, Australia, New Zealand. This is why the idea of leaving France and continuing the resistance from overseas possessions struck such a weak response.

One can understand the bitter resentment in Great Britain, and among British sympathizers in the United States, as the Vichy Government moved along the path of collaboration with Germany. Surrender has its own laws and these are inexorable. When the French Government decided to remain in France, to accept the decision of the war as final, it left no destiny for France except that of a German satellite.

At the same time neither Great Britain nor the United States made use of the means which were at their disposal to counteract German pressure on Vichy and to build up a fund of good will among the French people. The putting into effect both in occupied and in unoccupied France of a large-scale feeding plan, modeled on Mr. Hoover's Belgian Relief during the first World War, accompanied, of course, by stringent provisions against diversion of the food to German use, would have immensely raised British and American prestige in France and would have made it almost impossible for the Vichy Government to have engaged in an anti-British policy. Such a policy would have represented both good humanity and good political strategy. But extremely little was done in this direction. Some Americans, whom history will probably judge as equally obtuse and inhuman, even went out of their way to protest against any sending of food to France and worked themselves up into a state of false emotionalism where they believed, or professed to believe, that the issue of the war would be seriously affected by the sending of oatmeal and bananas to hungry, undernourished French children.

The sentiment that would have seemed most appropriate in relation to fallen France was one of profound sympathy, the sympathy that one would feel for an old man who, after a long and distinguished career, wished to retire and cultivate his garden in peace and retirement but who was forced into a struggle for which his physical strength no longer sufficed. France was an old nation and the French of all classes possessed many qualities of maturity, a high degree of critical intelligence, skepticism, moderation, lucid rationality.

How happy the French could and would have been if France, like Sweden, could simply have gracefully retired from the burdensome glory of being a "great power" and maintained its culture and its way of life in independence without seeking foreign conquests. But such an abdication is apparently seldom feasible. After the deep and unhealed wounds of the first World War, France made the most des-

perate efforts to avoid another, first by the policy of maintaining armed preponderance in Europe, then by the policy
of isolation and disinterestedness in European concerns. Both
policies failed; the second was not given a genuine test. France,
to its eternal misfortune, was drawn into the infernal cycle of
war and revolution from which, as one of the most eminent
French scholars and publicists said to me shortly before the
beginning of the war, it had everything to lose and nothing
to gain.

When that stormy petrel and tireless apostle of *la revanche*,
Paul Déroulède, called on Renan to request a contribution to
some nationalist cause the old scholar looked at him sadly
and said:

"Young man, France is dying. Do not trouble her agony."

Renan's pessimism was premature; there would seem to be
more reason for it today. But history affords a multitude of
examples to show that the permanent fruits of victory are not
always to the violent and to the strong. Whether France will
ever again be a great power, the arbiter of Europe's destiny,
is doubtful.

But there is an immortal France of mind and soul and spirit
that will survive triumphantly all the vicissitudes of French
temporal history. It is the France of creative artists, of the
great believers and the great doubters. It is this eternal France
and its immortal creations in stone and painting and books
that is today the surest refuge of many French men and women
who might otherwise be overwhelmed by their country's
disaster. For this France there will always be an honored place
in the community of European nations when the dawn of a
still unseen renaissance breaks over Europe's Iron Age.

Chapter Twelve

THE ORDEAL OF BRITAIN

THERE HAS NEVER BEEN an ordeal quite like that of Great Britain—an island besieged from sea and air, an uninvaded country devastated by explosive and incendiary bombs. After the fall of France, England was left in the position of an isolated island, facing a much larger continent, exposed to air attack from several directions, while German submarines, issuing from bases from the North Cape to the Pyrenees, preyed on its shipping.

There were three main reasons, I think, why England fought on after France had surrendered. The first of these was geographical. Germany's superiority in land and air power was overwhelming. Of the many explanations advanced for the fall of France the simplest is also the most correct: decisive advantage in men, tanks, airplanes and capacity for modern warfare.

But Germany's unsurpassed military machine stopped functioning at the water's edge. Airplanes could spread havoc but could not, by themselves, break a resolute will to resist. England's precious moat, the absence of any land connection with the continent, was its best and surest defense.

A second cause of British steadfastness was the sense of solidarity with the empire overseas and, to a lesser extent, with the United States of America. When Churchill vows to go to Ottawa rather than surrender, the idea seems feasible, even though it is terrible to imagine what would happen to the population of the British Isles if they were left as hostages in the hands of Hitler. On the other hand, there would have been something grotesque, exotic, unreal, about a government calling itself French and located in Senegal, or Madagascar, or French Indo–China, or Tahiti. There was no overseas France which could serve as a base and a rallying point for the French who desired to continue the war. For 99 per cent of Frenchmen life began and ended in their own country.

The third reason why Great Britain stood while France fell is that now, as in the past, the Englishman has not been swept off his feet by revolutionary ideas coming from the continent. Macaulay, referring to England's stability in the stormy year 1848, boasted that, because England had liberty in the midst of despotism, it had order in the midst of anarchy. And the tradition of gradual change, of peaceful progress under law, to which England adhered more consistently than any other great power after its most revolutionary century, the seventeenth, was never seriously disturbed by the storms of the continent. There was a good deal of truth in the old familiar joke that when an unusually heavy fog interrupted the normal communication between England and Europe the characteristic British newspaper headline was "Continent isolated."

Even such a tremendous near-by shock as the French Revolution failed to excite any corresponding repercussion of insurrection and civil war in England. There was an ebullition of what would now be called parlor bolshevism. There was a little futile plotting. There was some extra repressive legislation. But the British system of government, then a tight oligarchy so far as political representation was concerned, tempered by a very considerable respect for individual liberty, stood up to the double impact of the Revolution and the Napoleonic Wars without sustaining any serious cracks.

So it is not surprising that communism and fascism, which had eaten like twin cancers into the body of French national unity, left England comparatively little touched. Some British workers and intellectuals were attracted by the idea of communism, often without the slightest realistic idea of what Soviet practice was. A few young men and women of well-to-do and middle class families professed admiration for Mussolini and Hitler and paraded in black-shirt uniforms. But, as against the seventy-two Communists who sat in the last French Chamber of Deputies, there was never more than one Communist in the British Parliament. The French Fascist forces were strong enough to incite serious riots, with considerable loss of life in the heart of Paris. The British Fascists never got beyond the stage of hawking their little-read publications on street corners and occasionally becoming involved in petty scuffles.

The British Liberal party disappeared as an effective political force—a casualty of the first World War. But England remained a liberal country. Its national unity was a fact, not a phrase. Its Conservatives, with negligible exceptions, were not Fascists. Its Labor members of Parliament, in the great majority, had no sympathy with communism. This was especially true after the trade unions had obtained some practical experience in dealing with the underhanded Communist tactics of disrupting and "boring from within."

Perhaps the most vivid illustration of essential British liberalism was the course of the general strike in 1926. A general strike is about the most serious political weapon that can be brought into play, short of armed rebellion. In any other country such a movement would almost certainly have been accompanied by violent clashes between the strikers and soldiers, police and volunteer strikebreakers. In England this whole great industrial drama was played out without fighting, without even as much outward show of bitterness as characterized the discussion of the adoption of a revised Prayer Book for the Church of England. There were no reprisals after the defeat of the strike. And there was a typically British sequel. Several years later two of the leaders of the strike, Walter Citrine and Arthur Pugh, were knighted by the King.

A people that could settle a grave internal crisis so peacefully was pretty well assured of solidarity in the event of war. And this was especially true because public opinion was ahead of the government in recommending a bellicose policy after the occupation of Czechoslovakia.

The instinct of the Cabinet, headed by Neville Chamberlain, to avoid war by all means consistent with the independence and integrity of the British Empire was entirely sound. Great Britain was at the same disadvantage in a world of hungry totalitarian states that a civilized country always faces when confronted by barbarians. It had everything to lose and nothing to gain from war.

And defeat for Great Britain carried with it an element of terrific finality. Defeat in modern war is a major tragedy for any state. It almost certainly means acute impoverishment of all classes, serious social dislocations, a revolutionary change of government. But defeat for Great Britain would be little short of national extinction because, of all great powers, it is least adapted to self-sufficiency. A very large proportion of its 47,000,000 inhabitants depend for their livelihood on the maintenance of sea communications with the far-flung empire and with other overseas countries. For England there is no question of a voluntary abdication, of a stepping down from the pedestal of power. She must be a great power with command of the seas or she will be reduced to nothingness.

The penalty of defeat for England in any major war was,

therefore, tremendous and irrevocable. And there was an implicit risk in victory, as well as in defeat. British prosperity and the livelihood of great numbers of British people of all classes are bound up with the preservation of the delicate mechanism of trade and exchange which may broadly be called the international capitalist system.

Now a kind of national socialism had been instituted after the First World War in Russia, and later in Italy and in Germany. All these countries established economic systems which were less and less in contact with the outside world. The value of their currencies, for instance, was fixed by executive fiat and not left to the impersonal judgment of a free exchange market. Trade was strictly controlled in the supposed interests of the nation and in some cases became a matter of barter, not of sales for money.

These systems of national socialism imposed great hardships. They certainly did not make for higher and more comfortable standards of living. Yet, after a fashion, they worked. Germany was even able to use such a system as the economic basis of a prodigious war machine.

But it is extremely difficult to imagine England, isolated in its islands, being able to maintain national existence, even on a much reduced standard of living, under any such system. The disproportion between population and home-grown foodstuffs and domestic sources of raw material is too great. Again and again one is brought back to the inescapable conclusion that England can exist only as an imperial power with assured maritime access to its Dominions and colonies.

And it can exist comfortably and securely only in a world where there is some kind of international economic order, where there is some common denominator for currency exchange, where business transactions with the far corners of the world can be executed with smoothness and facility, where the flow of British capital into countries that require development can be unimpeded and stimulate a return flow of interest and dividends for the benefit of the considerable number of Britons who live on incomes derived from abroad.

As the shadows of the Iron Age fell more heavily on the world Great Britain was faced by a tragic dilemma. And it is against the background of this dilemma that what seems to be the weakness, irresolution and vacillation of British policy during the thirties must be understood and interpreted. There were limitations, of course, in the personalities of the British leaders at this time. Mr. Baldwin was an incurable wishful thinker. Mr. Neville Chamberlain was handicapped in foreign relations by the fact that he knew little of foreign countries and less of the new winds of totalitarian doctrine, so alien to everything which he had taken for granted in the town council of Birmingham.

But the dilemma was difficult enough to have challenged the mind of a Pitt, of a Gladstone, of a Disraeli. International capitalism furnished much of the lifeblood of British economy. It was a delicate organism which had been jarred and deranged by one World War and might well be completely destroyed by another. Hence the categorical imperative not to resort to war except in case of the most urgent necessity. Yet Great Britain's very life depended on control of the sea routes of trade and imperial communication. It had to face war, with all its perils, if a real threat to this control should develop.

When the dilemma itself was so baffling it is not surprising that the proper solution was not found. There was no halfway house with Hitler. One had either to crush him or to concede to Germany a land empire comparable in size and resources with the overseas empires of Great Britain and France. A few minor frontier rectifications in Europe would not suffice.

The opportunity to crush Hitler in 1935 or 1936 was allowed to slip. But the alternative, the acceptance of German hegemony in Eastern Europe, was also not accepted. Retrospective "might have beens" are inevitably inconclusive. No one can say with certainty what would have occurred if a different turn had been taken at a historic crossroads of decision. The date when Great Britain gave its unconditional guaranty of support to Poland, March 31, 1939, marked such a crossroads. What would have happened if Great Britain had continued the policy of aloof disinterestedness in Eastern Europe which was a logical consequence of the failure to prevent Hitler from remilitarizing the Rhineland and which seemed to be foreshadowed in the Munich settlement?

In such a case it is very unlikely that Poland would have fought. It would probably have reached an agreement with Hitler on the basis of surrendering former German territory in the West for Russian and Lithuanian land in the East. Like Hungary and Bulgaria, it would have swung into the orbit of German influence. It would have been a point of departure for Hitler's march toward the East, for the acquisition of that land empire which Hitler, in "Mein Kampf," described as a basic objective of German foreign policy. There is no proof, and certainly no certainty, that Hitler, with his desire for a secure source of foodstuffs and raw materials satisfied with the livestock and cereals of Ukraina, the oil and manganese and timber of the Caucasus, would have launched a war against the West.

So the British Government had not exhausted the possibilities of a policy of nonintervention which would not have sacrificed British vital interests when it made its decision for war by giving its guaranty of Poland's frontiers. Thus far there has been no conclusive explanation of why this decision, involving a complete reversal of the previous policy of the Chamberlain Cabinet, was made. There was undoubtedly some pressure of public opinion because of the occupation of Czechoslovakia. Communist and semi-Communist propaganda played its part, because Communists and the far more numerous fringe of sympathizers with communism were convinced, up to the moment of the signature of the Hitler–Stalin pact, that the Soviet Union, if only properly propitiated or "appeased," would be a reliable ally against Hitler.

Barring the publication of positive evidence of an intention on Hitler's part to attack the West, the British decision to fight on the Polish issue seems to have been a mistake. Once the opportunity to crush Hitler in the early years of his regime had been missed, the most intelligent and realistic course for Great Britain and France would have been to write off Eastern Europe as lost, to view with indifference the probable German drive against the Soviet Union, to make their own continental and imperial possessions as safe as possible against attack and to commit themselves to the policy of fighting only if their own frontiers or those of the small adjacent countries of Western Europe should be attacked.

It is difficult to see what benefit Great Britain rendered either to unfortunate Poland or to its own interests by giving a guaranty which, when put to the test, could not be implemented. There was only one figure on the European political scene who could derive satisfaction, although it proved to be both short-lived and shortsighted, from the British and French decision to intervene on behalf of Poland. This was Joseph Stalin, who took advantage of Europe's preoccupation with war to swallow temporarily eastern Poland, Latvia, Lithuania, Esthonia, Bessarabia and Bukovina, although Soviet possession of these spoils was not left unchallenged very long.

The Charge of the Light Brigade is only one of many instances in British history when the slip of an anonymous "someone who blundered" was offset by the heroism of the men who carried out the mistaken order. The spirit of the British people in their unprecedented ordeal was magnificent. Once plunged into the war, they displayed a determination to see it through at any cost and they did not waver when the fall of France left them facing the hostile resources of a continent.

The British resolution to fight on after the collapse of France found expression in many ways. There was a dramatic cartoon which showed Great Britain in a posture of defiance and bore the caption "Well, then, alone." There was the more or less legendary story of the charwoman who remarked, "That 'Itler; 'ee'll not give up without a struggle, I'll be bound." One of England's finest economic scholars, R. H. Tawney, pointed out in a remarkably eloquent letter that England could expect no gain from the war, could indeed anticipate great all-round impoverishment, but elaborated the familiar slogan "We would rather die on our feet than live on our knees."

And words were followed by deeds. The modern war that placed every civilian in the larger towns within range of possible death brought out in these civilians qualities of courage and self-sacrifice as high as any soldier's. The British proved again, in the face of an even greater test, what the Chinese and the Spaniards had already shown. The science of destruction has not become so inhumanly perfect that it can break the eternal spirit of man.

There is no need here to dwell on the courage of the British people in the face of the terror by night and the destruction that sometimes stalked at noonday. There is an abundance of eyewitness descriptions of this courage.

What is perhaps less appreciated and is even more remarkable is the extent to which the classical British qualities of liberalism and tolerance maintained themselves under the ordeal of a type of war which might well have conduced to hysteria. In the face of constant imminent peril there was no approach to the methods of a Cheka, of a Committee of Public Safety.

Two incidents of which I have personal knowledge are

highly illustrative in this connection. They would not be
likely to be paralleled, I think, in any other country which
was engaged in a life-and-death struggle. An American author had published a book which was sharply critical of
British policy in the prewar years, was pessimistic about the
outlook for England in the war and was strongly isolationist
in its recommendations about American foreign policy.

The author was amazed when his regular British publishers
brought out this book after the beginning of the war and still
more surprised when he received several reviews, lucid, tem-
perate, sometimes even more favorable, perhaps, than the
book deserved. And the book was published and the reviews
were written to an accompaniment of the crash of bombs and
the glare of incendiary fires in London and many other British cities. One wonders whether such superbly cool intellectual detachment would have been possible in any other country. It would certainly be unwise to count on it in America.

An Englishwoman of my acquaintance, living in America,
is convinced that England is being lured on to fight beyond
its strength, to reject possibilities of compromise peace, by
hopes of American aid that will not and cannot be of decisive
importance. She wrote an article based on this idea, an article
which would have been infuriating to American interventionists, and showed it to a British acquaintance, an elderly
scholar whose home and many precious possessions had been
destroyed in a bombing raid. He read it over and observed
very calmly and judicially:

"Well, there is much here that I do not agree with. But
you have a definite point of view. It ought to be presented."

No perfervid denunciation; no frantic invocation of God,
King and country. Just a display of the unruffled rationalism
with which a certain type of British mind will doubtless greet
the sounding of the trumpet of the Last Judgment.

That quality of humane rationalism, of liberalism in the
deepest and truest sense of the word, is probably England's

greatest contribution to civilization. Should it perish in a world of ever increasing violence and irrationality, the loss to humanity would be even graver and more irreparable than the destruction of some of the oldest and grandest and most beautiful material monuments of civilization.

Every nation at war erects a more or less convincing façade of national unity. The cracks and fissures in the French structure were obvious to all but the most superficial observers. Any weaknesses that may exist in dictatorships are concealed behind an iron mask of censorship and propaganda until they are brought into the open by the inescapable test of war.

Repression in England during the first two years of the war has been moderate. A number of Fascists have been interned; two Communist publications were suppressed. But candidates who advocate a negotiated peace have been able to contest elections and the proposition has been freely debated in Parliament. Pacifist literature is permitted to circulate (specimens which I have seen would certainly not seem calculated to exert any mass appeal) and the claims of conscientious objectors to alternative service are given careful consideration. Public opinion, as reflected in the attitude of employers and fellow workers, is often more intolerant of the conscientious objector than is the state itself.

Judged by every available means of testing sentiment, the British people as the second year of the war draws to a close are firm in their support of Prime Minister Churchill's program of fighting to an uncompromising victorious finish, regardless of the human and material cost involved. This British morale is a tremendous asset. But it would be unwise to assume that it is absolutely unchangeable.

In order to stand the ordeal of pounding that will presumably go on indefinitely and the privations which are increasing and must continue to increase so long as ships are being sunk and damaged faster than they can be replaced, there must be some positive hope of ultimate victory. There must be either successes in some field of hostilities or a firm faith that larger and more effective help will arrive from America. England is a small compact country where opinion can turn over very quickly. Leaving aside the possibility of a successful German invasion, the time may come when the reconquest of the continent from Hitler may appear an impossible task; when a compromise peace would seem preferable to the doubtful prospect of American aid that might arrive "too little and too late," to quote Lloyd George's phrase about England's own aid to the countries of the continent.

Such a compromise peace, based on recognition of Germany's domination of Europe but providing for the maintenance of the integrity of the British Empire, with perhaps some modification of the status of Gibraltar and Suez, has been available to Great Britain at any time. Hitler made it clear in July, 1940, that he had no territorial claims against Great Britain and there is good reason to suspect that the spectacular and mystifying parachute descent of Rudolf Hess was connected with efforts to open up peace discussions along these lines.

It is perhaps not sufficiently realized that Hitler has nothing to gain from the breakup of the British Empire. The British Isles themselves would be a liability rather than an asset to the German dictator's empire, which is already top-heavy with man power and industrial plant but short of foodstuffs and raw materials. And the British Dominions and colonies are so far away that they would most probably either find a refuge in affiliation with the United States or fall a prey to some other conqueror before Hitler could muster sufficient sea power to take them over.

So Great Britain is not fighting for its own territorial integrity or even for that of its empire. It is fighting primarily because it believes that a Europe dominated by a single power, and by a power so aggressive and dynamic as Nazi Germany, would be an intolerable threat to its peace and security.

Will England be more or less democratic after the war is ended? Is it predestined by the war to adopt some socialist form of economy? These questions have been raised and hotly debated. But there is still no evidence on which a certain forecast could be based.

England could certainly not retain democracy in defeat. In such an eventuality Sir Oswald Mosley or some other British Fascist would presumably emerge from prison to take over the leadership of a regime that would be closely akin to the Vichy Government of France in spirit and policy. The active figures in the war would flee across the Atlantic, if they could. England would have no future except as a German dependency.

Democracy would be exposed to a severe strain if the war should end in a compromise peace. The sacrifices and sufferings which are bearable so long as the prospect of victory at the end of the road remains would seem futile and intolerable if peace were made on terms which would acknowledge Hitler's conquest of the continent. There would almost certainly be a violent reaction against everyone prominently associated with the origin and conduct of the war. And England after such a peace would be obliged to choose between two hard courses.

It might give up the struggle as hopeless, in which case the consequences of compromise peace would not be very different from those of total defeat. Or it might arm feverishly, building as many ships and airplanes as possible against the day when the war might be resumed. But a state of high-tension armament would not be very different from a state of war, and would be equally inimical to the practice of democracy.

In the event of victory the democratic ideal would seem to be vindicated. England soon regained its characteristic liberalism after the strain of the last war. One should not assume too readily, however, that this process will be repeated, even if complete victory should prove attainable.

The problems of reconstruction in every country, and not least in Great Britain, will be colossal. In the heat and passion and consecration of the struggle the bombs that fall impartially on the mansions of the rich, in the West End, on the City, nerve center of British business and finance, and on the slums of Whitechapel may create a sense of a community of suffering, may produce a welding and unifying effect.

But when the war is over there will be a sudden shock of recognition that everyone, or almost everyone, is much poorer and the struggle as to which classes should bear the burden of paying for the conflict will almost certainly be bitter. There can scarcely be any illusion this time about the possibility of "making Germany pay." Even today Germany is so lean, so devoid of all transferable values, that little could be squeezed out if Hitler should surrender tomorrow. And before Germany could be conquered it would most probably have to be largely wrecked, with its industrial centers and means of transportation laid in ruins.

The postwar British Government will face a staggering load of debt, a currency system shaken to its foundations, a derelict system of international exchanges and world trade channels blocked by many obstructions—among which perhaps the most formidable is represented by the prodigious loss of shipping, actual and probable for the future. There will be the strongest impulse to continue in peace the war system of coalition government and political truce. The government would probably preserve many of its exceptional war powers for the period of reconstruction. All this might well be justifiable in terms of necessity. But it would not be democracy, in the full sense of the term. Parliament would tend to lose vitality when there was no genuine give-and-take between a government and a strong opposition, even if freedom of discussion should be preserved.

Before the beginning of the present war political democracy in England was experiencing a severe crisis, although social democracy had made gains since the last war. The system under which a large number of the most desirable posts in the state service were, in practice, a preserve for a limited class of "gentlemen" had been modified, but by no means abolished. The doors of opportunity for the more capable aspirants from the poorer classes had been pushed somewhat more widely open. There had been two Labor governments —something which would have seemed unthinkable in the time of Gladstone and Disraeli.

But politically the period from the fall of the second Labor Cabinet in 1931 until the beginning of the war was one of stagnation; of rule by a small clique of Conservatives, of whom many were dull and undistinguished. The reason for this stagnation was that the Labor party, because of the doctrinaire socialism of its program, did not offer a practical political alternative to conservatism. The two brief Labor Cabinets existed on the sufferance of the Liberals. In a country where capitalism had struck such deep roots as was the case in England it proved impossible to persuade the majority of the voters to commit the government exclusively to the hands of a party which was avowedly out to destroy capitalism.

Had the Labor party expressed the mood of many of its members, made its appeal on a program of progressive social reform and shelved or dropped the controversial proposals for wholesale nationalization it would have attracted far more voters and there would have been a healthier alternation of power between Labor and conservatism. Theoretically, in a country which, like Great Britain, has no written constitution, it would be possible peacefully to vote the system of private property out of existence. But in practice so much bitter resentment and sense of injustice would be aroused that it would be only a short step to civil war, and civil war under modern conditions, as Russia and Spain have demonstrated, sounds the death knell of democracy.

The outlook for democracy in England, therefore, depends in some measure on whether the traditional British genius for compromise will make it possible to avoid a head-on collision between doctrinaire socialism and the instinct for private property. One promising means of adjustment, which had come into practical application before the war in such industries as electrical power distribution and transportation, was the establishment of a system of public board management. Under this system public control of the development of the industries was assured; but the functions of management were left in the hands of independent experts, and not turned over to bureaucrats.

Undiluted state socialism, following the total uncompensated expropriation of all forms of private property, has proved such a grandiose fiasco in Russia that one grave possible danger to democracy in Great Britain and in other highly industrialized countries may not materialize in the world after the present war. This is the danger that a small majority would vote for a series of confiscatory measures which a large minority would regard as outright robbery.

On the other hand, war is a potent psychological stimulus to violent shortcuts. It is not impossible, perhaps not improbable, that the mere effect of the war, of the economic dislocations which it has caused and will cause, of the mood which it will evoke, will wipe out many characteristic features of the individualist economic order.

Unless all signs fail, there will be much less to go around for Englishmen of all classes after the war is over, even if it ends in victory. Claims to income based on interest and dividends may be among the least secure. The war necessity of rationing, in order to insure that everyone has a minimum of bread before anyone has cake, may be a peacetime necessity for a longer period than one can now foresee. And rationing, if applied to industries as well as to individuals, would be a deep opening wedge for some form of socialism.

War often hastens social and economic processes which would have taken place in any event, but at a slower, more gradual pace. One of the results of the present conflict may be a huge transfer of population from the British Isles to Canada or to other parts of the empire overseas. For the ability of the United Kingdom to support its present population depends on conditions which were changing for the worse slowly before the commencement of hostilities and which will change for the worse at catastrophic speed if the war leads to defeat or even to a very prolonged stalemate.

Every additional month of world conflict makes the whole system of international credit more insecure and England was a primary beneficiary of this system. While England's own factories are turned to war uses the factories of Canada and Australia and India will be turning more and more to satisfy the needs of those countries for consumption goods. With the progressive loss of Great Britain's position as the workshop and financial center of the world will disappear the livelihoods of great numbers of Englishmen.

There are two aspects of the British Empire. Some of the countries which it includes are equal members of a voluntary association. Canada, Australia, New Zealand, South Africa, are entirely self-governing. Great Britain has long possessed no right of interference in their domestic concerns. Since the first World War these Dominions have maintained their own embassies in foreign capitals. This is also true of Eire, which acquired its independence by guerrilla revolt and has exercised its right to remain neutral in the present war.

The parts of the empire which are mainly inhabited by brown and black men are governed in authoritarian fashion. Some progress has been made in granting provincial autonomy in India. But the key points of military, police and financial control in the central government are kept firmly in British hands. Many thousands of Indian nationalists, including the leader of the movement, Jawaharlal Nehru, are in prison.

⌐ There is a ferment of nationalist discontent in India. Yet most Indian nationalists would recognize that British rule, with all its faults, would be preferable to German or Russian or Japanese. Both Mahatma Gandhi and Nehru have been repeatedly imprisoned by the British authorities. But Gandhi's moral philosophy is known to the whole world and Nehru made good use of his time in prison to write a brilliant and sympathetic autobiography. A Czech or Polish Nehru would have been extinguished without a hearing. A Soviet Gandhi would have perished inarticulate in a concentration camp.

It is glib and superficial to dismiss the war as merely a clash between sated and hungry imperialisms. It is this, of course. But there is a difference not only in the degree but in the character of imperialisms. There is a fundamental difference between the British form of rule, which almost encourages the intelligentsia of the subject races to become rebels by the Western education which it gives them, and the all-crushing totalitarian type of rule over conquered and colonial peoples.

The impact of the war on the states which are voluntarily associated with Great Britain and on the colonies and possessions of the empire will probably be different. Canada, Australia, New Zealand, South Africa (with reservations for its strong Boer minority), may be expected to stand by the mother country until the end. Should there be a tragic end, a collapse and surrender, these far-flung Anglo-Saxon outposts would presumably seek some kind of affiliation with the United States.

⌐ The fall of England in Europe would spread anarchy over a considerable part of the globe. There seems to be no single force in India strong enough to fill the vacuum which would be created by the fall of the British Raj. So all sorts of racial and religious feuds might break out and a period of widespread disorder would perhaps be the prelude to a new foreign intervention and conquest. There might be a race between Japan, Germany and the Soviet Union (if it survives the present war) to reach India. Many of the subject peoples of the British Empire, the Malays, for instance, and many of the African Zulus, Bantus and other tribes, would most probably be too backward and lacking in political consciousness to make any move toward independence and would fall into the hands of any power which was strong enough to drive out the British.

It is sometimes suggested that Great Britain should impart a revolutionary character to its war against the Axis powers by foregoing sovereignty over India and giving up all special privileges in China. Such suggestions may look attractive on paper, but they are not easily reconciled with political realities. One shrewd observer remarked that it would be impossible to go to the sons of well-to-do and middle class families who constitute most of the personnel of the Royal Air Force and propose the liberation of all subject nations, such as India, as a war aim. Their reaction would be:

"What are we fighting for, if not to keep the empire?"

Its whole history and social, economic and psychological background would seem to make it impossible for Great Britain to fight a revolutionary war, to step forward as an apostle of drastic change. When a British diplomat does recognize the need for postwar change in general terms he is quick to take refuge in platitudes when pressed for specific details.

Great Britain is fighting for the maintenance of its position as a great power, for an empire and a *status quo* out of which not only its ruling class but its whole population, in varying degree, have done rather well. The dole, liberal by European standards, which is paid to the British unemployed is partly covered by the additional proceeds from trade and investment which are associated with the possession of the world's largest empire.

There is no reason why England should be ashamed of fighting for an old order which, with all its faults, was far more humane and attractive than such modern alternatives as communism and fascism. The question is rather whether it is possible to restore this old order where it has been destroyed; whether British power, even if it should be vindicated by means of the war, will not require stronger, more brutal, more direct, means of self-assertion than gold and sea power and the diplomacy of the balance of power, of keeping Europe perpetually divided.

Again and again one is impressed by the difficulty of Great Britain's dilemma. Its leaders believed that it was necessary to fight a Second World War in order to ward off the danger of disintegration of the empire. This war deals blow after blow to the system of international capitalism, of far-flung trade, credit and investment on which Great Britain, that little island off the coast of Europe, has prospered and grown rich. There is symbolic as well as physical destructive power in the bombs which fall on the City of London. If the war proceeds a very long time and unlooses many subsidiary political and economic upheavals the bonds and shares which repose in the vaults of the great London banks and which formerly represented vast fortunes may be reduced to little more than waste paper in value.

Whatever may be the outcome of the ordeal of Great Britain, the British people have passed through the valley of the shadow of death without flinching. History will give its judgment as to whether the cause for which England fought was a lost one. But the British people have vindicated the judgment of their most implacable enemy, Adolf Hitler, who said:

"The English people must be looked upon as the most valuable ally in the world so long as its leaders and the spirit of its great masses permit us to expect that brutality and toughness which is determined to fight out, by all means, a struggle once begun to the victorious end."

And they have risen to the spirit of the glowing peroration which their leader, Winston Churchill, pronounced in one of his speeches during one of the darkest hours of the struggle:

"Let us so bear ourselves that, if the British Empire and its Commonwealth last for a thousand years, men will still say: 'This was their finest hour.'"

Chapter Thirteen

AMERICA FACES THE IRON AGE

IT HAS BECOME a commonplace to say that America is facing a crisis of its destiny. The Iron Age that began in Russia, that spread by revolution and war over Europe and much of Asia, could not leave America unaffected. Somehow its challenge must be met.

As I have tried to show, it has been one of the most familiar tragedies of the European democracies to have got the worst of two clear-cut alternative policies by wavering between them. And this, I fear, may also prove to be a tragedy for America.

The clear-cut alternatives for Great Britain and France were to have stopped Hitler by decisive action in 1935 or 1936 or to let him expand at the expense of the Soviet Union and build up a land empire which would have been comparable in wealth and resources with their overseas empire. They did not fight when there was every prospect of success; they finally put themselves in the anomalous position of fighting under very unfavorable circumstances and thereby making it possible for Stalin to remain aloof and cherish the dream of winning the war by staying out of it. It is true that this dream was shattered by Hitler's own action, but this does not invalidate the criticism of the British and French tactics in selecting 1939, not 1935 or 1936, as the time to strike at Hitler.

America's position is not analogous, and yet in some respects it has been similar. The clear-cut alternatives for America were to have thrown its whole weight into the war from the day when it began or to have adhered to a policy of hemisphere defense, eschewing power politics and especially avoiding the heavy responsibility of ruling out any suggestions of negotiated peace in Europe and in Asia. The first alternative was clearly ruled out by the state of public opinion; the second has certainly not been adopted. And one cannot be blind to the danger that America may drift and blunder into a war for which there is no popular mandate, for which the psychological and material preparation of the country is inadequate. Here the recent French example of what may happen when a reluctant people is pushed into war by its government without the stimulus of direct attack should certainly exert a sobering influence. My own sense of emphasis and values differs from that of the largest or at least of the most articulate body of public opinion in the United States at the present time. I think the risks of entering a war of unlimited liability are greater than those of a policy of strict hemisphere defense. I think America's crisis is less serious internationally and more serious internally than is generally assumed. I think the term "mortal danger" which has been used even by officials in responsible positions to describe America's position in the spring of 1941 is a gross exaggeration and is regrettable because it will deaden the effect of such strong words if the time should ever come when America will be in mortal danger.

I cannot share the extraordinary prophetic insight into Hitler's intentions of those individuals who predict with absolute assurance that he will be on his way to attack this continent thirty days, sixty days or ninety days after the end of the war in Europe. I am not impressed by the sensational forebodings of a mercurial ex-diplomat that Hitler may be in Philadelphia, making fun of the Liberty Bell, or that all our churches may be closed by the fiat of Dr. Goebbels.

I have yet to see a sober factual military argument proving the feasibility of a physical invasion of the United States, even in the event of the most unfavorable turn of the war in Europe. Germany at the present time has one first-class battleship and two pocket battleships as against nineteen of these capital ships for the United States. Throw in the remnants of the French and Italian navies and the picture of an invincible armada coming to our shores is still far from convincing.

For the carrying out of landing operations over three thousand miles of ocean in the face of the most powerful navy in the world would require superiority, not parity, in naval strength. And such superiority could not be attained within any predictable future, because the construction of a battleship is a matter not of months, but of years, and there are bottlenecks in the supply of skilled labor, in shipyard facilities (all badly battered), in Europe and in the number of trained sailors.

Even the capture of the British Navy would not make an invasion feasible; Hitler would still not possess enough naval strength to undertake a sea-borne invasion. And, while the Japanese Navy is a serious factor in the Western Pacific, it is no menace to this hemisphere, because the cruising range of its ships is too small to permit an ocean-crossing operation which, in the Pacific, would involve distances twice as great as those in the Atlantic. And Japan has no bases in the Eastern Pacific.

The roots of the American crisis are not in any peril of invasion. They are to be found rather in the failure of American democratic institutions to respond adequately to the needs of the situation, to permit the American people to choose freely and consciously and intelligently between the two policies which were open to them as the Iron Age loomed up on the international horizon.

The first of these policies was the one which the overwhelming majority of the American people certainly desired before the fall of France. Since that time opinion has become more evenly divided, yet between 75 and 85 per cent of the American people, on unofficial but regular polls without suspicion of isolationist bias, have been, up to the time of writing (July, 1941), opposed to entering the present war. It is sometimes disingenuously suggested that, as everyone prefers peace to war, these polls are without value. It may be noted that the question, as posed, was not "war" in general, but this particular war.

The first American crusade to make the world safe for democracy was an obvious and unmitigated political failure, even if it had been a military success. The world had become safe not for democracy but for communism and fascism. America, which desired and obtained no territory from the war, could cast up the following balance sheet from its participation. Some fifty thousand dead, several times that number wounded, crippled, disabled; a gigantic increase in the national debt and an economic crisis, greatly aggravated by the war, which assumed for America the proportions of a national disaster.

It was in this mood that Congress passed, by a virtually unanimous vote, neutrality legislation which deliberately tried to remove the most probable causes of involvement in future wars. American ships were forbidden to enter combat zones. Loans to belligerent governments, rightly regarded as unrepayable, were prohibited. Notice was served on the world that the American people, without "isolating" themselves from constructive forms of cooperation with other nations, proposed to isolate themselves from wars which were not of their making so long as the Western hemisphere was not attacked.

This policy was a practical attempt to implement the deep desire of the American people for peace, not at any price, but so long as there was no attack on American independence or territorial integrity or on regions which were vital to American security. Abused from the beginning by those who consciously or unconsciously placed the interests of other countries ahead of those of America, it was a thoroughly feasible policy for a country in America's singularly well-protected geographical position. It deserved a fairer test than it received. It was evaded and sabotaged and has now been largely scrapped. Yet it is interesting to note that it was not considered politically expedient to propose the outright repeal of the Neutrality Act to Congress, even when its spirit was being violated in every way.

"Might have beens" are never conclusive. But to me it has always been an interesting speculation what would have occurred if the enforcement of the Neutrality Act had been in the hands of a President who believed in its underlying philosophy, in the possibility of insulating America from Europe's and Asia's war; in the hands of a political leader from the socially democratic and pacific Middle West, of a man like Bryan or the elder La Follette.

It is quite conceivable that America might then have faced the Iron Age with a maximum degree of unity. For, whatever criticism might have been voiced of this policy of noninvolvement in overseas war, it would certainly have been simpler, both in conception and in execution, than the alternative policy of all-out intervention.

There would have been no harassing anxiety, for instance, as to whether to strike for Dakar, for the Azores, for the Cape Verde Islands, for Singapore, for Batavia, for Vladivostok or for other places in distant parts of the world which have been more or less convincingly represented as essential to the security of Kansas and Nebraska. A plan for the defense of the Americas in the Atlantic along the line of the bases which were acquired from Great Britain, in the Pacific along the Alaska–Hawaii line, would certainly be far easier to implement than the unlimited liabilities in Europe, Asia and Africa which are implicit in the assumption that American interests are vitally identified with the outcome of all the wars which are proceeding in various parts of the world.

Not one American in a hundred would hesitate to support, with his life if necessary, the policy of defending his own country and adjacent areas in America against hostile aggression. But when it is a question of plunging into the complicated vortex of European and Asiatic power politics, with its many bewildering and incalculable shifts, public opinion is deeply divided, as every poll on the subject shows. In short, it is the simpler, easier and safer military and naval policy which would have attracted much the higher proportion of popular endorsement.

It is fashionable to represent the policy of hemisphere defense as selfish and cowardly and impracticable into the bargain. We shall probably never know whether it was impracticable or not. For it was never honestly tried. But the ideal of an America concerned with the making of a better democracy within its own frontiers, remaining an island of reason and sanity in a world darkened by war and revolution, preparing to exert a healing and mediating influence when the madness of the Iron Age shall have passed, was not an unworthy one. For there is much truth in the words of Dr. Harry Emerson Fosdick:

"There are worse things than war, and war brings every one of them."

One need not be a pacifist, one need only be a democrat and a liberal, to recognize how many things that are worse than loss of life and destruction of property are inseparable from war. Mass hysteria, for instance, and an almost total abdication of the rational faculty. A mania for witch-hunting and spying on one's neighbor. Intolerance and bigotry in their crudest forms. Dangerous aggravation of race and class tensions. The fate of the German Jews is only one of many illustrations of how easily the dark passions aroused by a disastrous war and the subsequent misfortune of inflation can be canalized against an unpopular minority.

The word Fascist was not known at the time, but America was never in its history so close to the pattern of a Fascist state as when Woodrow Wilson was engaged in his crusade to extend the blessings of democracy to the whole world. The number of lynchings was abnormally high; whole areas of the Middle West were given over to mob rule; the rights of labor were systematically infringed. America was never such a happy hunting ground for petty would-be local dictators like the Mayor of Seattle, Ole Hansen, who announced, when he closed the headquarters of an unpopular labor organization:

"We didn't have any law, and we didn't need any. We used nails."

Every civilized man and woman would subscribe heartily to President Roosevelt's ideal of the four freedoms: freedom of religion, freedom of speech, freedom from want, freedom from fear. But every thoughtful man and woman must be haunted by grave doubts as to whether war is a hopeful means either of establishing these freedoms abroad or of maintaining them at home.

The pacifist minister or layman often experiences little tolerance for his religious convictions in time of war. Freedom of speech tends to sink to the level of a dictatorship, not of a democracy. Freedom from want is not the usual result of modern warfare, with its terrific economic dislocations—culminating either in inflation or in mass unemployment. Nor does freedom from fear prevail at a time when amateur imitations of the GPU and the Gestapo spring up like mushrooms.

The alternative to the policy of hemisphere defense, of nonintervention in the wars of Europe and Asia, is the policy of all-out participation in foreign conflicts. In the long run there will scarcely be any tenable middle ground, any maintenance of the "aid short of war" principle.

The arguments for complete involvement are varied, ranging from what purport to be considerations of enlightened national selfishness to pleas which attain a stratospheric pitch of emotionalism. The most familiar argument of the former type is that the world has become too small for the coexistence of democracy and totalitarian dictatorship. It is assumed that Hitler is bent on world domination, that he will inevitably come into conflict with the United States and that it is in America's interest to check him as soon as possible.

The interventionist does not rest his case entirely upon the military menace represented by the Third Reich, although he is disposed to take a dark view of America's strategic prospects in the event of a British defeat. He also stresses economic and moral considerations.

It is contended that trade would become a formidable weapon in the hands of a Hitler who dominated Europe and parts of Asia and Africa. It could and would be used to exert political pressure in the United States, to promote intrigues in Latin American countries. There could, it is said, be no *modus vivendi*, no point of contact, between the trade of a gigantic totalitarian empire and that of a democratic country.

Moral grounds are also widely invoked. We cannot, as one prominent public man tells us, maintain the American way of life unless we also maintain the British way, the Chinese way, the Greek way. So far as I know this prophet has remained silent on the somewhat delicate point of whether the American way of life is also dependent on the maintenance of the Stalinite way. And he was not very explicit as to what he meant by the Chinese way of life, old-fashioned Confucianism, for instance, or Kuomintang nationalism, or the Chinese brand of communism.

America, it is argued, would be under strong pressure to adopt some form of fascism itself in a totalitarian world. It would be obliged to transform itself into an armed camp, always in danger of attack. This would curtail or eliminate any possibility of social progress.

Sentiment has generally worked on the side of the interventionists. American civilization is predominantly Anglo–Saxon. Far more individual Americans are bound to England than to any other foreign country by family ties, friendships, cultural associations.

This factor was important in shaping the American decision to intervene in 1917. A new factor for intervention was created when Hitler set out on his program of social and economic extermination of the Jews. Indignation felt in Jewish and non-Jewish circles over the brutal measures of racial persecution adopted by the Nazi regime was reinforced by resentment against repressive measures which Hitler applied against Catholic and Protestant churches and against the peoples of the conquered countries.

In short, the interventionist plea touched on a whole gamut of themes, ranging from the contention that defense of America would become difficult, if not impossible, in a totalitarian world to emphasis on the supposedly insatiable nature of Hitler's revolutionary movement for conquest. High-pitched emotionalism has also been characteristic of interventionist psychology. Among innumerable specimens I select the following excerpts from an article in a leading monthly:

"In man the refusal to fight save in self-defense may be not only profoundly immoral but morally catastrophic. For man is a willing and purposeful creature. He can make his world. He can lift up his eyes to the hills and achieve the summits. Sometimes he decrees golden domes to arise upon the flat plains of his existence. And whenever he has done so he has been at peace with himself and approached a little nearer to the angels. . . . There is something, I believe, for which Americans will fight: our souls' repose and a world made in our own splendid image."

Now sincere patriotic Americans can and do differ as to whether a program of limited liability, restricting military action to cases of definite hostile action against this hemisphere, or a policy of unlimited intervention would best serve America's national interests. What is most unfortunate is that this question, the most important, probably, which has confronted the American people since the Civil War, was never put up to the people to be settled, in the democratic way, by an election.

The Presidential election of 1940, when America was clearly approaching a historical crossroad, would have afforded an ideal occasion for a plebiscite on this question. Had one candidate straightforwardly advocated intervention, the other nonintervention, the voters would have heard every argument on both sides and an unmistakable national verdict, which the minority would certainly have loyally accepted, would have been rendered.

Unfortunately both major candidates acted like politicians maneuvering for office, not like statesmen conscious of a moral obligation to tell the voters what policy they proposed to follow after the election. It would require a very skillful casuist to establish a line of harmony and continuity between some of the election speeches of both candidates and their words (and Mr. Roosevelt's actions) after the election.

Mr. Willkie, to be sure, shrugged off comment on one of these discrepancies with a remark about "campaign oratory," which may not be remembered very favorably if it is ever necessary to write a book on the decline and fall of American democracy. Nothing could have a more disastrous effect on the preservation and vitality of democracy in America and anywhere else than the spread of a cynical belief that elections are useless because of the complete discrepancy between the statements of candidates before the election and their performances after they come into office.

Mr. Roosevelt said at Philadelphia on October 23, 1940:

"I repeat again that I stand on the platform of our party; we will not participate in foreign wars and will not send our Army, Naval or Air Forces to fight in foreign lands outside of the Americas except in case of attack."

He said at Boston on October 30:

"And while I am talking to you, fathers and mothers, I give you one more assurance. I have said this before, but I shall say it again, and again, and again: your boys are not going to be sent into any foreign wars."

This was a few days before the election. But after the votes were counted Mr. Roosevelt did not give these assurances "again," at least with the same explicitness. On the contrary, in his first message to Congress, he made a statement which was difficult to reconcile with any prospect of permanently staying out of foreign wars.

"We are committed to the proposition that principles of morality and considerations of our own security will never permit us to acquiesce in a peace dictated by aggressors and sponsored by appeasers."

Here was certainly interventionism in its strongest terms, a proclamation by nonbelligerent America of a veto against any compromise peace. The logical corollary of this assumption was certainly a policy of aid to Great Britain which could scarcely stop short of war. England, bolstered by American support with munitions and supplies, could conceivably create a stalemate; establish a basis for a compromise peace, perhaps on the basis of a German evacuation of Western Europe accompanied by a free hand for Germany in the East. But only a most daring flight into wishful thinking could count on Great Britain, singlehanded, or even with such aid as the Soviet Union could give after being kicked into the war, winning the total victory over Germany which it had required a combination of six great powers and a number of smaller ones to accomplish in 1914–1918. Indeed since the beginning of the war in Europe there has been a steady graduated stepping up of British claims on American aid. First it was represented that the sale of munitions would be enough. Then it was decided to give Great Britain all needed munitions and supplies and Premier Churchill gave the assurance: "Give us the tools and we will finish the job." "Give us the tools" was soon altered to read "Bring us the tools"; that is, engage in a shooting naval war if necessary to assure supply. And early in July, 1941, the prominent British General Sir Archibald Wavell, seconded by his successor, General Claude Auchinleck, confirmed a theory that had been set forth by the much abused Colonel Lindbergh two months earlier. They frankly stated that the war could be won only by an invasion of Germany and hinted that American man power would be required for such an invasion.

American democratic institutions have not functioned as they should during this critical period in the shaping of American foreign policy. There was no real choice as to the vital issue of foreign policy between the two leading candidates in the last election. And very few of those who have advocated American intervention in the war have emulated the courage and honesty and farsightedness of Winston Churchill, when he told his countrymen that all he had to offer them was "blood, sweat and tears." America has been deluged with books, pamphlets, articles, inevitably highly speculative in character, painting the American prospects of existence in the darkest colors if Hitler is not destroyed. But the price of crushing Hitler in his own country, of invading a European continent which is buttressed by aircraft and guarded by one of the most efficient military machines in history, has seldom been stated straightforwardly to the unknown soldiers of the future and their parents.

Some curious *non sequiturs* began to gain widespread currency. Because it would be difficult and inconvenient to adjust American foreign trade to dealing with a totalitarian regime it was assumed that all totalitarian regimes must be destroyed. As if the material (to say nothing of the human) costs of a very short period of all-out war would not be greater and would not inflict more present and future dislocations on our economy than a generation of trading under difficulties! Because Hitler overran small countries like the Netherlands and Belgium, which were contiguous with Germany and were exposed to the full weight of the overwhelming Nazi land and air power, it is often assumed that he could and would attack with equal ease and certainty the United States, the strongest industrial power in the world, with a first line of defense consisting of two oceans and the strongest navy in the world. One is bombarded with analogies that are not analogous, with warnings that sound hollow if they are subjected to careful analysis.

The pages of ancient history are ransacked and I don't know how often the example of Demosthenes, vainly appealing to the Athenians to act more quickly against Philip of Macedon, has been trotted out as a horrible example for American anti-interventionists. Without discussing how far one can safely trust such remote precedents, it is not difficult to find other events in Greek history which seem to point quite different morals. The expedition of the Athenians to Sicily, the turning point of the Peloponnesian War, shows that very disastrous results can follow from the "offensive spirit" which is sometimes uncritically recommended as the sure guaranty of victory under all circumstances. And, if there had been more "appeasers" in the Athenian Government, peace in that ancient war could have more than once been arranged on terms more advantageous than those which were finally imposed.

When the time comes (if it ever does come) to write the

history of America's involvement in the Second World War, the critical historian, I think, will describe the fundamental interventionist technique as superficially clever, but not deeply wise. This technique consisted of taking one step after another toward belligerency under the guise of keeping the country out of war. Then, at a given moment, after the passing of the Lease-Lend Act, the technique was suddenly reversed. The pretense of keeping the country out of war was dropped. The new line of argument was that America had gone too far to turn back.

Superficially this method was clever. Not a few anti-interventionists, without being in the least convinced that their views were mistaken, abandoned the struggle as hopeless. A new class of "reluctant interventionists," to use the expression of one man who had changed his outward position without losing his doubts, appeared.

But it is doubtful whether this maneuver was wise in the deeper sense. It produced uniformity, not unity. Despite the prodigious barrage of interventionist propaganda, more than three fourths of the American people, by the evidence of a regular unofficial poll, remained opposed to entrance into the war. The American Constitution vests the right to declare war in Congress and a declaration of war is a boomerang if it is not very nearly unanimous. But it would be a grotesque parody of democracy if Congress should vote by a large majority in favor of a step which only a minority of the people desire.

It is too soon to attempt to give a detailed and authoritative analysis of Mr. Roosevelt's foreign policy during a period when he was beset by many conflicting pulls both in the international situation and in domestic politics. Perhaps events may so shape themselves that he may remain poised on the brink of the abyss. Perhaps he can limit himself to an undeclared naval war. Yet the inner logic of the policy which he has followed seems to demand ultimate American intervention, unless there is some unforeseeable miracle like a Soviet successful resistance or an internal collapse in one or more of the dictatorships. How the awkward hurdle of unmistakable popular reluctance to repeat the experiment of 1917 is to be surmounted remains to be seen. But perhaps the necessary preliminary bloodletting will emerge from the occupation of Iceland or from some other overseas adventure.

I sometimes like to appeal, in imagination, from the increasing heat and the diminishing light of 1941 to the judgment of the American historians and publicists of 1950 or 1960. Assuming something that is by no means certain, that we shall emerge from the Iron Age with our traditional freedom of speech and writing, I am convinced that the decade 1950–1960, perhaps even an earlier period, will produce a spate of books with such titles as "The Road to War" and "Now It Can Be Told."

Perhaps I might venture now, in that curious twilight zone when Americans are disputing, according to their wishes and preferences, as to whether the country is in or out of the war, to suggest a few current intellectual phenomena that might deserve more detailed study by these historians of the future.

One of the most familiar features of the totalitarian technique is the substitution of standardized abuse and invective for rational discussion. There is no discussion of the dissenter in a dictatorship on the merits of his ideas. In Russia he will be called a "Trotskyist mad dog" or a "Bukharinite viper." In Germany or Italy he will be described as a "Jewish liberal," a "plutodemocrat" or a "Bolshevik."

This same stupid tyranny of words has been establishing itself in America. Anyone can be damned and sometimes cowed into silence by simply calling him an "appeaser" or, better still, a "fifth columnist." Appeaser would have been a legitimate term of reproach for an American who was willing to forego American territory or American national independence before a threat of foreign aggression. But appeaser, 1941 definition, is anyone who expresses a doubt as to whether America should or could attempt to impose its standard of righteousness on the whole world.

The widespread use of the sinister-sounding epithet "fifth columnist" is ironically amusing, in view of the realities of the situation. To judge from many speeches, broadcasts and articles, one might imagine that America was flooded with German, Italian and Japanese agents, all endeavoring to sow disunion, to obstruct defense efforts and to influence the public mind against participation in the war.

Now of course no one can say with certainty how many secret emissaries various foreign countries may have maintained in America. But if there was a single alien who was active in speech or print on the anti-interventionist side of the argument, I do not know his name. The men who led the struggle against American involvement in the war, Colonel Lindbergh, Senators Wheeler and Nye and Clark, Norman Thomas, John T. Flynn, General Robert E. Wood, to mention a few of the more conspicuous, were all native Americans who had long been identified in one way or another with American public life. Not one of them, by the wildest stretch of partisan imagination, could be represented as the agent of a foreign country. Right or wrong in their judgment, they were Americans responding to American motives and impulses.

This was also doubtless true of the majority of the prominent interventionists. But the real "fifth column" of foreigners who were trying to influence American public opinion was entirely on the interventionist side. It would be difficult, perhaps impossible, to name one alien who exerted any perceptible influence in favor of isolation from war. It would be easy to mention scores or dozens of members of an interventionist "Foreign Legion," of men and women who were not American citizens and who, with varying degrees of tact and finesse and camouflage, devoted themselves to the cause of trying to persuade America to enter the war.

Some of these advocates of intervention were British; some were refugees from Germany and Austria and German-occupied countries on the continent. One could understand and sympathize with their motives, although it is seldom wise for aliens to attempt to influence the policy of the country which they are visiting or where they have found a refuge. But it is a grotesque inversion of the facts to suggest an imaginary fifth column of enemy agents, endeavoring to influence American opinion along the lines of "appeasement," and to ignore the very real "fifth column" of foreigners who were working for intervention.

During our trek from Paris to the Spanish border my wife and I were often touched by the kindness which simple French men and women, themselves in the shadow of a national catastrophe, showed to us, along with other refugees. There was an innkeeper in Tours who, with his wife, took the greatest pains to provide what comfort was possible for the refugees who jammed his inn, to see that no one was turned away to sleep in the streets. There was an old peasant who ran back and forth with heavy buckets of water from his well to give drink to a trainload of hot and thirsty refugees. There was the wife of a postal employee in St. Jean de Luz who gave us shelter in her little apartment and would accept only the smallest pittance for rent, although she was already finding it hard to get food and shoes for her children.

I hoped that America would find some means of helping these people and millions of others like them, not only in France but in other occupied countries, in Belgium, where distress was especially great because of the highly industrialized character of the country, in the Netherlands, Norway and Denmark. The vast relief work organized by Herbert Hoover during and after the last World War began under similar circumstances in occupied Belgium. When Mr. Hoover proposed a plan for feeding the occupied small democracies, under American supervision and with stringent safeguards against German misappropriation of the food, I felt that here was a practical humanitarian enterprise in which all Americans, and especially those identified with the Christian faith, would be glad to cooperate.

It scarcely seemed credible to me and perhaps it will scarcely seem credible to some future age that the Hoover Plan aroused a storm of abuse and misrepresentation. Some prominent Church leaders were most active in opposing this or any other plan for relieving distress in occupied countries. From ministers of a gospel of mercy they transformed themselves into armchair military and naval experts and specialists in the strategy of a hunger blockade the main weight of which inevitably fell not on the German aggressors but on the unfortunate peoples whose only crime was that they had not been strong enough to resist invasion.

This reaction to the Hoover Plan, not universal, fortunately, but very general, first gave me the measure of how far the psychology of the Iron Age had taken hold of a considerable part of the American educated classes. Never since I had argued with Soviet and foreign Communists about the man-made famine in Russia in 1932–33 have I heard so much sophistry about how suffering, malnutrition, possible starvation of tens of millions of human beings, is really only a minor incident, regrettable, perhaps, but necessary in the interests of a higher good—the "building of socialism" in Russia, the winning of the war now.

Just how Germany's defeat was to be compassed by creating conditions which would make for the growing up of a stunted, undernourished younger generation in the German-occupied countries was never made very clear or convincing. As it is obvious, in view of the present distribution of power, that the Germans would be the last to starve, the chief result of a completely effective blockade would be to increase the numerical preponderance of the Germans over the people of the democratic countries.

In fact, the whole reaction to proposals for the feeding of the occupied countries was emotional, rather than reasonable. Many people, normally kind and charitable, although perhaps their lives were too sheltered to make them fully conscious of the responsibility which they were assuming in opposing plans to relieve starvation, had so far lost all sense of reality and balance and proportion that they apparently believed the issue of the war would be seriously affected by the dispatch of limited quantities of food, to be distributed under strict American supervision.

Watching the Iron Age come closer to America as propaganda for war, cautious and camouflaged at first, became more strident and insistent, I could understand better the rise to power of Hitler. So many Americans who did not in the least believe that Kansas and Nebraska had to be defended in Dakar and Singapore or that fighting would be conducive to their "souls' repose," to cite the more poetic interventionist argument, became silent or passively accepted the idea that war had been made inevitable. It was the attitude all over again of many non-Nazi Germans in the last stages of Hitler's campaign against the Weimar Republic. Fear of economic reprisals, of social ostracism, of being called an appeaser, a defeatist, a fifth columnist or some other bad name, was causing many people to hide their honest convictions. To me, a long-term resident of dictatorially and semidictatorially governed countries, it was a familiar, and an unpleasant, psychological pattern.

More than once, in lectures and in conversations, I have told what I think is the best story of the technique of dictatorship. It is about the dictator who goes to a moving picture show, incognito, remains seated when his picture is thrown on the screen while everyone else rises to applaud and receives from the man next to him an assurance of secret sympathy, coupled with the admonition: "Just the same, it would be much safer for you to get up and join in the applause." I never thought I would find a practical illustration of that anecdote in America.

But after I had spoken before a Midwestern audience and set forth the reasons why, as I believed, belligerent participation in the war would be a grave mistake for the United States, a man came up to me afterward, looked around to see whether anyone was listening (I was familiar with that attitude from Russia and from Germany) and said:

"Many people in this part of the country believe as you do. But we don't dare say so any more. We would suffer in our business, in our social relations; we might be persecuted by government agents."

Perhaps this man was timid and inclined to exaggeration. Yet if this attitude can be found (and this was not an isolated example) in the prewar period, what will remain of democracy and liberalism if a formal state of war, with a revived Espionage Act, should come into existence? Few, if any, genuine spies or enemy agents were prosecuted under this act. But it was utilized to inflict barbarously long prison sentences on war critics, including religious pacifists and economic radicals.

As war hysteria rises in America one can discern more and more frequently one of the most characteristic features of the psychology of the Iron Age, of war and violent revolution. This is the illusion that humane and rational ends can be achieved by means which are inhuman and irrational. Woodrow Wilson, after putting aside the wisdom of his "peace without victory" ideal, succumbed to the fallacy that the world could be made safe for democracy by the unlimited use of what he chose to call "righteous force." The Russian Communists, those of them who were sincere, believed that an ideal order of liberty, justice and equality would on some millennial date emerge phoenixlike from a long preparatory period of terror, violence and oppression. The German Nazis, those who were sincere, believed in an ideal race community, to the accompaniment of brutal persecution of and hostility to other peoples.

Now one can see this same moral and intellectual confusion in America. The very persons who are most insistent that America should launch a crusading war to save, restore or impose liberty and democracy in the whole world are most contemptuous of democratic processes at home. It is just these ardent interventionists who express delight when the President finds means to "by-pass" Congress; who indignantly reject the idea that the people should vote on the question of whether war should be undertaken when no question of direct national defense is involved; who urge warlike activities without consultation of the authority in which the Constitution vests the power to declare war, the United States Congress.

A vivid illustration of this tendency in time for war or revolution to achieve a total divorce between ends and means was furnished by a zealous interventionist in Cincinnati. On being invited to attend an anti-intervention meeting he sent the following extraordinary reply:

"I am not grateful to you for sending me notice of the traitorous assemblage to be held on June 16. I do not care to listen to Nazi agents, even when United States Senators and their wives. If I had the authority I would bomb and machine gun your meeting. I am a member of the Fight for Freedom Committee."

This gentleman's desire to fight was obvious; his conception of freedom was, to put it mildly, muddled. To be sure, the local Fight for Freedom organization repudiated this idea of directing bombs and machine guns against fellow Americans and it might be possible to dismiss the author of the letter as a psychopathic crank who had been thrown completely off balance by reading too much superheated war literature. But one should not underestimate the potential future danger of such an isolated case. For, as Nietzsche says, "insanity in individuals is something rare—but in groups, parties, nations and epochs it is the rule." It is certainly apt to be the rule for considerable sections of the population in time of war.

This same confusion of ends and means finds amusing illustration in a letter which I recently noticed in a Washington newspaper:

"The sooner the mouths of isolationists are closed, the better. We need to be 100 percent Americans now, and that means liberty not only for ourselves, but for all the world."

This unknown letter writer, who apparently believes that by denying liberty to his own countrymen he will somehow contrive to extend it to "all the world," was following, no doubt unconsciously, in the intellectual footsteps of the general of French revolutionary armies whose first order, after he had occupied a part of Germany, read substantially as follows:

"I bring you perfect freedom. Whoever makes an unauthorized move will be shot."

The greatest danger confronting American democracy at the present time is not Hitler, but Hitlerism—if one uses that term as synonymous with the political, economic and moral characteristics of the totalitarian state: militarism, suppression or thwarting of democratic processes, destruction of civil liberties, regimented economy, abnormal fear of imaginary or greatly exaggerated dangers which at times approaches paranoia. There is no danger of a foreign attack on this continent provided that elementary prudence is shown in reserving our naval forces for defense, properly so-called, and not risking a serious depletion of these forces in long-distance conflicts undertaken primarily for the benefit of other powers. But there is a very real danger that we shall more or less voluntarily assume many features of the totalitarian state. Indeed this process is already visibly advancing. The late Huey P. Long, who was by no means devoid of political perspicacity, once observed that if fascism should ever come to America it would call itself antifascism.

It would have been utopian folly to imagine that America could have altogether escaped the impact of the Iron Age. Candid students of the situation would agree that any policy which the American Government might have followed in a period of swift and violent change in international relations would have had its element of risk and danger.

But I think the impact of the Iron Age would have been much less formidable than it seems likely to be, that much more genuine national unity could have been achieved, if certain facts of the international situation had been viewed in more realistic, if less moralistic, terms, if more limited objectives had been set in strategy and diplomacy and more care taken to assure that these objectives could and would be achieved, if the American people had been treated more frankly and given more voice in determining their own destiny. Hanson W. Baldwin, the very able military critic of the "New York Times," uttered a profoundly true political comment when he wrote:

"If a minority—vocal and vigorous and strident—leads the majority to a war it does not want, the minority and the nation will live to regret it."

One hopes that these words will be seriously pondered by the small group of men with whom the decision of war or peace rests. They may well stand as an extremely euphemistic epitaph on the consequences of unpopular war.

No doubt if America should be tricked, maneuvered, pushed, into war without a much more compelling case for self-defense than has yet been presented, there would be plenty of hack writers to exalt the spirit of grim sullen determination with which American youth was setting about its job. There were writers who wrote in just these terms about France in 1939 and 1940.

But to anyone who is not an incurable wishful thinker the

cleavage of viewpoint between age groups is or should be one
of the most sobering considerations affecting American foreign
policy. Bellicose sentiment in America, in the main and with
a few inevitable exceptions, is in inverse ratio to fitness for
military service. The typical American advocate of all-out
participation in war is almost never a young man. He is far
more likely to be an aged Senator, a septuagenarian Cabinet
member, a venerable bishop, a ripely mature college president.

Where the Iron Age will take America no one can predict
with certainty. Barring some such miracle as a Soviet military
victory over Germany or an internal collapse in Japan, America would enter the war, if this decision should be finally
taken, under vastly less favorable circumstances than in 1917.
Then Germany already counted its casualties in millions and
America was entering a world coalition, of which France,
Italy, Japan and several smaller powers were members. At the
present time England would be America's only major ally and
the perplexing problems of a two-ocean war without a two-
ocean navy,[1] nonexistent in 1917–18, would very probably
arise from the beginning.

The American economy and financial structure are far less
well adapted to the strain of a prolonged war than was the
case in 1917. The national debt in the summer of 1941 was
approximately fifty times the 1917 figure. The huge expenditures of a war (swollen by the decision to subsidize the British
and Chinese war effort) are likely to produce economic dislocations of which we experienced only a hint in the earlier
European conflict. To be sure, there are some bright, not to
say overbright, young men who have been exerting some influence on public policy and who are committed to the pleas-
ing theory that if a big enough deficit can only be achieved in
the national budget everyone will find employment and live

[1] America already has a "two-ocean navy" for purposes of the defense
of its own shores. But it does not have a two-ocean navy for an offensive
war against Germany in the Atlantic and against Japan in the Pacific.

happily ever afterward. The charm of this theory is undeniable. But inasmuch as inflation, bankruptcy and repudiation have been the unfailing consequences of its numerous applications in past history one must regard it with considerable reserve.

Thoughtful economic observers are increasingly inclined to regard inflation as a genuine danger. And, next to war itself, there is no such stimulus to violent discontent as inflation, with the general chaos and impoverishment which it brings and the economic wiping out of the middle class. Its effect in America would be all the more explosive because there has been no case of this particular economic disease in the United States since the Civil War. The Germans waited for ten years after their tragic inflation until they received the additional stimulus to despair of a gigantic industrial slump, with mass unemployment. Then they succumbed to Hitler. Americans might not be so patient. An unpopular war, leading up to inflation, would open up some very grave perspectives of internal dissension, of setting class against class and one group in the population against another.

There has been much speculation about America's place in the future world. It has been suggested that the "capital of the world" after the war will be either Washington or Berlin. I think there is strong reason to doubt whether the world will ever have a capital, implying a single power whose will is sovereign all over the globe. Both the bogy of German world rule and the idea of an "American century," in which America, with some assistance from Great Britain, would rule the entire globe, for its own good, of course, will prove to be unreal fantasies, I suspect.

Without assuming the futile role of a crystal gazer or trying to draw up a blueprint for a world which has seldom been in a more fluid state I would suggest that America's political relations with the rest of the world are certain, in the long run, to be largely predetermined by three geographical facts.

First, there is a great area in the Western hemisphere where America's industrial and military predominance is unchallenged and which can be and should be made impregnable against hostile invasion. Second, there is a vast overseas land mass, the continents of Europe, Asia and Africa, where America can never permanently make its will prevail by force. Third, there are certain borderline areas, notably some of the large islands and archipelagoes of the South Pacific, which America might seize or "protect," in a burst of neo-imperialism, and hold by sea and air power. It is doubtful, however, whether the human and material costs of such an adventure would not be out of all proportion to its economic and strategic advantages. It is to be hoped that these common-sense facts will be recognized before there has been an unnecessary outpouring of "blood, sweat and tears" in an inevitably futile effort to disregard them.

How far America can and will cooperate economically and financially with other countries in the future depends on the kind of world that emerges after the end of the war. I think the idea that it is only necessary to beat Hitler and then expect the whole world to live happily ever afterward is based on a misconception of the extent to which the old liberal civilization has been undermined, not only by Hitler's career of conquest, but by other forces and trends which can scarcely be reversed by the method of war.

A factor that is both disturbing and profoundly significant is the failure of British and American statesmen to set forth any war aims except in the most general terms, to give any convincing assurance that the peace settlement after the total victory which is so far the sole war aim will be any more stable, any more free from seeds of disintegration, than the settlements after the First World War. It is disturbing because it indicates that all-out American participation would be one of the blindest of crusades, one of the greatest gambles with human lives and with the stability of our democratic institutions and our relatively successful free economy. It is significant because it seems to confirm the diagnosis that our civilization is sick with more than one disease for which no cure has been found.

Whether an ordered world economy can be rebuilt in any near future, regardless of the course of the war, is doubtful, to say the least. America is so self-sufficient that it has felt remarkably few inconveniences from the virtual cessation of trade with the European continent. Americans, therefore, are slow to understand and to accept the implications of a cataclysm which has destroyed the value, as a means of international exchange, of every currency in the world except the American dollar, which has depleted shipping on an unprecedented scale, which has created a fantastic situation where the livelihood of men in every large country except beaten France is dependent on turning out weapons of destruction.

For a time the fuller employment of labor and plant as a result of the American armament program may feed the illusion here that an unprecedented diversion of national resources to unproductive ends is a road to prosperity. But the bloom will soon be off this inflationary peach and America seems destined soon or late to choose between two hard alternatives. It may go in for large-scale militarism and imperialism, both of which are quite inconsistent with the American tradition, with the inevitable accompaniment of a regimented economy and controlled speech and thought. Or a terrific crash will follow the war boom and the demobilization of the war industries will be attended by a gigantic new unemployment problem. As wars become bigger, more expensive and more industrialized this problem of postwar adjustment becomes formidable, if not insoluble, for every country, because the modern war, besides the men whom it takes out of production and places in uniforms, requires such an enormous number of workers in industry and in transportation.

The picture I have painted is not a cheerful one and I sincerely hope, as an American, that unforeseen new factors, perhaps some fortunate accidents in the international field or some eleventh-hour reconsideration of the risks, external and internal, of plunging into a war for which there is no popular mandate, will soften the tints and refute some of the apprehensions.

But there has been so much soothing syrup of wishful thinking on tap in America that it will do no harm, I think, to look the Iron Age in the face and see what may well be the stark realities of two or three or even five years hence, unreal as they seem in the still relatively sheltered and happy America of 1941. I have always felt that some of the "debunking" books about the last war should have been published before or during the struggle. The authors would doubtless have made themselves unpopular and might have done some time in jail. But later they would have gained credit for a foresight that is always more impressive than hindsight. The time to be disillusioned about an unnecessary war is before it happens.

But it is not on the note of pessimism that I should wish to end this chapter. For there is no country whose future is, or could be, brighter, even in an age of world disorder and disintegration. It has new frontiers of technological progress, of diminution of poverty, to conquer. And it has the means to conquer these frontiers in the inventive spirit and restless energy of the people, the material base in home-produced raw materials and in industrial plant and mechanically equipped agriculture.

Human and social relations in America are far from perfect, but now especially these relations could be considered almost ideal against the grim background of the rest of the world. One could search far to find a better illustration of homely everyday working social democracy than one takes for granted in many American communities, especially in the Middle West, where distribution of wealth is least uneven and people of many racial stocks have been most successfully integrated into an American pattern. Members of races which have hated and despised and oppressed and killed each other with monotonous regularity for centuries in Europe have now, in the main, forgotten these senseless feuds and merged themselves voluntarily in the community of American citizenship.

It is in the building of a new and ever better democracy at home, not in adventures abroad, that America's true mission lies. I would like to see the young men of America not dying in some Arctic waste or tropical jungle for a vague and undefined cause, but living for democracy in their own country, filling the universities and technical schools, mastering the physical and intellectual tools of every trade and profession, approximating ever more closely to the ideals of our great democratic thinkers and dreamers—of Jefferson and Tom Paine, of Lincoln and Walt Whitman.

It is the faith in an independent national destiny that America most needs today. I believe America will return to this faith, perhaps after a period of wandering in the wilderness. It is in the realization of this independent national destiny, to be realized in cooperation with like-minded nations if possible, alone if necessary, that America can best serve itself and humanity. For recent experience has shown that a nation which embarks on a crusading war is far more likely to endanger its own liberty than to implant liberty anywhere else. But the steady light that would shine from a country that was making democracy work effectively would ultimately make its way into the lands of tyranny and contribute to the downfall that has always been tyranny's fate in the past.

Chapter Fourteen

THE TOTALITARIAN CHALLENGE

BY A COMBINED PROCESS of internal revolution and military aggression the totalitarian idea has conquered almost the entire continent of Europe. First came the revolutions in Russia, in Italy, in Germany. Then came the ordeal by battle, in which the totalitarian side has so far been invariably victorious except for the Italian misadventures in Africa. Germany swallowed up Czechoslovakia, the most democratic state in Eastern Europe, in two installments, without an armed clash. It overran the small democracies of Northern and Western Europe, Norway, Denmark, the Netherlands, Belgium. It crushed France, the sole surviving large continental state with a democratic form of government.

The Soviet Union, playing jackal to Hitler's lion, took over the helpless little Baltic peasant republics. It wrested strategic territory from gallant Finland. Later the two Fascist dictators partitioned the Balkans. And now the stronger and more efficient totalitarian state, Germany, has turned on the weaker and more backward, the Soviet Union.

Meanwhile the exigencies of war have been forcing on Great Britain and its Dominions many of the financial restrictions and extensions of state control over the personal and economic life of the individual which were previously characteristic only of the totalitarian systems. This same tendency is growing in the United States.

Must one, therefore, regard the totalitarian society as something inevitable—as a "wave of the future," to use a phrase which has been much used and much abused in America? Is it logical to assume that the totalitarian technique is unavoidable, regardless of which nations emerge victorious in the war? This question of who owns the future is too large and too complex to be answered with a simple Yes or No.

When two ways of life, two social and economic systems, are in sharp conflict, the superficial view is to insist that there must be a fight to the bitter end, that one or the other must go down. The longer historical view is to anticipate that there will be a process of compromise and adjustment, that international order will absorb some features of the new system without breaking all its links with the past. The outcome of the dramatic conflict between the French Revolution and the conservative and monarchical states was certainly not a complete victory for either. And the last half of the twentieth century will quite probably witness a compound of democratic and totalitarian ideas and practices.

At the present moment, however, the totalitarian sweep represents a challenge which is both unmistakable and many-sided. There is a moral challenge. There is a politico-military challenge. And there is an economic challenge.

The moral challenge is rooted in the psychological fact, rediscovered by Communist and Fascist leaders, that man is neither so rational nor so self-controlled nor so dominated by material interests as the utilitarian moralists of the nineteenth century believed. Our contemporary revolutionaries have exploited passions and instincts which were repressed under the "bourgeois" type of civilization, the passion for violent action, the instinct for race and class solidarity, the instinct, under prompting, to make sacrifices for nonmaterial ends.

It is easy to prove that democracy, in the overwhelming majority of cases, has provided a higher and more comfortable standard of living than dictatorship. But all the facts and figures that can be marshaled in support of this proposition are not of decisive importance in measuring the strength and appeal of the totalitarian regimes.

In the first place, the German, the Italian, the Russian, is pretty effectively insulated against any knowledge of these comparisons. Even if he distrusts his own newspapers, books and magazines, he seldom possesses any positive, definite knowledge of his own to set against the flood of propaganda, favorable to the regime and disparaging to its rivals, in which he is submerged.

Moreover, and this is perhaps of still greater importance, the totalitarian systems create for their subjects a sense of function and status which is sometimes denied to the less fortunate members of a democratic society. The ruling parties and their affiliated youth organizations carry on a variety of activities which provide an outlet for the energy and sense of self-importance of their members.

In an age when unemployment and the fear of unemployment have been the curse of democratic states the ability of the totalitarian systems to provide occupation for all, or almost all, cannot be underestimated as a factor for relative contentment, even though full employment is accompanied by low real wages. Moreover, both Communist and Fascist organizers possess some of Tom Sawyer's gift of making work seem attractive. Prizes, competitions, songs, speeches, meetings, help to relieve the terrific strain of monotony in an industrial era when the old joy of craftsmanship has largely been displaced by the robot methods of mass production.

It is perhaps not sufficiently realized that the typically American ideal of giving everyone as comfortable a standard of living as possible has never been put into practice or even widely accepted intellectually in Europe. Sacrifice, austerity, deliberately hard living, may also appeal to the imagination, especially of the young.

The totalitarian movement, in both its forms of expression, has taken advantage of some of the limitations and weaknesses of classical liberalism. It is by no means a scientific law, for instance, that the sum of individual selfishness will add up to the common good.

Liberalism certainly carried within itself the seeds of its own reform. The wide development of social services in such economically individualistic countries as Great Britain and the United States cannot be ignored. But in maintaining massive enterprises designed to promote public health and recreation the totalitarian state carried out a most effective form of propaganda for itself.

The very nature of the modern industrial system places a severe strain on the sense of individual liberty which gradually gained ground in the Liberal Age. There is little sense of liberty for the mechanized human being of our time who must repeat the same motions, leading up to the same process, without variation on every working day of the year. And this is true even if wages are relatively high and hours are relatively short. Industrialism in its full-blown stage has posed problems which were undreamed of by Marx and by more orthodox economists, problems of psychology rather than of economics. And there is little sense of liberty, or of security and dignity, for the unemployed.

Liberty for certain groups and classes, even for certain peoples, may become a burden, rather than a precious possession. There is an amusing and true story of a party of German tourists who were being taken to see Niagara Falls by the representative of an American travel agency. One of the tourists got out on a dangerous rock, whereupon the guide constituted himself the *Fuehrer* of the expedition, insisting that the members of the group stay together and not stray off. The scheme was remarkably popular; the tourists marched in step, singing songs, and several of them later told the guide that this was the most enjoyable day of the excursion.

This is only a typical illustration of how the Germans enjoy order and discipline more than peoples with a larger mixture of individualism in their national character. But under the impact of war, of political and economic upheaval, of the stress and strain of industrial life, there is a strong tendency for the average man simply to renounce his faculty of individual judgment; to feel a positive sense of relief in surrendering all responsibility to those new secular gods, the Leader and the Party.

Perhaps the most powerful element in the moral challenge of the totalitarian idea is its capacity to persuade and coerce a far greater measure of sacrifice from the peoples who are subjected to its influence than free peoples will usually give except under the compulsion of a generally recognized supreme emergency. In this capacity to extract sacrifice is an implicit element of capacity, through persistent indoctrination, to instill a sense of purpose and unity which is often lacking in citizens of democratic countries.

The moral challenge of totalitarianism is not to be confused with an ethical challenge. Life under the most defective of free systems is a hundred times more civilized and humane than it is or can be under systems which authorize the darkest methods of terrorism to maintain their power. The French were leading an infinitely more sensible and desirable type of life than the Germans during the years immediately before the fall of France. Yet France fell. And one of the reasons for its fall was a German moral superiority in the sense that the Germans were psychologically better equipped for struggle and survival in the World's Iron Age.

Along with the moral challenge there is a politico-military

challenge. It is almost inevitable that our age of the airplane should render obsolete or greatly modify certain political practices which originated in the days of the railway, or even of the stagecoach.

It is not merely in deference to the memory of Mr. Kellogg, for instance, that declarations of war are now customarily omitted. Such a declaration was an act of courtesy which cost neither combatant anything in the time when war, like dancing, was slow and formal. But it is a handicap, and is consequently usually dispensed with, when days, even hours, are of the greatest strategic importance in the competitive bombing of the enemy's air bases, railway stations and other military and industrial objectives.

Amid all the fighting in Europe and in Asia during the last years one notes only two declarations of war, those of Great Britain and France against Germany in 1939. And by declaring war these two countries served notice on Germany and on the world that they had no immediate intention of waging it.

On the long historical view dictatorship has usually involved atrophy of the vital faculties of a people. The Roman Empire is the classical illustration of a vast political creation perishing from internal dry rot because a despotic government gradually assumed all the functions which had formerly been left to private individuals.

But on the short view dictatorship confers certain practical advantages in an era when events move at a speed which suggests the airplane capable of flying several hundred miles an hour. Decisions can be put into effect instantaneously, without waiting for the slow crystallization of public opinion. Indeed an independent public opinion does not exist in the totalitarian state. It is manufactured from above.

While Hitler found it advantageous to prepare the ground for some of his moves by a systematic working up of sentiment, achieved by means of sensational presentation of false or greatly exaggerated "atrocity stories," he felt able to carry out two of his most spectacular shifts of policy, the agreement with the Soviet Union in August, 1939, and the break with Russia in June, 1941, without any advance preparation of the popular mind.

The totalitarian method makes it possible to insure greater continuity of administration and to retain experts in office regardless of their popularity. As against this, of course, must be set the slackness and corruption that can develop in an administration that is not subject to control from below.

Formerly this disadvantage would probably have outweighed the advantages of more continuity of administration and greater utilization of experts. But government is becoming more functional and more specialized. In an age when politics is clearly dominating economics, in the democracies as in the dictatorships, there is more urgent need for high standards of technical efficiency for state officials. Many an American community has found its affairs more satisfactorily administered when an expert city manager has replaced an elected mayor.

It is obviously necessary to have trained experts in government service when the state is taking over so many important and complicated functions which were formerly left to private initiative, private charity or the automatic working of the gold standard. Among these functions may be mentioned management of the currency system, protection of the worker against unemployment, protection of the farmer against low prices, with regulation of foreign trade and foreign investment looming up as not unlikely features of the economy of the future.

Along with the moral challenge and the politico-military challenge, the Iron Age of the dictatorships presents an economic challenge. Two of the ends which have been attained in the totalitarian states, removal of artificial restrictions on full employment of labor and industrial plant and elimination of stoppages of production through labor disputes, are, in themselves, desirable. The means by which these ends have been realized, however, are so abominable that they more than offset the gain implied for an economic society where there is a steady flow of production without slumps and strikes.

The means are coercion of the mind and of the body, espionage, repression, indoctrination—all designed to create a robot type of personality. Any normal human being would rather live in the most slovenly home than in the neatest, most modern prison. This is why democracy at its worst is more satisfactory, in terms of human values, than dictatorship at its best.

Moreover, there is a very genuine pragmatic value in freedom. A government that is responsible to the voters, that can be called to account, is unable to commit a fraction of the outrages against human freedom and human personality that are just the normal stock in trade of a dictatorship.

But there is no reason why one should not learn from a hostile system. There is every reason why democracy, in a world where it is being violently challenged, should make every effort to put its house in order by the method of common counsel and voluntary persuasion.

We are so used to the society in which we live that we take its processes and motivations pretty much for granted. But if we could step outside certain limitations of time and space and view the business civilization of the twentieth century through the eyes of a spectator from another era or another planet, certain structural weaknesses would be very obvious.

What occurred in the United States between 1929 and 1933 is a graver indictment of the individualist order in economics than any amount of theoretical Communist or Fascist criticism. The richest, best equipped, most favorably located large country in the world experienced an attack of acute economic paralysis. There was no element of external misfortune, war, violent revolution, great natural catastrophe, to account for this immense disaster, this folding up of productive forces, which presented for so long a time the disgraceful spectacle of abject poverty in the midst of plenty, of idle men and idle plant, and no means of bringing the two together.

The dispassionate observer would instinctively feel that the happiest results for the general welfare could scarcely be anticipated in a society where it was one of the hard laws of economics to get as much as possible by giving as little as possible. He would observe that enjoyment of work for its own sake was restricted to far too small a part of the population. And he would be frankly puzzled by the frequent experiments in trying to multiply fictitious wealth in the form of money by diminishing real wealth, in the form of goods and commodities.

A searching examination of the weaknesses of what may be called a business civilization, accompanied by an equally clear perception of the intolerable evils of the practical alternatives which have been offered up to the present time, communism and fascism, brings one to the heart of the fundamental social problem of our century. This is the reconciliation of the right of man, the individual, to fullest freedom of thought and speech and expression with the right of man, as a member of society, to security against unemployment, accident, illness, destitution in old age.

We are living in a far less self-sufficient age than that of the agricultural civilization which preceded our industrial era. The demand for security has its dangers and its weaknesses. But it is both justifiable and unavoidable under an economic system where even farmers, proverbially able to "live off the land," find it more economical to buy all their clothes and much of their food.

Of the making of blueprints for a perfect society there has

been no end since Plato conceived his scheme of an ideal Republic. No philosophers and only a few rulers and revolutionaries have been able to impose with any success changes in institutions and living habits by executive fiat. Many of the most profound historical changes have been a consequence of impersonal and accidental events, such as scientific inventions which altered ways of life and habits of thought.

It is unlikely that a democratic society will ever be able to reorganize itself completely by means of thought and discussion. There will have to be an impact of external pressure. Yet the problem of adjustment to the high-speed industrial age is ever present and ever insistent.

It is conceivable that much could be done in realizing the goals of a steady, even, balanced rhythm of production and consumption and of a diminution, if not a complete cessation, of industrial strife by applying the parliamentary method in the economic sphere. Side by side with the political organs of self-government there should be national and regional economic councils, in which men and women would be represented not as citizens but as producers and consumers. In these councils delegates of trade unions, employers' associations, farmers' organizations, consumers' unions, professional associations of engineers and physicians and other technical and intellectual groups, should sit and deliberate on important questions of national economic policy.

In the beginning, to avoid confusion, these economic councils should possess only advisory powers. But any unanimous or nearly unanimous recommendations of these bodies, which should be well staffed with technical experts, would certainly carry great weight in the national and state legislatures. And the discussion and debates in these economic parliaments would have substantial educational value.

The economic councils would afford a natural forum for contact between capital and management and labor in an atmosphere less strained than that of disputes over wages and hours and working conditions. There is no more to be said, in principle, for class war than for international war. It is wasteful and impoverishing to both sides. When carried, as it was in Russia, to its extreme logical conclusion of violent revolution and expropriation of all property, it led to the clamping down on the workers of a bureaucratic dictatorship which was more ruthless and more inescapable than any system of capitalist oppression could be.

One might hope, therefore, that the establishment, within the democratic framework, of the principle of economic, occupational and professional representation would do much to cure the imperfections and solve the contradictions of a system where too often one sees only the competing pull of various forms of individual and group selfishness. When businessmen, engineers, industrial workers, farmers and representatives of other groups would meet regularly and become familiar with each other's viewpoints and problems there would be a far better chance for a coordinated effort to reach the generally beneficial goal: ever expanding production at ever lower costs.

There is still another threat of the totalitarian systems to the democracies, although its character has been modified by the constantly expanding war which tends to throw every governmental system into a gigantic testing crucible. In time of peace the dictatorship enjoys an unfair and yet unavoidable advantage over the democracy.

The totalitarian form of rule cannot be changed except by violent revolution. And in time of peace it is just about as proof against organized revolt as any type of government ever devised, thanks to its far-flung network of organized supporters and spies and its dreaded secret police, combined with the systematic suppression of any expression of critical opinion and any independent organization among its subjects. A democratic state, on the other hand, by its very nature, must permit the advocacy of theories of radical change. If it did not, it would cease to be democratic. A democracy can actually be voted out of existence, as the German experience shows.

Parties with Communist and Fascist programs can exist in democratic countries, contest election after election unsuccessfully and still continue to function. But if a single election, most probably held under circumstances of extraordinary strain and crisis, should yield a totalitarian majority democracy would be permanently lost, unless and until it should be restored by violent revolution. It would be useless to appeal to the verdict of the next election. For there would be no more free elections, only farcical plebiscites.

Every student of economics knows of Gresham's Law: that bad money will drive good money out of circulation. And there might have been a Gresham's Law of Politics; bad government might have driven out good government, simply because a democratic form of administration can be voted out of existence and a dictatorship cannot be, if the two systems had coexisted during a prolonged period of peace. But this did not occur. And now both the totalitarian and the democratic systems are being subjected to the most merciless and searching of tests, that of large-scale war.

This test has become more inclusive because of the German attack on the Soviet Union. Whatever may be the outcome of this gigantic new move on the world chessboard of war and diplomacy, it has most probably eliminated the possibility of the ending of the war which Stalin was hoping for and which would have been an irretrievable disaster for European civilization. This was an all-round collapse of social order and cohesion in an atmosphere of universal hunger, misery and despair, as the climax of a prolonged military deadlock and a futile competition in destruction from the air. Then the Soviet dictator, had he been able to remain aloof from the conflict and to keep his forces intact, could have stepped into the vacuum as the arbiter and master of

Europe's destiny. He would have won the war by staying out of it.

This possibility would now seem to be ruled out, although one cannot know with certainty what outbursts of revolutionary despair may yet occur in a Europe that has not yet drunk its cup of bitter torment to the dregs. But as from June 22, 1941, Stalinite communism has been pretty definitely eliminated as Europe's "wave of the future." It had already been deeply discredited, even in the eyes of many former apologists, by the many executions of old revolutionaries, the pact with Hitler, the unprovoked attack upon Finland.

Military defeat may be considered almost a certainty,[1] because of the great inferiority in efficiency of the Communist to the National Socialist type of dictatorship. Even though the Red Army occupied a privileged position in the Soviet political order and war industries received preferential treatment, it would be impossible to isolate the army altogether from the weaknesses of the Soviet industrial and transportation system. And military defeat time after time has been the prelude to revolution in Russia. This is why Stalin during the two years between the pact with Hitler and the invasion of Russia showed himself prepared to pay almost any price in "appeasement" to induce Hitler to stay his hand.

But Hitler, for several reasons, refused to be appeased. Stalin was not given a chance to accept or reject any demands. The German blow fell suddenly and without warning. This German–Soviet war, a struggle for the mastery of

[1]To venture the prediction that Stalin will be defeated is not to commit oneself to the broader and more debatable proposition that Hitler will win. Military victory over the Red Army will be the beginning, not the end, of Hitler's problems in Russia. Such questions as how much resistance, organized and unorganized, can still be offered, how much destruction will be wrought in evacuated territory, how successful the Germans will be in restoring and increasing industrial and agricultural production, must be answered before Hitler's Russian adventure can be pronounced a success.

Eurasia, a titanic clash of the two mastodons which had between them devoured almost every independent state on the European continent, is of such immense significance that its main implications must be discussed, even though the conflict, at the time of writing (July, 1941), is in an early stage of development.

Why did Hitler attack the Soviet Union, the power which he had immobilized at the beginning of the war and which was only too willing to remain immobilized? His move has been widely and variously interpreted, as a desperate drive for food and oil, as a confession that England could not be conquered—at least in any near future. The Fuehrer himself and his Foreign Minister, Von Ribbentrop, cited as an excuse for the invasion a series of pinpricks in Soviet–German relations, cases of Soviet overstepping of the bounds of the original agreement, subterranean intrigues in the Balkans.

There is a measure of truth in all these explanations. But the main reason why Hitler struck at Russia was perhaps too simple and too obvious to be readily recognized. The Soviet Union, or, to be more specific, the more productive regions of European Russia, Ukraina and the Caucasus, represented far and away the richest economic prize within Hitler's reach. Here, and here alone, he could hope to find the rich colonial empire, capable of being held by land and air power, which would fill out the requirements of highly industrialized Germany.

Ukraina contains iron and coal and manganese and, under efficient management, which Germany would hope to furnish, could produce a substantial surplus of almost all the staple foodstuffs, wheat and livestock and sugar beets and vegetables. The adjacent North Caucasus, which includes the fertile valleys of the Don and the Kuban, traditional home of the largest communities of Russian Cossacks, is or could be rich in herds and flocks and wheat, grapes, oil seeds and other farm products.[2] Farther to the south, in the mountainous Caucasus area between the Black and Caspian seas, are two of Russia's main sources of oil, Baku and Grozny, together with the rich manganese deposits of Chiatouri, in Georgia. The Caucasus also produces timber and molybdenum and a variety of miscellaneous products—fresh and dried fruits and nuts, for instance.

Nowhere in Europe is there a storehouse of natural wealth comparable with southern and southeastern Russia. I am convinced that this storehouse was always Hitler's basic objective; that his whole war against the West was an interlude, an unwelcome interruption in the process of empire building in the East. This viewpoint can be supported by one of the most emphatic references to foreign policy in "Mein Kampf":

"We terminate the endless German drive to the south and west of Europe and direct our gaze toward the lands of the east. We finally terminate the colonial and trade policy of the pre-war period, and proceed to the territorial policy of the future.

"But if we talk about new soil and territory in Europe today, we can think primarily only of Russia and its vassal border states."

Some individuals who insist that not a word of Hitler's can be believed are simultaneously convinced, for some reason, that every word he wrote in "Mein Kampf" is absolutely valid and authentic. But my own belief that Hitler's basic orientation is eastward, not westward, is based not so much on the authority of "Mein Kampf" as on the immutable facts of geography, economics and modern imperialism.

---

[2] The North Caucasus in 1933, as I know from personal observation, had suffered terrible desolation from the forced collectivization of agriculture in 1933. Whether and how far it has recovered is difficult to say with certainty, in view of the extreme paucity of firsthand foreign reporting of the Russian countryside in recent years.

Of what permanent benefit to Germany is the physical possession of small, highly industrialized countries like Belgium
and the Netherlands, so dependent on sea trade and colonial
empires? These empires would indeed be welcome acquisitions; but Hitler, in view of his weakness in sea power, cannot hope to anticipate Japan (or the United States) in the
Dutch East Indies. And it is still a long way to the Belgian
Congo. Even France, apart from the Lorraine iron, possesses
no natural resources which would tempt a German invasion.

Until Germany becomes a commanding naval power (and
this may well be a matter of many years) its interests are
bound to lie in the direction of land expansion. And the only
theater of land expansion large enough and rich enough to be
worth a major war is Russia.

There is another consideration that points in the same direction. Hitler, one of the chief architects of the Iron Age,
has the strongest reasons for doubting whether the old system of far-flung international trade and investment, based on
the gold standard or at least on some common denominator
of commercial confidence, will ever be restored. Even in the
event of peace Germany's supply of overseas foodstuffs and
raw materials would always be precarious. Consequently the
German leader must have felt that it was a matter of vital
national self-interest to possess under the direct control of
the German Army and Air Force a reservoir of supply which
did not depend on control of the seas.

After the beginning of the war I expressed the opinion in
my book "The Confessions of an Individualist" that France
and England could easily have canalized Hitler in an eastward direction. Some critics took issue with me on this point
and pointed to the Soviet–German Pact as proof that Hitler
had no intention or desire to attack Russia. The more recent
turn of events, I think, bears out my own belief that Hitler's
basic interest is in overland expansion to the East.

Another significant element in Hitler's decision was his desire to put some ideological cement into a union of Europe which had hitherto been entirely a product of German military force and threat of force. Three countries, Finland, Hungary and Rumania, were induced to take part in the war and a movement to recruit volunteers for the crusade against communism was launched in France, in Spain and in other lands. The military value of such volunteer contingents would be negligible.

But Hitler reckons with the possibility that anticommunism may prove an attractive slogan to conservatives throughout Europe and may diminish the antagonism aroused by German methods of rule. It remains to be seen whether this reckoning will be justified by events.

One of the paradoxes of this war is that Hitler has mustered at least a semblance of international support, while the Soviet Union, always inclined to boast of the supposed sympathies of the working classes of other countries, has been left to its own resources. Indeed Soviet appeals have been significantly phrased largely in terms of Russian nationalism. There have been notably few references to world revolution or even to the achievements of the Russian Revolution. Perhaps it would be too much of a mockery to call on the peasants, reduced to a status of state serfdom and mercilessly exploited under the new agricultural system, to defend "their" collective farms.

The German–Soviet conflict is the greatest single war in history, if measured by the number of men and of modern weapons engaged, by the vast extent of the field of hostilities and by the size of the stakes involved. If one keeps in mind that the Soviet Union is the largest land area under a single sovereignty in the world, with the most numerous predominantly white population,[3] that it covers between one

---

[3] The population of the Soviet Union within its original frontiers was about 170,000,000. Between fifteen and twenty million people were annexed in the Baltic states, eastern Poland, Bessarabia and Bukovina. But these regions were quickly lost before the German advance.

seventh and one sixth of the surface of the globe, that it is about forty times the size of France, the magnitude of the struggle and the size of the stakes for which Hitler is playing become evident.

After the first ten days of fighting the German advance at many points had reached a depth of two hundred miles. A similar advance in France would have brought the Germans to Paris. A second advance of equal length would have implied the total defeat of France. But after the preliminary rush the Germans had not reached any major Soviet industrial center. And the Red Army could retreat a thousand miles and, if it retained cohesion and fighting spirit, still have a vast hinterland and a number of industrial centers in its rear.

One aspect of the war is almost certain to be a bitter struggle of trained, experienced "fifth columns." Jan Valtin, the German ex-Communist who has described so vividly his career as an underground Communist agitator and his maltreatment at the hands of the Gestapo and the GPU, speaks with unusual authority on the character of these opposing armies of secret agents. The Germans, as one might expect, according to Valtin, possess the qualities of order, system and thoroughness. But the Russians have the advantages of longer experience in illegal work and of being able to draw on a more cosmopolitan group of spies and saboteurs. Practically all the reliable Gestapo agents are of German origin.

In Germany itself and in the German-occupied countries there is a Soviet fifth column, consisting partly of secret agents from Moscow, partly of local Communists. The chief mission of this fifth column will undoubtedly be to stir up all possible trouble in the rear; to play on every anti-Nazi feeling, from the orthodox Marxism of the French or Belgian industrial worker to the Pan-Slav sentiments of the Bulgarian and Yugoslav peasant; to commit as many acts of sabotage as possible.

Germany has its fifth column, partly conscious and partly unconscious, behind the Soviet lines. Along with such German spies and outright sympathizers as have escaped the wide dragnet of the Soviet political police there is a number, difficult to estimate accurately, of Soviet citizens who are so embittered by the ruthless policies of the existing regime that they would do anything in their power to promote its downfall.

Just as there have never been so many tanks and airplanes engaged in conflict, so there has never been such a fierce, desperate, merciless battle of wits, where the penalty of failure is usually death, as went on behind the German and Soviet lines. To one who, like the writer, has lived for many years in the Soviet Union there is a tremendous fascination about the war, because it will almost certainly soon reveal the authoritative answers to many questions which could never have been answered with finality and certainty if Stalin's regime had not been subjected to the ordeal of a large-scale war.

In Russia, as in every dictatorship, it is quite impossible to know, except in the case of a few intimate friends (and it is highly unsafe to be known as the friend or associate of a foreigner), how many people go through the prescribed motions of loyalty to the system with enthusiasm, how many with bored indifference and how many purely out of fear and with hatred and bitterness in their hearts.

But masks fall off under the stress of unsuccessful war. In the confusion and breakup of a retreat there is little possibility of compelling the population to carry on guerrilla war, to resist on their own initiative. The first honest election or plebiscite to be held under Soviet rule will be the experience of Ukraina or any large region which may fall under German military occupation. If there is passionate resistance by the local population, motivated by the desire to restore the fallen Soviets, this will be more impressive than any of the

99 per cent majorities registered in Soviet "elections," where there was only one list of candidates to be voted for. If there is apathetic acceptance of the change, even some willing cooperation with the invaders, this will be a negative verdict on the Communist dictatorship.

I doubt whether Stalin will be vindicated by the great assize of history which he must now face. When I read his appeal to "comrades, citizens, brothers and sisters" I thought of the millions (the figure is sober truth, not rhetorical exaggeration) of ghosts of his victims who might rise and respond in mocking derision. I thought of the villages of Ukraina and the North Caucasus, decimated by the state-organized famine of 1932–33. I thought of the freight cars packed with wretched kulaks and their wives and children and old men, driven from their homes and dispatched, many of them, to cruel lingering deaths in the serf labor concentration camps of North Russia and Siberia. I thought of the many eminent Russian intellectuals who were broken on the wheel of fraudulent sabotage trials. If Stalin's victims could rise from the dead and march in close order through Moscow's spacious Red Square it would be several days before the ghostly procession would come to an end.

It has been one of Stalin's whims to pose as a lover of Shakespeare. "Macbeth" would have been suitable reading for him after the German invasion put his regime to the supreme test. How many Banquos, old comrades whom he had murdered, would rise up accusingly before his eyes: Trotsky, Zinoviev, Kamenev, Rykov, Bukharin, Tomsky, Karakhan, Yenukidze—but here again the list is almost endless.

It seems doubtful whether a regime which has committed so many acts of ruthless cruelty against its own people could survive a severe military defeat. Disaffection on the Right and on the Left was an important cause of the fall of France. And no Frenchman had a fraction of the reason to hate the

Third Republic that large numbers of Russians, Ukrainians and members of other national minorities have to hate the Soviet regime. The French Republic never "liquidated" whole classes, never created famine conditions, never rounded up enormous numbers of people for forced labor in concentration camps.

Yet I am frankly conscious of the need for a certain diffidence in predicting Russian psychological reactions. There is always, for the foreign observer, the danger of seeing Russia and the Russians too much "under Western eyes," to borrow the title of Joseph Conrad's interesting novel about Russian revolutionaries. It may be that there is something Asiatic, atavistic, masochistic, about the Russian character that instinctively rebels against mild humane liberalism, that is not only subdued but captivated by extreme forms of brutality. It may be that Russians will not react to extremely cruel forms of tyranny as one would expect a Western people to react, if it were given the opportunity. Under the shock of a great defeat almost anything might happen in Russia. There might be an upsurge of nationalist feeling. There might be a terrific explosion of long suppressed thirst for revenge that would tear the vast country to pieces.

Stalin's regime is not identical with Russia. And there is a possibility, the most hopeful, perhaps, for Russia and for the whole world, that the war will prove fatal to Stalin's personal dictatorship and to many aspects of communism, but not to the national existence of the Russian people. It may be that there are healthy nationalist forces, in the Red Army and in the Soviet administrative system, waiting to be released by the explosive force of this foreign invasion. After a period of initial defeats had thoroughly discredited the existing regime these forces might prove strong enough to sweep away Stalin, to abolish the modern equivalents of serfdom which exist in Soviet farm and factory, to tear down the barbed wire around the many grim and forbidding concentration camps and to rally the whole Russian people for a true war of liberation, directed equally against Stalin's GPU and Hitler's Gestapo.

It is hard for even the strongest advocate of war to the bitter end against Hitler to regard Stalin as a desirable or trustworthy ally. In the light of the experience of the last two years there can be no guaranty that the Soviet dictator, if he were given the opportunity, would not make a peace of surrender and assume the role of a *Gauleiter*, carrying out Hitler's orders.

But free peoples everywhere would feel a warm upsurge of sympathy with a genuine Russian peoples' struggle against German conquest and oppression, a struggle which had nothing to do with the sinister fantasy of world revolution or with a new crucifixion of Russia on the cross of the obsolete and fallacious dogmas of Marx. The essential prerequisites of any such popular struggle would be the liquidation (to use the favorite Communist term) of Stalin and his coterie and the transformation of the collective farms into voluntary peasant cooperatives, from which peasants who preferred individual methods of farming should be free to withdraw.

There are three broad perspectives for the outcome of the new great war which has begun in Russia. By far the least likely of these, except perhaps to Mr. Bernard Shaw and the Dean of Canterbury, is a Soviet military victory. Such a victory would be little short of a miracle. It would run counter to every ascertainable fact about the comparative military and industrial strength of the two combatants. It would also transform immediately and sensationally the whole atmosphere of international politics. It would let loose the fiercest kind of civil war all over Europe. It would signify the end of Hitler. And England, incredible as the prospect may seem at the moment, might find itself in the position of aiding whatever conservative forces might emerge from the Nazi wreckage in Germany to dam the tide of triumphant bolshevism.

Much more plausible, although by no means completely certain, is the perspective of a complete victory for Hitler. Suppose that every doubt about the course of this Soviet–German war resolves itself in Germany's favor. Assume that the better trained and better equipped units of the Red Army, after a few months of hard fighting, are smashed to pieces. Suppose that the Russians, Ukrainians and other peoples of the Soviet Union are too apathetic, too depressed by Stalin's own technique of tyranny, to offer much effective resistance in the form of guerrilla warfare or sabotage.

Hitler would then have made a very profitable political and military investment. He would possess, along with the man power and industrial plant of Western and Central Europe, new and rich reserves of many of the most essential foodstuffs and raw materials, so located as to be almost inaccessible to bombing attack. With the German legions established in the Caucasus, Hitler would possess a new base from which to launch military and propaganda offensives against the British position in the Near and Middle East. Should his conquest extend to Soviet Central Asia he could threaten India.

The German dictator would be in an advantageous position either to offer peace, perhaps on the basis of an evacuation of Western Europe in return for a free hand in the East, or to prosecute the war against Great Britain in the Isles, in Africa and in Asia more relentlessly than ever. Should his sway extend, through the medium of puppet governments, all the way across Siberia he would be in a position to intervene in the affairs of Japan and China. Most definitely he would have escaped from the prison of his European conquests, in which the British blockade has sought to contain him.

It would be doubtful whether Great Britain and the United States together could muster enough land and air power to break this huge Eurasian empire, this "Union Now" of the totalitarian mastodons under the hegemony of the stronger. At the same time sea power would preserve America and the outlying parts of the British Empire from any serious danger of attack.

There is a third possible outcome of the war, less improbable than the first, less spectacularly decisive than the second. This would be a protracted struggle, following the general outline of the Sino–Japanese War. Germany would win the big battles, occupy many large towns and considerable stretches of territory. But some kind of front would continue to exist, perhaps in the Urals or even farther to the East. A Soviet Government, or a new Russian nationalist government, would remain in being. The countryside would be laid waste before the armies of occupation. Oil wells and industrial plants would be damaged and destroyed. Guerrilla war would be waged in the occupied regions.

Should such a situation arise and be maintained indefinitely, Hitler's victory would not be worth its price. His empire would begin to bleed to death, as Napoleon's bled to death in Spain and in Russia. It seems doubtful whether England possesses the man power and material to initiate a two front war in 1941. By 1942, however, if a Russian army was still in the field, this nightmare of German strategists might become a reality.

Whatever may be its outcome, the German–Soviet war certainly represents a most important turn of the wheel of history. It opens up probabilities of vast new changes, in Asia as in Europe. For Japan will scarcely remain aloof if there should be a Soviet collapse. This, in turn, may seriously affect the policy and strategy of the United States.

The cycle of war and violent revolution, each promoting the other, advances further. The two hardest, most ruthless and most powerful regimes which have emerged in the Iron Age are now themselves being subjected to the supreme ordeal of total war. One of them almost certainly, both of them possibly, will break under the strain. Then the question will become insistent: What can replace the gigantic vacuum which the totalitarian power machine creates around itself? *Note*

Chapter Fifteen

TOWARD A NEW CIVILIZATION?

FEW OBSERVERS POSSESS the prophetic vision and the sense of balance and proportion which are necessary if one is to write of the present in terms which will prove acceptable to the future. Most of the books and essays which are written in the heat of epochs of violence are valuable only as psychological curiosities for the next generation. One must always guard against exaggerating the evils of one's own time.

Yet it seems reasonable, in view of the extraordinary series of wars and revolutions, of violence and disorder, which our generation has seen, to suggest that Western modern civilization is experiencing its third major crisis. The first of these crises was reflected in the Protestant Reformation and in the series of wars and internal upheavals which are more or less directly associated with this movement. Many of these wars and upheavals had little to do with religion; their causes were dynastic, national, economic. But in a Europe that had just emerged from the Middle Ages, where religion was such an overmastering preoccupation of the mind and the soul, it was natural that most actions should outwardly assume a religious motivation.

The second crisis was heralded by the French Revolution

and the Napoleonic Wars. Then, as now, it seemed that the very bases of society were crumbling. The accepted political and social and economic forms, absolute monarchy, feudalism, some aspects of private property, were challenged. Old thrones were falling. Historic boundary lines were being changed overnight.

When the fury of Napoleon's career of conquest was spent the groundwork had been laid for the Liberal Age. The nineteenth century was not without its wars and revolutions. But the former were not of a devastating character and the latter did not tear up established human relations by the roots. The revolutions were political and national, rather than social, in character. They took comparatively few victims.

It seems easy, in retrospect, to identify the two previous crises of civilization with the new ideas and new ways of living which began with the Reformation and the French Revolution. But in the troubled times of that most destructive of religious conflicts, the Thirty Years' War, or during the era of Napoleon's lightning campaigns, it must have been extremely difficult for the most intelligent observer to discern with any sureness the trend of the time.

And it would still perhaps be premature to define too narrowly and too dogmatically the causes and issues of the great crisis of our own times. That it is a major crisis, more serious probably than its two predecessors, is not open to doubt. For the epoch between 1914 and the still unknown date when the forces of destructive change will have spent themselves and peace of some kind will return has been packed with violence of the most spectacular kind, the violence of war, the violence of social revolution.

An outstanding cause of all this turmoil has certainly been man's inability to adjust himself to a mechanical age. There is an unmistakable correspondence in rhythm between the greatest wars and the fastest means of communication, between rapid changes in thought and habits and sweeping social revolution.

Moreover, there has been a grave and portentous schism between the growth of man's moral stature and the multiplication of the means of power, and hence of destruction, which science has placed at his disposition. There has been no ethical advance to keep pace with the march, or rather with the rush, of science and invention.

A future historian may regard it as one of the most disheartening features of our age that so many people bore stoically the immense and essentially futile sacrifices of war, while there was little inclination to make the far slighter sacrifices, in abatement of national sovereignty, in economic concessions, which would have made for peace. Right ends have seldom enlisted a fraction of the fanatical energy and devotion that have been enlisted for wrong ends.

Quite apart from the complex political and economic factors which lead to war and revolution there is a self-generating, self-perpetuating, self-aggravating quality about the familiar moods and passions with which every observer of a country at war or in revolution becomes familiar: hatred, vindictiveness, intolerance, irrationality, suspicion, hysteria, fear that is so exaggerated as to carry a suggestion of paranoia.[1] It is quite probable that much of the history of the last three decades can be written accurately only by experts in abnormal psychology. Perhaps, indeed, it is a question, in an age of turmoil, as to what may be considered normal and what abnormal. For war and revolution produce states of mass exaltation, mass hatred, mass suspicion and mass credulity which would be characteristic only of psychically deranged individuals in more tranquil periods.

---

[1] A woman in a New England community became convinced that German agents were going about poisoning wells and was vastly crestfallen when a young man who asked to inspect her well, and whom she subtly detained for investigation, proved to be an employee of the municipal water department.

One can trace a fairly consistent pattern of interpretation of the cycle of war and revolution in terms of political and economic causality. But there are points in which the pattern fails to satisfy, where one feels that the explanation is rooted in the deep-seated and perhaps ineradicable wickedness of man.

The Russian physiologist Pavlov, who hated and despised the Soviet regime, even though it lavishly subsidized his experimental work in the field of conditional reflexes, once privately expressed the hope that the human race could be scientifically immunized against what he called "wars, revolutions and other bestialities." But no such quarantine has yet proved feasible. Man has learned to protect himself against wild beasts, against typhus and smallpox and bubonic plague. But he has not yet learned how to protect himself against man.

That profound and brilliant devil-worshiper and extoller of the darker passions Friedrich Nietzsche, one of the prophets of the decline of the Liberal Age, expressed the belief that "severity, violence, slavery, danger in the street and in the heart, everything wicked, terrible, tyrannical, predatory and serpentine in man, serves as well for the elevation of the human species as its opposite."

However one may define "the elevation of the human species," it seems certain that much that is "wicked, terrible, tyrannical, predatory and serpentine" is deeply imbedded in human character. The crust of humane civilization is very thin. Periodic explosions of war and revolution are perhaps an inevitable discharge of the evil passions which are more or less repressed in periods of calm and order. The future may demonstrate that the deep disease, the positive disintegration, which has eaten so far into the body of civilization is moral and psychological, rather than political and economic.

This suggestion may open up a new approach to the problem of how the crisis is to be resolved. A marked feature of

American thinking during the period when the country was slipping closer and closer to actual belligerence was a demand for books, essays, lectures, dealing with the problems of the future, with blueprints for a new world organization. One could understand this curiosity and sympathize with the desire to plan for a better future.

Yet there is something very hollow about all paper schemes for international cooperation unless there is an underlying common denominator of accepted moral standards. This is why the emergence of communism and fascism as dominant creeds over large areas of Europe and Asia portends such a serious schism in the unity of civilization.

It is certainly a striking paradox that, just when air communication was making physical contact between the most distant continents constantly easier and simpler, political and economic and ideological conflicts were more and more dividing the world into several more or less clearly marked compartments. Until the German invasion the Eurasian Soviet Union had been almost hermetically sealed against foreigners. There were large cities in this vast realm where a foreigner would be as rare as in Kabul or Timbuctoo.

The simplest transactions between America and Europe, the remittance of money, the exchange of letters, have become extremely difficult. I know the typical case of a Russian woman in America who has completely lost touch both with her father in Russia and with her relatives in France. It would be dangerous for the father in Russia to receive letters from abroad. The relatives in France have been lost in the general dislocation and confusion.

If some of the deepest roots of the crisis are moral a spiritual solution would seem to be required. But one looks in vain for the source of the saving word. The churches march closely in step with the state and go to war, apart from individual pacifists and objectors, when the state goes to war.

It is perhaps inevitable in modern times that churches

should become more or less identified in outlook with the general body of their parishioners and with the citizens of their countries. Yet this tendency goes far to deprive them of any role of leadership, of the sort of independent authority which the medieval Church claimed and exercised, sometimes for good, sometimes for evil.

Will there be perhaps a spectacular turn toward an old or a new faith after the peoples are sickened of the slaughter and destruction which an age that has worshiped material gods has endured? This is one of the many great incalculables of the future. But without some spiritual change, either in the wider acceptance of some supernatural faith or in a revival of the spirit of intellectual liberalism, with its qualities of humanism, skepticism and tolerance, there can be no unity and little vitality in modern civilization.

The tremendous agony of our time should inspire the most searching examination of the values of the Liberal Age. Where did civilization miss its road of further progress? What was so far amiss in the predominantly liberal social and economic order that prevailed before 1914 as to provoke the ferocious, far-flung revolt against civilization of which we are the horrified spectators?

It is easy, in the retrospect of history, to understand the causes of the schism in the Catholic Church. One can appreciate the appeal of the French Revolution, the desire of the common man to rid himself of the curbs imposed by absolutism and feudalism. But a revolt against liberalism, a revolt against freedom itself? It is hard for those who have been bred in a liberal tradition to conceive, much less to understand, such a phenomenon. And yet it is here, before our eyes.

It should not be forgotten that democracy, the theory that every man should have a voice in the conduct of public affairs, is a new and experimental proposition. And liberty, as indispensable as air to some individuals, conveys to others a sense of unwanted strain and responsibility. Some Germans felt as if the doors of a prison had closed on them when Hitler came into power. But there were others, apart from active Nazi partisans, who breathed a sigh of relief when the difficult necessity of choosing between a score of wrangling parties in the Reichstag was taken away from them and they were assigned a definite place in the new regimented order and told authoritatively what to do.

Liberty, if not balanced by discipline, whether imposed from within or from without, carries seeds of disintegration, for individuals as for nations. A foreign observer of long experience in France once said to me:

"One finds the best types of Frenchmen in the Church and in the Army. The French mind is so quick, so agile, so versatile, that the Frenchman without some profession that gives him orders, in some sense, that places him under definite responsibilities, is apt to become a dilettante, an intellectual Jack-of-all-trades."

When one considers the apparent contradiction in terms of the phrase "revolt against liberty" one must consider that human destinies are often shaped by impersonal and often uncontrollable forces. It is hard to see how any conscious effort could have prevented or greatly modified the shift from an agricultural to an industrial basis of economy in the larger countries and the consequent growth of the cities at the expense of the country.

Yet this shift, combined with the mechanization of agriculture and the trend toward larger units of farm production, weakened one of the surest foundations of a stable democracy: a large class of independent farm proprietors. All over the world, under every form of government, the increasing complexity of economic life has led to steady extensions of governmental subsidies, governmental controls and bureaucracy. *Laissez-faire* economic liberalism gradually became as extinct as the dinosaur, even in countries where there were no uprooting revolutions.

Power has become more centralized, not more diffused, irrespective of the system of government. The coming of a type of warfare in which comparatively small elite groups of aviators and of operators of mechanized units, not masses of infantry, are of primary importance has also strengthened the possibilities of dictatorship at home and abroad.

The all-questioning liberalism of the nineteenth century possessed its element of self-destruction. When reason became the supreme authority it questioned all values and ended, naturally enough, by doubting and denying reason itself. An attentive observer of the European scene toward the end of the nineteenth century would have recognized the first flashes of a coming storm not only in mounting armament expenditures and the scramble for colonies but in the antirationalist reaction symbolized in such thinkers as Nietzsche and Sorel. Man was apparently too restless, violent and predatory a being to remain pent up indefinitely within the confines of a rationalist world.

It is perhaps a historical anachronism to speak of the fall of the Roman Empire. Fall implies a sudden crash. It is doubtful whether the population of the empire could have recognized the precise date when it ceased to exist, because what happened was a process of disintegration which continued for centuries.

And it is doubtful whether most Americans realize the extent of the fall of liberal civilization in Europe, the thorough sweep of old standards and values. The process has been most complete in Russia, where the two formerly opposed worlds of the Imperial officialdom and of the liberal and radical intelligentsia experienced a common ruin.

A similar collapse in a milder way, on a milder scale and for a different reason, foreign conquest rather than internal revolution, took place in France in 1940. In the bedlam of confusion at Bordeaux, where all Paris seemed to have crowded into the old provincial town, with its huge statue of the

Girondins, one stumbled on prominent businessmen, politicians of all groupings, Socialists and trade union leaders, members of opposed camps before the war, now involved in an all-embracing disaster.

The years before 1914, when capitalism was taken for granted in economic life, when government budgets were regarded as something to be balanced, when the convertibility of paper money into gold was no more questioned than the Ten Commandments, seem much farther off in spirit than in actual time. The old disputes between capitalism and socialism seem quite obsolete. For the totalitarian wave has washed away both the old-fashioned capitalism and the old-fashioned socialism and in their place has come an economy which is an amalgam of both.

What is perhaps most characteristic of our age is the loss of the sense of measure, of restraint. Here the influence of ever changing wonders of scientific technique can be felt in politics. Sovereigns formerly schemed for decades in order to round out their frontiers by the addition of a province. Now it seems to require less effort to subdue a continent. It is a period when the impossible becomes the commonplace, when the supernatural becomes the normal.

Cultures are no longer permitted to die slow, lingering deaths. They are cut off with the merciless speed of a shock of electric current, whether by revolution or by war. The barbarians had more respect for the traditional majesty of Rome than the Communists, with their long list of demolished churches and monasteries, showed for these landmarks of the old Russian civilization. And the youth of Russia, of Germany, of Italy, offer many examples of how energetic indoctrination with a new credo can obliterate old moral and intellectual patterns.

We live in a time when a fantastic mind might imagine that the earth is revolving around its axis more rapidly than nature prescribes. The ends of many beginnings are written large before our eyes. Many cycles have run their course.

The access of individual freedom, for instance, during the nineteenth century, the shedding of the restrictions which feudalism and mercantilism imposed on production, made possible an unprecedented accretion of wealth, at least for limited classes of individuals. This accumulated wealth facilitated the progress of invention and the spread of technical and general education. But the very fertility of invention, the greater wealth of all states, generated an antithetical process. More destructive and more exhausting wars were made possible. War became more destructive because it was constantly waged with more ingenious and more powerful weapons. It became more exhausting because the modern state and the modern economy lend themselves to total mobilization for military purposes. So both freedom and wealth melted away as a result of wars and social revolutions.

Nationalism reached its ultimate absurdity in autarchy, in an attempted self-sufficiency which inevitably led to impoverishment and hardship. But this very excess of nationalism led to an attempt to break down the restricting barriers of independent state sovereignties, to the creation by force of the larger economic units which fit in with modern production needs but which had not been established by voluntary agreement.

The principle of the competing national state, pushed to its uttermost limit, ended in a trampling on the rights of nationality on an unprecedented scale. The reaction against the self-determination which led to such a multiplication of European frontiers after the first World War took the form of conquest and a unification of Europe by violence.

The restless urge for profit caused European businessmen to part with many of the secrets of Europe's industrial hegemony to the peoples of Asia and Africa. The sequel has been a formidable industrialization, based on extremely low labor costs, of Japan, and it is only a question of time until a similar process will be realized in China and in India. Then the whole material basis of Europe's position of privileged superiority will be seriously undermined.

The world has seldom been so uprooted, so far cut adrift from customary moorings. Beneath the surface turmoil a sensitive intelligence could perhaps detect a spirit of groping for adjustment to an uncertain present and an unknown future. There has been a break in the continuity of the old civilization. Of this there can be no doubt. And the break will become more and more irreparable with every additional year of war and with the social upheavals which will follow the war, unless all historical precedents are upset.

Are we on the threshold of a Great Chaos or of a new civilization? Europe's downward slide from a state of relative order, prosperity and security for individuals and for nations between 1930 and 1940 was one of the swiftest than can be recalled. But there have been historical illustrations of capacity to recover fairly quickly from a low ebb of decline. Both the Roman and the Byzantine empires knew such periods of recovery and it was not so long after the conclusion of the Hundred Years' War, one of the dreariest, bleakest and apparently most hopeless in French history, that France experienced the first glow of Renaissance literature, architecture and thought.

The human race has great powers of adaptation, survival and regeneration and one should not take the present agony of Western civilization as necessarily the beginning of a new Dark Age. During each of the two previous crises of civilization there were moments when some of the most thoughtful observers must have been tempted to cry havoc and yield to despair. Yet from each of these troubled times Europe emerged with a broadened base for cultural life and material progress.

It may turn out that some of the methods which have been

horribly perverted to achieve bad ends may ease the way to the attainment of good ends. The method of universal state planning, tried out under the Soviet dictatorship, proved a ghastly bureaucratic fiasco, a producer not of abundance but of innumerable shortages and dislocations.

Yet planning (democratically controlled from below, for without this qualification it is certain to turn into dangerous tyranny) may be the key that will unlock new doors of technological progress. The war and semiwar controls which exist in every large country in the world, regardless of political and economic systems, will prove easier to establish than to dispense with.

National socialism in Germany achieved a transition from vast unemployment and much unused plant to labor scarcity and maximum utilization of existing industrial resources. This was done for a thoroughly evil purpose, the preparation of a war which has brought inestimable suffering to the European continent. But the technique, financial and economic, of realizing this maximum production should be carefully studied. Some features of it might prove serviceable for the realization of the economic ideal of every democratic society: steady, expanding production without hectic booms and disastrous slumps.

The dictatorships have subjected human character to a cruel ordeal. Often in Russia and in Germany it has required the highest kind of moral and physical courage not to be a scoundrel, not to turn informer, not to bear false witness.[2]

---

[2] The following anecdote illustrates the Russian popular judgment of the credibility of the confessions which are a feature of every Soviet public political trial. A GPU official meets a professor of music who complains that none of his students could identify the author of Tschaikovsky's well-known opera "Eugene Onyegin."

"That looks like counterrevolution and sabotage, professor; just leave the matter to us." And two weeks later the exultant GPU official reports to the professor: "We arrested all the members of that class and, after we put them through a few examinations, we got signed confessions from six of them that they had written 'Eugene Onyegin' themselves."

The flesh has naturally often been weak, but there have been some splendid victories of the spirit. When one thinks of what some of the more devoted victims in the prisons and concentration camps of the GPU and the Gestapo have endured, the lack of moral backbone of those who, in democratic countries, surrender the expression of their honest convictions to fear of unpopularity or loss of social prestige or business advantage appears in a very unfavorable light.

Hitler has united a large part of Europe by the brutal and indefensible method of conquest. But it is conceivable, although not certain, that experience under this forced unification may reveal many economic advantages and may pave the way for the ultimate realization of the dream of many great Europeans: a voluntary Pan-European federation.

Black as the European prospect is today, it is hard to believe that the glorious old continent, built out of the dust of many past civilizations, is without a future. What man has achieved once man must be able to achieve again, and to surpass. If in the dark days of the present and the still darker days which may lie ahead European culture may seem dead, there are many voices that will surely call to renaissance, to resurrection. There is the Germany of Beethoven's Ninth Symphony and Goethe's "Faust." There is the France of the great mystics and the great skeptics, of Chartres and Notre Dame, of Voltaire and Anatole France, of Pascal's God-seeking and Montaigne's soft pillow of eternal doubt.

One cannot, however, be blind to the fact that many circumstances are working against the liberty of the individual which was so widely realized in the last century. In retrospect one must recognize that the Liberal Age was an exceptional era in the freedom which it assured to the ordinary man to live and travel and spend money and speak and write as he pleased. It intervened between a period when the common man was inarticulate and conscious thought was largely restricted to a small well-to-do educated class and the present Iron Age, when the common man is articulate enough, sometimes too articulate, but when he has fallen into the grip of a new streamlined type of tyranny, working through mass propaganda and indoctrination. The impact of Europe's Iron Age has already robbed Americans of their traditional freedom from military conscription, of their right to travel freely, and other losses of liberty will not be slow in following.

The effect of war on democracy has been much debated. The two extreme viewpoints are that war inevitably destroys democracy and that war exerts a strengthening and invigorating influence when it is waged for a democratic cause.

There have been many wars with many aftermaths and no oversimplified formula will cover the problem. Much depends on the character and political traditions of the people engaged in war, on the outcome of the conflict and on the circumstances in which it originated. Wars have been fought for an infinite variety of real and ostensible causes, for religion, for trade, for empire, for defense against invasion, for territorial gain, for ideological slogans, for racial hates.

There has been more freedom of criticism during the American Civil War and in England during the present war than there is in a totalitarian state in time of peace. Here the influence of Anglo–Saxon political habits is obvious.

On the other hand, the American record in maintaining democracy and civil liberties at home while it was crusading, ostensibly for these ideals, abroad in 1917–18 was not a good one. There was a considerable number of cases of mob violence, winked at if not instigated by the authorities. Lynchings of Negroes increased and there were never so many cases of illegal repression of radical labor groups as during the war and its immediate aftermath. The Socialist leader, Eugene V. Debs, received a sentence of ten years in prison for saying no more about a war which was being fought three thousand miles away than many critics of Abraham Lincoln said with impunity about a war which was being fought on American soil.

Another consideration comes into play in this connection. A war that is not generally recognized by the great majority of the people as unavoidable in the cause of national self-preservation will require more terrorism, official and unofficial, to keep the people in line than a war which is regarded as a struggle for elementary self-preservation.

It is interesting to compare the recent experiences of France and Great Britain. The French people, despite all the drums of propaganda, went to war reluctantly and unwillingly. They did not want to die for Danzig or for Poland, or for anything except the preservation of France's own frontiers. From the beginning the police were rounding up persons accused of antiwar agitation and the courts were imposing severe sentences. But all this had no constructive effect on morale, which remained low and collapsed completely under the shock of the great German offensive.

In Great Britain, especially after the fall of France made the peril seem so much more imminent and more real, there was no serious popular opposition to the war. Arrests were few and a very fair measure of civil liberty was maintained. A people with a collective sense of fighting for its life does not require drastic measures of repression to compel it to put forward its full effort. It is in the psychological condition of a community that is fighting a flood or a forest fire. To this proposition one exception must be taken. Real national unity presupposes a reasonable measure of trust and good feeling between the classes within the nation. Ruthless terrorism is a familiar accompaniment of wars after violent revolutions, when the party in power fears its disaffected fellow citizens more than it fears the foreign enemy.

Revolution is more likely to follow defeat than victory. War in any case imposes heavy losses in human lives and in property. Even victorious countries emerge poorer in substance and confronted with the serious problem of returning millions of soldiers and munitions workers to normal employment. The mere sense of being victorious, however, exerts some stabilizing influence.

The defeated country bears a heavier burden of losses, aggravated and often made intolerable by the consciousness that all its sufferings and sacrifices were in vain. So the psychological stage is set for violent upheaval. All the defeated countries in the first World War experienced revolutions, although in Germany the fundamental upheaval which grew out of the war took place almost fifteen years after the Armistice.

Victory, however, is no certain guaranty against subsequent political convulsions. Italy sat in at the Peace Conference in 1919 as one of the victorious powers. But the strain of a war which was unpopular from the beginning with large numbers of Italians was too severe to be shaken off. Italy fell into a condition of chronic disorder which ended in the triumph of fascism. Italian liberals who pressed for Italian involvement in the war on the theory that this would strengthen democracy and liberalism in Italy had little reason to be satisfied with the results of their handiwork.

Russia would have been on the winning side if it had held out until the end in the first World War. But in Russia, even more than in Italy, the strain of modern war on a relatively backward political, economic and social system was too great to be borne. Russia collapsed. There were Russian liberals and moderate Socialists who supported the war policy of the Tsarist Government in the hope that Russia would become more progressive through its association with the Western democracies. This hope was not realized. The result of the war, for Russia, was a break in the continuity of its cultural development, the blotting out of the thin overlay of Western liberalism in the country.

So, while defeat in war is obviously more conducive to

violent change than is victory, such considerations as the amount of social and economic dislocation which war involves and the degree of wholehearted acceptance of the conflict by the masses of the people are also of great importance. There is no factual basis for the statement that war positively strengthens democracy. Great Britain, France and the United States were all democracies and were victorious in the first World War. But an ardent militant faith in democracy was certainly not characteristic of any of these countries during the interval between the wars.

The rather loose assertion that war never settles anything is perhaps rather too easy a strawman to knock down. There have unquestionably been issues that have been settled by the instrumentality of war. The independence of the United States and the abolition of slavery are cases in point.

At the same time war often "settles" a good deal more than its promoters either foresee or desire. When Woodrow Wilson led America into the first World War he certainly did not anticipate, much less desire, that communism and fascism would dominate large parts of the postwar world. War is an extremely unreliable weapon and often acts as a boomerang when it is employed not for direct national defense, not for some specific territorial acquisition, but for some vague dream of determining the complex, changing and elastic pattern of international affairs.

In trying to answer the question "Toward a New Civilization?" one cannot overlook the possibility that several types of civilization may be in the making. For the dissolution of normal contact between the various continents has been a conspicuous feature of the war. It is not difficult to imagine political and military developments which might lead to pretty complete isolation of considerable sections of the world, one from another. In this event one could foresee the growth, in more or less hermetically sealed compartments, of several civilizations, with varied economies and standards of living and ways of life.

Should events move toward the restoration of a complete or at least of a greater unity of world civilization three questions will certainly demand the most careful study from those who are responsible for making and preserving the future peace. These questions may be as difficult to solve as the Riddles of the Sphinx. But the quality and the durability of any new civilization that may emerge from the travail of our time depend upon the realization of some tolerable approximation to solutions.

Somehow a means must be found to reconcile the liberty of man, the most precious inheritance of the Liberal Age, with the social security that is an imperative necessity of an industrial era. Some economists may regard this problem as comparable in difficulty with the squaring of the circle. But solved in some fashion it must be. And much of the future political life of the world, one may predict, will revolve around the search for the solution.

Just as inequality of wealth between classes within a country, if it becomes too sharp, sometimes leads to an explosion, in the shape of a revolution, so inequality in distribution of natural resources and raw materials, when aggravated by policies of extreme protectionism, leads to an explosion, in the form of war. Class struggle between "proletarian" and "bourgeois" nations is just as natural, if just as disastrous, as class struggle between the rich and the poor within a nation.

For this situation there are two possible remedies. There could be a redistribution of the world's colonial areas, with more attention to the population, industrial capacities and economic needs of the countries possessing the colonies. The other remedy, which would be much sounder and more desirable, would approach the problem from another angle. It would call for a diminution of existing imperialist privileges, not for the establishment of new imperialisms. It would involve a steady extension of self-government to all but the most primitive colonial peoples, equality of commercial opportunity for all countries in colonies and mandated areas and an attempt by international agreement to cut through the jungle of tariffs, quotas, managed currencies and other restrictions on the freest possible movement across frontiers of men, of goods and of capital.

And, if the pitfalls of Versailles and its disastrous aftermath are to be avoided, there must be another reconciliation of two principles. Cultural autonomy, administrative self-government, for all peoples, large and small, must be combined with the creation of those larger economic units which are the only alternative, in an age of mass production, to chronic impoverishment and discontent.

The world will indeed be fortunate if the situation at the end of the war makes possible the application of these principles or, indeed, of any clearly thought-out program of reconstruction. One must hope that a new civilization is in the making, amid all the fearful tragedies, the breakup and confusion, that mark the fall of an old one. But one still waits in vain for a sign of salvation. The infernal cycle of violence, of war and revolution, has not yet run its course.

INDEX